The Antiquers

Elizabeth Stillinger

The Antiquers

The lives and careers, the deals, the finds, the collections
of the men and women who were responsible for the
changing taste in American antiques, 1850–1930

Alfred A. Knopf New York 1980

THIS IS A BORZOI BOOK
PUBLISHED BY ALFRED A. KNOPF, INC.

Copyright © 1980 by Elizabeth Stillinger
All rights reserved under International and Pan-American Copyright Conventions.
Published in the United States by Alfred A. Knopf, Inc., New York,
and simultaneously in Canada by Random House of Canada Limited, Toronto.
Distributed by Random House, Inc., New York.

Grateful acknowledgment is made to the following for permission
to reprint from previously published material:

The Curtis Publishing Company: Excerpt from "Antiquing" by M. L. Blumen-
thal. Reprinted from *The Saturday Evening Post*. Copyright © 1924
The Curtis Publishing Company.
E. P. Dutton: Excerpt from *Days of the Phoenix* by Van Wyck Brooks.
Copyright © 1957 by Van Wyck Brooks.
Reprinted by permission of E. P. Dutton, publishers.
Random House, Inc.: Excerpt from *The Americans: The National Experience*
by Daniel J. Boorstin. Copyright © 1965 by Daniel J. Boorstin.
Reprinted by permission of Random House, Inc.

Library of Congress Cataloging in Publication Data
Stillinger, Elizabeth. (date)
The antiquers: the lives and careers, the deals,
the finds, the collections of the men and women who
were responsible for the changing taste in American
antiques, 1850–1930.
Includes bibliographical references and index.
1. Antiques—United States—History. 2. Americana—
History. I. Title.
NK805.S72   1980   745.1′0974   80–3525
ISBN 0-394-40329-0

Manufactured in the United States of America
First Edition

To Dick
and
To Alice and Amy

Contents

Acknowledgments

DAN O'KEEFE STARTED ME ON THIS BOOK. ALTHOUGH HE ORIGINALLY SUGGESTED a somewhat broader treatment of the subject, he has been encouraging and enthusiastic about this variation. Debby O'Keefe provided, as she always does, sympathy and humor during the trying times, and excellent advice when asked.

Alice Winchester was unfailingly generous with time, information, and reminiscences. My many conversations with her on the subject of collecting and collectors have helped to shape the ideas embodied in this book, and I am very grateful for her advice and encouragement.

Wendell Garrett not only directed me to source material in the beginning, but has been most generous in lending me books from his own collection and in suggesting people for me to interview.

Richard Saunders made the first study of collecting in New England for his Winterthur thesis. He has been extraordinarily kind in sharing with me sources, ideas, and photographs. I am extremely grateful to him.

Karen Jones lent me a room to write in, and her ear whenever I needed it— for both of which I am more appreciative than I can say. My mother furnished a grant which paid for a year's baby-sitting, and for that, too, I am deeply grateful. Bill Guthman very kindly searched out and lent me photographs of special interest from his own collection.

Nearly everyone in the libraries, archives, historical societies, and museums I used was more than helpful, and many of those to whom I am indebted are mentioned in footnotes.

I would like to thank particularly Richard Barons, Robertson Center for the Arts and Sciences; Bland Blackford, Archivist, Colonial Williamsburg; David Blaney; Kathryn Buhler, Museum of Fine Arts, Boston; Devere Card; Jan Christman, Historical Services, New York State Museum; Wendy Cooper, Assistant Curator, Museum of Fine Arts, Boston; Mrs. G. Frank Cram; Abbott Lowell Cummings, Director, Society for the Preservation of New England Antiquities; Marshall B. Davidson; Dean Failey, Christie's, New York; Jonathan Fairbanks, Curator, Museum of Fine Arts, Boston; Barry Greenlaw, Curator, Bayou Bend Collection, Museum of Fine Arts, Houston; Thompson R. Harlow, Director, The Connecticut Historical Society; Elizabeth Hill, former Archivist, Downs Manuscript Library, Winterthur Museum; Arthur Holden; J. A. Lloyd Hyde; Edward C. Johnson III; Phillip Johnston, Chief Curator of Decorative Arts, Wadsworth Atheneum; Patricia Kane, Curator, Garvan and Related Collections, Yale University Art Gallery; Mrs. Stephen T. Keiley; Bernard Levy; Nina and Bertram K. Little; Dr. Jane Lockwood; Patricia Maccubbin, Chief Audio-Visual Librarian, Colonial Williamsburg; Jerry M. Mallick, Museum Specialist, Photographic Archives, National Gallery of Art; Sr. Marie Joseph, Librarian, St. Thomas Aquinas College; Mrs. Hans Miller; Pauline Mitchell, Research Staff, Shelburne Museum; the late Charles F. Montgomery, former Curator, Garvan and Related Collections, Yale University Art Gallery; Robert Nikirk, Librarian, Grolier Club; John Page, Director, New Hampshire Historical Society; Ruth Page; Donald Peirce, Associate Curator of Decorative Arts, Brooklyn Museum; Patricia Pellegrini, Archivist, Metropolitan Museum of Art; Diane Pilgrim, Curator of Decorative Arts, Brooklyn Museum; Jeannie Rengsdorff, Associate Archivist, Metropolitan Museum of Art; Norman S. Rice, Director, Albany Institute of History and Art; Mr. and Mrs. Reginald P. Rose; Harold Sack; Karol Schmiegel, Associate Registrar, Winterthur Museum; Josephine Setze; Caroline Stride, Director, Concord Antiquarian Society; John Sweeney, Coordinator of Research, Winterthur Museum; Charlotte Wilcoxin, Research Librarian, Albany Institute of History and Art; and John Wright, Assistant Curator, Essex Institute.

Barbara Buff, Carol Gibbon, Pat Murphy, Judy Slane, and my brother, Dick Johns, listened patiently and affectionately during the years I was working on the manuscript. My editor, Jane Garrett, never failed to be helpful and supportive, or to give skilled editorial advice. Sandy Wright typed the final version cheerfully and competently.

Alice and Amy endured, and for that they have my very special thanks. My husband, Dick, not only helped me to formulate the ideas presented here, but was always willing to worry with me over specific smaller problems until we found a solution. He devoted weeks to editing the manuscript; no one else could, I think, have done so thorough, informed, and caring a job.

February 19, 1980   E.S.

Introduction

ONE OF THE MOST GRATIFYING ASPECTS OF WRITING THIS BOOK HAS BEEN THE amount of enthusiasm expressed for its subject. From college professors to Wall Street brokers, the history of collecting American antiques has aroused curiosity and interest. Museum people have always been fascinated by the great collections, but questions about who started to collect, and why, seem never to have occurred to most others. What has surprised and sustained me is how quickly the subject took hold with almost everyone to whom it was mentioned.

The enormous popularity of American antiques today makes the study of its origins doubly interesting. The key to understanding the opposite attitude, with which the pioneer collectors of the nineteenth century lived, is in Holger Cahill's introduction to the *Index of American Design* (1950):

> In one sense the Index is a kind of archaeology. It helps to correct a bias which has tended to relegate the work of the craftsman and the folk artist to the subconscious of our history where it can be recovered only by digging. In the past we have lost whole sequences out of their story, and have all but forgotten the unique contribution of hand skills in our culture.

The nineteenth-century tidal wave of machine-made furnishings, sweeping handmade objects from the domestic interior, also erased the techniques of hand craftsmanship. Factory goods were cheaper, and considered by many to be more fashionable, than handmade ones. Early pieces were banished to the kitchen, attic, or barn. And there they remained, frequently undergoing severe or irreparable damage, until one day the first stranger—apparently somewhat deranged—appeared at the door and offered to buy some.

Not only did this earliest collector spend long days tracking down a rumored chest or teapot but he also had to discover its original purpose and name, and try to guess where it had been made. For many years it was generally thought that fine old furniture and silver were English, imported at an early date for American use. The publication of Dr. Irving W. Lyon's *Colonial Furniture of New England* in 1891 was a revelation to collectors, and families with inherited colonial furniture. They were surprised and pleased to be informed that antiques found in New England had actually been made there, and to learn the correct names and original uses of many of their objects. Clearly, Dr. Lyon's generation of collectors were true pioneers; for they were exploring uncharted country, relying for success on their instincts.

The territory covered in this book is also, to a large extent, uncharted, because by now the attitudes and motivations of these early collectors have approached the kind of oblivion once occupied by the antiques they sought. This is an attempt to identify and explore the patterns characteristic of the collecting movement from about 1850 to 1930. Before 1850 there was very little collecting of what we call antiques—furniture, ceramics, silver, pewter, and other decorative arts—while the year 1930 saw the end of a great collecting era. The onset of the Great Depression concluded the wild buying associated with the American antiques craze of the 1920s.

Instead of trying to compile an all-inclusive catalogue of collectors and to cover all geographical regions, I have attempted to give the flavor of successive generations by picking out people who exemplify them. New England figures most prominently, because New England is where collecting American antiques really began; and it was the traditions and legends, as well as the antiques, of New England that stimulated collectors from other regions. A representative selection will, I hope, convey each era's attitude toward the possessions of our ancestors.

Who collected, why, what, how, and with what result are the questions I have asked. I have read letters, early articles, books, and other materials, and I have interviewed or corresponded with friends and descendants of collectors. In many cases, that meant grandchildren who are by this time grandparents themselves. For other important collectors, the links seem to have disappeared entirely. The answers I arrived at are the subject of this book.

.   .   .

The earliest interest in American antiques stemmed from patriotic or romantic sentiments, or from curiosity about the unfamiliar. The chairs, cups, and coffeepots of colonial and Federal America were not admired for themselves so much as for their associations with famous—or infamous—people, and with a far-off way of life that seemed both heroic and quaint. The organizers of mid-nineteenth-century charity fairs and bazaars found that a booth of curiosities, relics, memorabilia, and souvenirs always attracted an interested audience. At the Albany Army Relief Bazaar of 1864, George Washington's hair, cane, pistol, and writing bureau were described as "of priceless value and great national interest." But at the same fair, and also a great attraction, were Franklin's gold-headed cane, Napoleon's garden chair, Voltaire's blanket, an American Indian pipe, nails from a Pompeiian house, and a host of other curiosities. The common denominator was association with a famous person, place, or event, or with the foreign and exotic.

A general interest in history and its famous participants expanded to encompass one's own family, town, or region. People began to have what might be described as a genealogical orientation toward old things. They were valuable because they represented the family or a distinguished family member, or because they had been made or used long ago in one's home town, county, or state. The realization that many of the arts of early America were beautifully designed, constructed, and finished had simply not developed.

Beyond the initial stage of regarding antiques with nostalgia or curiosity, a small group of serious collectors took shape—mainly in New England, where the history was long and vivid, and collectible objects relatively easy to find. These men and women, too, were influenced by the historical and associative aspects of the things they collected. But, affected by the arts-and-crafts insistence on simplicity and honesty, they also regarded early American furnishings as morally and aesthetically superior to most new household goods then available. So instead of settling for a house full of comfortable and fashionable overstuffed furniture, the collector of American antiques surrounded himself with what were to him beautiful, evocative furnishings of a satisfying extra dimension.

His wainscot chair had been in the vicinity of Hartford, Connecticut, for over two hundred years. His gateleg table had stood in the center of a room which, tradition asserted, served as an important Revolutionary War headquarters. The collector relished the sense of history—of *American* history—his chairs and tables imparted. At the same time, he liked the feeling that at least in his own home he was escaping the increasingly pervasive influence of the machine. He was going back to a time when hand work—given a special moral significance by arts-and-crafts writers such as John Ruskin, William Morris, and Charles Eastlake—produced all household effects. The spirit of the worthy craftsman and his honest, brave patron lived again in the imagination of the collector.

In the 1890s, collectors of American antiques moved into another phase. This was the heyday of pleasing furniture groupings and room arrangements. Fanciful Turkish corners, sybaritic Moorish divans, and exotic trappings from other Mediterranean spots transformed fashionable parlors. Pleasure in creating a romantic atmosphere carried over to American antiques, which were sought increasingly by casual collectors to add to the effectiveness of a "colonial" corner or hallway. An old chair or mirror in the front entry, a row of antique plates high on the dining room wall, were thought to lend quaintness and interest to the house. This was also the colonial-revival period in architecture; and colonial furnishings, either authentic or reproduction, carried out the theme.

During this period the beauty of American antiques began to be stressed by collectors, but their history and associations remained very important. Patriotic feelings were strong in the 1890s, when societies such as the Daughters of the American Revolution, the Sons of the American Revolution, and the Colonial Dames were formed. It became increasingly desirable not only to have American antiques but to establish that one's family had been in America long enough to have handed them down.

With the expansion of collecting American antiques after the turn of the century, more and more printed material appeared on the subject. Most of it was aimed at the novice. Among these general, sometimes vaguely organized books were *The Furniture of Our Forefathers* (1900), *Chats on Old Furniture* (1905), *The Lure of the Antique* (1910), *The Quest of the Quaint* (1916), and *The Charm of the Antique* (1916).

Increased popular interest in American antiques gave rise to a spate of museum exhibitions in the early 1900s. The sorting, cataloguing, and displaying customary in other museum departments in the United States began to be applied also to American decorative arts. An attempt was made to show the range and progression of styles, and to illustrate which chairs and tables belonged stylistically with which silver tankards and ceramic mugs. Increased exhibition led to greater popular understanding and interest, which in turn spurred even more exhibition and study. A peak was reached in the exhibit of American decorative arts held at the Metropolitan Museum during the grand Hudson-Fulton Celebration of 1909. Furniture, silver, ceramics, glass, and pewter lent by collectors from Boston to Philadelphia were displayed in the museum's galleries. They were so favorably received that the Metropolitan took the then-amazing step of purchasing Eugene Bolles's entire collection of American antique furniture.

Other developments resulted from the success of the Hudson-Fulton exhibition. One was the founding of the Walpole Society, a select collectors' group that had its first meeting in 1910. Another was the elaborate plan that slowly took shape for proper display of the Bolles collection; it culminated fifteen years later in the Metropolitan's American Wing, which opened to extraordinarily enthusiastic acclaim.

Thus, in this period from 1890 to 1915, the appreciation of American antiques was extended from their associational aspect to include their artistic qualities as well. It was also a time when the institutionalization of collectors and collecting began. Several other museums and institutions held exhibitions of American silver or furniture during the early years of the century.

As World War I drew nearer and immigrants continued to pour onto American shores, people began to appreciate American antiques still more keenly. Anything foreign seemed threatening to the American way of life, and even to the dominance of Americans in their own land. Early indigenous furnishings were now employed by museums as educational and propaganda tools. Designers could find inspiration in their simple lines, careful workmanship, and pleasing proportions. The immigrant hordes crowding urban tenements could view them and find basic American virtues: simplicity, honesty, and usefulness.

Conceived as a teaching exhibit, the American Wing contained several intended lessons. Its period rooms were an attempt to re-create as accurately as possible the interiors of colonial and Federal America. Their chronological arrangement provided a historical survey of the development of style in America from the seventeenth to the early nineteenth centuries. The Wing was to be both a lesson in history and evidence of an American artistic tradition. It was further meant to represent the early American spirit: the simplicity and purity of line of its architecture and objects were counterparts of the simplicity and purity felt to be characteristic of the forefathers.

The American Wing had an enormous impact on the collecting movement. Its presentation of antiques as tangible symbols of the American character appealed to most Americans in the nationalistic 1920s; its combination of antiques and architecture of the same period was an inspiration, giving collecting a method and a focus; and its acceptance of American antiques as worthy of a major museum confirmed their artistic merit.

As a result, collectors could now be found in many walks of life. Henry Ford, who became a committed collector in the booming 1920s, had made it possible for his less affluent countrymen to compete with him—at least in mobility. His inexpensive cars allowed the middle classes to spend leisure time antiquing in the country. American antiques also became at last a hobby for the very rich, whose collections had previously been largely European.

The period-room idea appealed to people at many economic levels. Enthusiasm for creating atmosphere with American antiques—generated by the simplicity and harmony of the American Wing—was widespread. Different collectors produced different kinds of atmosphere; but no one surpassed Henry du Pont in creating charm and romance—unless it was Henry Sleeper, who helped Du Pont with his earliest rooms.

Although most collectors couldn't hope to compete either aesthetically or financially with Sleeper and Du Pont, thousands tried to furnish their houses tastefully and charmingly with American antiques. They wanted to have the right piece in the right place. Gracious living was stressed; and the heavy seventeenth-century oak that reminded nineteenth-century collectors of their hardy pioneer ancestors gave way to later and lighter pieces in comfortable, appealing arrangements. Early Duncan Phyfe was sought avidly in New York, while Boston and Philadelphia collectors concentrated on elegant eighteenth-century furniture from their respective cities.

Magazines, newspapers, and more books fed the public appetite for information about antiques. The super-rich collectors who entered the field in the twenties created a dramatic climate through their intense competitive buying in the shops and auction rooms. More broadly, the antiques boom was reflected in the mushrooming reproduction business, influential loan exhibitions, other shows, frequent auctions in both town and country, and the emergence of magazines devoted entirely to American antiques.

The decade ended with two of the most spectacular auctions of Americana ever held; prices reached heights not scaled again until the 1960s. By the early 1930s, however, the antiques craze had dwindled, like so many enthusiasms of the glittering twenties. Even so, American antiques had been firmly established as having not only historical but also artistic value. From then on, although receding temporarily into the background, they would never relinquish a place of importance in the national consciousness.

The Antiquers

I

Antiques as Emblems: Patriotism, Heroism, and History

We are so young a people that we feel the want of nationality,
and delight in whatever asserts our national "American" existence.
We have not, like England and France, centuries of achievements
and calamities to look back on; we have no *record* of
Americanism and we feel its want. Hence the development, in
every state of the Union, of "Historical Societies" that seize on and
seal up every worthless reminiscence of our colonial
and revolutionary times.

George Templeton Strong, *Diary,* November 8, 1854

IT TOOK UNTIL THE END OF THE NINETEENTH CENTURY TO PRODUCE A RATIONAL, unified history of America. Before that the American story was told only disjointedly, through heroes, patriots, and their accomplishments. The Pilgrims and the Puritans were regarded as models of bravery and determination in their lonely battle to create a civilization out of treacherous wilderness. The Revolutionary War, with the men who took part and the surrounding events, was also held up as an inspiration to later, seemingly less idealistic generations. Washington, Franklin, and Lafayette had been American heroes—almost deities—since early in the nineteenth century.

"We crave a history, instinctively," wrote the diarist George Templeton Strong in 1854, "and being without the eras that belong to older nationalities . . . we dwell on the details of our little all of historic life, and venerate every trivial fact about our first settlers and colonial governors and revolutionary heroes."[1] An antique, to Strong and his contemporaries, was not the product of a distinctive American culture, representing an identifiable period and style. Instead, it was regarded as a piece of history—appreciated in direct proportion to its degree of association with past events or persons, especially famous or heroic ones. Until the final quarter of the nineteenth century, there were few collectors of American antiques; and they prized most highly those objects that provided concrete and specific links to a past viewed as embarrassingly sparse.

In addition, antiques that looked outlandish were of interest as curiosities. They were often exhibited as such at the fairs—usually held to raise money for a patriotic or charitable cause—that were so popular in Victorian America. It was, then, either as relics of historical people and events or as oddities that American antiques first came to the attention of the American public. The early collectors generally reflected that attitude; in any case, they exerted very little influence on its ultimate modification.

Already, in many areas of mid-nineteenth-century America, vast and various changes had almost obliterated traces of the colonial and Federal periods. The result was a sense of rootlessness, of displacement. There was a widespread feeling that contemporary life, with its peripatetic population, crowded cities, developing West, and time- and energy-saving devices, was missing some of the basic pleasures and satisfactions of earlier days. The social order had changed radically over the course of the century, with money displacing the older prerequisites of birth and education. Religion had been undermined by the new scientific theories. So solid Victorians fixed on the family, often symbolized by fireplace and hearth, as the most reliable and enduring institution of their age. The yearning for a return to the apparent peace and comfort of the home fireside gave rise, at least among a small minority of the population, to an interest in "old-time" furnishings. The growth of American antiques' popularity during the nineteenth century has many of its roots in this sentimental longing for the simpler life of the past.

The tendency to look wistfully backward was reinforced by the Civil War and its aftermath, which heightened Americans' consciousness of their traditions, and what they stood for as a nation. In an effort to justify the conflict, many invoked the heroic patriotism of Revolutionary War times. Turning to a distant past lessened the pain of the more recent one. Dissension between North and South could be repressed by recalling the colonial unity behind the Declaration of Independence. Identifying with earlier patriots, people began to revere objects that could be associated with the Revolution or any of its participants. George Washington's belongings were far and away the most desirable.

In the 1850s, an interest in the decorative arts of the American past had become manifest in art and literature. The approach was often highly romantic. Thoreau, for example, like many New Englanders of his day, was disturbed by a perceived loss of the finest aspects of New England's character. He was consoled by old furniture:

The home fireside, in Clarence Cook's The House Beautiful, *1878.*

How much more agreeable it is to sit in the midst of old furniture like Minott's clock, and secretary and looking-glass, which have come down from other generations, than amid that which was just brought from the cabinet-maker's, smelling of varnish, like a coffin! To sit under the face of an old clock that has been ticking one hundred and fifty years—there is something mortal, not to say immortal, about it; a clock that began to tick when Massachusetts was a province.[2]

Longfellow, who immortalized a Boston silversmith in the poem *Paul Revere's Ride*, had affinities similar to Thoreau's. *The Old Clock on the Stairs* made an object with a history seem very attractive. In 1851, Nathaniel Hawthorne used a description of the House of Seven Gables to create the mood for a brooding, romantic tale set in a seventeenth-century dwelling in Salem:

Half-way down a by-street of one of our New England towns stands a rusty wooden house, with seven acutely peaked gables, facing towards various points of the compass, and a huge, clustered chimney in the midst. . . . The aspect of the venerable mansion has always affected me like a human countenance, bearing the traces not merely of outward storm and sunshine, but expressive also, of the long lapse of mortal life, and accompanying vicissitudes that have passed within.[3]

Most writers and artists presented the objects of the past less soberly than Hawthorne. The painter Edward Lamson Henry began to make nostalgic drawings of old buildings a few years after Hawthorne had published his word-picture of the House of Seven Gables. As early as the 1850s, magazines like *Harper's* and *Scribner's* were offering appealingly illustrated articles about quiet New England towns, where the atmosphere of harmony and spaciousness contrasted with urban chaos. "Lyme, a Chapter of American Genealogy," in *Harper's New Monthly Magazine* for February 1876, described the old houses of Lyme, Connecticut, and their furnishings.[4] The writer imagined illustrious past inhabitants in powdered wigs and high-heeled shoes—romantic apparel more characteristic of eighteenth-century London or Paris than a rural Connecticut town.

Such sentimental interweaving of events, lineages, and legends was probably the result of urban living. In summertime, well-to-do city dwellers could leave the crowded, steaming streets for shady, peaceful country lanes; the contrast provoked a longing for earlier days and customs. The great anonymity of the city blurred the neat sense of identity that seemingly remained intact in New England towns. An urban visitor felt that here, among fine old houses and furnishings, was a reassuring sense of stability and order. It was natural for city people to begin finding and buying the old china and silver, the tables and cupboards made and lived with in these towns. They took antiques home as symbols of small-town serenity, and used them to create urban oases.

During the Civil War, "sanitary fairs" (so called because they came under the auspices of the Sanitary Commission, a forerunner of the Red Cross) were held in cities as widely separated as Indianapolis and Bangor, Maine, to raise money for the sick and wounded. They nearly always contained some antiques and relics. At the Brooklyn, New York, Sanitary Fair, held early in 1864, one room was set aside for the display of "treasures of the past." Here, along with a Russian saber from the Crimean War and the full court dress of a "Nubian lady of quality," were objects that had belonged to William Bradford, Miles Standish, John Hancock, and George Washington. There was, as well, a tablecloth alleged to have crossed the Atlantic on the *Mayflower*. Many other fascinating items were listed in the *Catalogue of Arts, Relics, and Curiosities*, a publication that reveals the exhibition committee's willingness to accept nearly anything odd, old, or of associational interest. It was as curiosities that American antiques were often first exhibited.

The ladies in charge of the Brooklyn Sanitary Fair set to work with a will. As plans and work progressed, "nothing was talked of but the great fair. . . ." On opening day, Washington's Birthday, 1864, the city of Cincinnati sent a challenging gift: it was a great broom inscribed "Sent by the managers of the Cincinnati Fair, Greeting: We have swept up $240,000; Brooklyn, beat this if you can." Brooklyn, at the close of her fair, was able to retort, "Brooklyn sees the $240,000 and goes $150,000 better."[5]

An especially popular attraction in Brooklyn, and at many other sanitary fairs, was the New England Kitchen. This feature is highly significant as an indication of growing interest in colonial American life and objects. It is also noteworthy because the New England, or colonial, kitchen is generally considered to have first appeared twelve years later at the Centennial Exposition in Philadelphia.

The committee in charge of the Brooklyn kitchen set forth its goals in a preliminary circular:

> The idea is to present a faithful picture of New England farm-house life of the last century. The grand old fire-place shall glow again—the spinning-wheel shall whirl as of old—the walls shall be garnished with the products of the forest and the field—the quilting, the donation, and the wedding party shall assemble once more, while the apple-paring shall not be forgotten—and the dinner-table, always set, shall be loaded with substantial New England cheer. We shall try to reproduce the manners, customs, dress, and if possible, the idiom of the time; in short, to illustrate the domestic life

and habits of the people, to whose determined courage, sustained by their faith in God, we owe that government, so dear to every loyal heart. The period fixed upon is just prior to the throwing overboard of the tea in Boston Harbor.[6]

This evocation of the past as a stimulus to patriotism was sentimental and oversimplified. It was also an enormously successful device that has been used ever since.

The focal point of the kitchen was its big open fireplace, with antique utensils and tools hanging in or about it. On the mantel, and on shelves around the room, were the teapot of a Revolutionary War general, the pewter plate of a Signer of the Declaration of Independence, and other associational items. They were on loan, according to the fair's daily paper, "from all parts of the East, several gentlemen interested in the Fair having taken extensive tours through the New England States expressly to collect such specimens."[7]

The Brooklyn kitchen was a kind of *tableau vivant*—but with active participation by the viewers, who had the option of being served food and drink. Some of the spectators, it was reported, "seem to have confused notions as to what they came out for to see . . . satisfied with a good long stare at the old-fashioned costumes, they turn their wondering gaze upon those visitors who sit down to eat apparently under the impression that the latter are a part of the show, engaged to eat daily, and eat after the manner of past centuries."[8]

Curiosity was a definite factor in the Brooklyn kitchen's popularity. Visitors were interested and often amused to be shown the curios, customs, and costumes of earlier days. But the nostalgia and patriotism that motivated the kitchen's organizers also found an echo among those in attendance, both here and at comparable exhibits in contemporary sanitary fairs. According to the *History of the Brooklyn and Long Island Fair*, "Many, before leaving the New England Kitchen, howsoever well satisfied with the new ways about us, were fain to conclude 'the old is better.' "[9]

Patriotic emphasis was strong at local Centennial celebrations held all over the nation in 1875. Local history and local heroes stimulated interest in antiques as symbols of a departed era—especially in the East, where the American past was longer and livelier than in the rest of the country. The celebrations began on April 19, 1875, with two grandly planned commemorations at Concord and Lexington.

In June, the most illustrious of all was held to mark the centennial of the Battle of Bunker Hill. It received national attention. *The Cabinetmaker* reported that "articles of historic interest . . . were sent in from various points and formed a pleasing picture of antique customs and tastes,"[10] at the associ-

The New England Kitchen at the Brooklyn Sanitary Fair, 1864. (McCloskey's Manual of the Common Council of the City of Brooklyn for 1864)

ated exhibition. One antique that received much attention was a wineglass, sent to Boston by Dr. William S. Forbes of Philadelphia. It was accompanied by an affidavit stating that it had been brought to America in or about 1657; that it was used the day Washington was christened; and that Washington himself had drunk from it at a dinner in Fredericksburg. Whether the wineglass was a beautiful example of craftsmanship is unknown; its importance at the Bunker Hill observance was due to its associations.

Other Centennial celebrations followed. New Haven's included an exhibition of 811 items, encompassing among the American antiques "primarily portraits, silver, ceramics, and furniture with historical associations."[11] The celebration in Hartford, Connecticut, held in November of 1875 offered an exhibition of relics. It included decanters and wineglasses reputed to have arrived in America aboard the *Mayflower*. A contemporary account reported:

> The "relic room" was beautifully decorated with the national colors, and contained a large and varied assortment of treasures of the past. Glass cases down the sides of the room and the center, were filled with the more valuable and fragile articles, and grouped here and there were lay-figures in ancient costumes, antique furniture, portraits, and pictures.[12]

Salem, Massachusetts, held its Centennial celebration in December, with a remarkable exhibition of old furniture and other antiques. Mounted in the Essex Institute's Plummer Hall, it comprised furniture, silver, prints and paintings, books, dresses, and many other items. The lenders included several aristocratic Massachusetts families—Saltonstalls, Derbys, Cabots, and Peabodys. Among the other contributors were serious Salem collectors Henry F. Waters and George Rea Curwen, and early dealers James Moulton and M. A. Stickney.[13]

It must have been owing to the participation of the collectors and dealers that the exhibition was so well organized. The sizable furniture group was divided as follows: "The XVIth Century, or period of discovery, the XVIIth Century or Colonial period, the XVIIIth Century, or Provincial and Revolutionary period," and a miscellaneous section. This attempt to present American furniture chronologically, providing an idea of the progression of style, was sophisticated and forward-looking for its time. *Frank Leslie's Illustrated Newspaper* described it as "by far the most complete and interesting exhibition of antique furniture, we venture to say, ever held in this country."[14]

Despite the pioneering concept of display, association items—considered worthwhile solely because of their association with a famous person or event—were still very important. Some were touching, as well. Along with objects related to Paul Revere and George Washington, the exhibition contained a "Silver tankard into which Gov. Andrews' grandfather was put, and the cover closed over him, in 1731," and "The last piece of jewelry worn by Louis XVI.

While imprisoned he gave it to the jailer to buy files with, but was executed before he could liberate himself."[15]

Life in 1876 may have seemed increasingly complex and uncertain to many Americans, but they also enjoyed the fruits of scientific and technical advance. It was the latter aspect that the Philadelphia Exposition stressed and celebrated. This grand international Centennial fair, in contrast to the local observances, was oriented toward the future. The past was used as a foil, to demonstrate how far the nation had traveled along the path of mechanization. America was "voluble," as William Dean Howells wrote, "in strong metals and their infinite uses."[16] From its parochial beginnings, America was rising to prominence as a world power, and its citizens were congratulating themselves on the industrial achievement that had made it possible.

A selection from the exhibition of relics organized by the Ladies' Centennial Committee in Plummer Hall, Salem, Massachusetts. Shown in Frank Leslie's Illustrated Newspaper, *January 22, 1876. (Courtesy, Essex Institute, Salem, Massachusetts)*

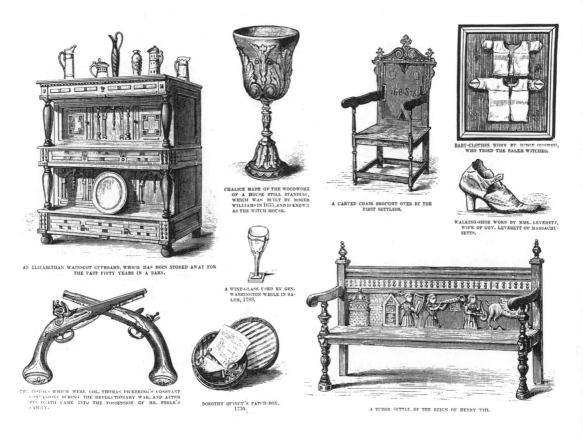

AN ELIZABETHAN WAINSCOT CUPBOARD, WHICH HAS BEEN STORED AWAY FOR THE PAST FIFTY YEARS IN A BARN.

CHALICE MADE OF THE WOODWORK OF A HOUSE STILL STANDING, WHICH WAS BUILT BY ROGER WILLIAMS IN 1635, AND IS KNOWN AS THE WITCH HOUSE.

A CARVED CHAIR BROUGHT OVER BY THE FIRST SETTLERS.

BABY-CLOTHES WORN BY JUDGE CURWIN, WHO TRIED THE SALEM WITCHES.

WALKING-SHOE WORN BY MME. LEVERETT, WIFE OF GOV. LEVERETT OF MASSACHU-SETTS.

A WINE-GLASS USED BY GEN. WASHINGTON WHILE IN SA-LEM, 1789.

THE PISTOLS WHICH WERE COL. THOMAS PICKERING'S CONSTANT COMPANIONS DURING THE REVOLUTIONARY WAR, AND AFTER HIS DEATH CAME INTO THE POSSESSION OF MR. PEELE'S FAMILY.

DOROTHY QUINCY'S PATCH-BOX, 1730.

A TUDOR SETTLE, OF THE REIGN OF HENRY VIII.

Visitors to the Centennial Exposition were surrounded by a vast number of material things, almost all of them new, or foreign, or strange. Antiques were definitely not prominent. George Eastman, a twenty-two-year-old visitor from Rochester, New York, wrote home from the fair:

> I intend to traverse every aisle, I have accomplished this in machinery hall & have got about half through the Main Bldg. . . . The ingenuity that exhibitors have displayed in arranging such things as tacks candles soap hardware needles thread pipe & all such apparently uninteresting articles is something marvelous—and they command the attention of the observer even against his will.[17]

The crowds that viewed this marvel on opening day made a lasting impression on the Japanese Commissioner to the Exhibition: "The first day crowds come like sheep, run here, run there, run everywhere. One man start, one thousand follow. Nobody can see anything, nobody can do anything. All rush, push, tear, shout, make plenty noise, say damn great many times, get very tired, and go home."[18]

In a study of early collectors in New England, Richard Saunders wrote: "The Centennial celebration has been thought of, for a number of years, as an exhibition place for colonial relics. It was not." There were only two major displays of colonial objects: the Old Log Cabin (or New England Kitchen) and the Connecticut Cottage. Furthermore, neither these nor the United States Government Pavilion's special collection of Washington and other patriotic relics indicated any "nationwide appreciation of colonial craftsmanship. They simply reflected the ongoing growth of interest in colonial history in New England and along the East Coast." Specific interest in colonial American art and antiques was confined to a relatively small group, even in the East. Most Americans were far more interested in modern advances and improvements than in artifacts of what one commentator, viewing 1776 through the eyes of the average Centennial visitor, has called "The Bad Old Times."[19]

Rodris Roth, in a study of "Centennial" furniture, makes the point that while there was some antique American furniture at the Philadelphia fair, there were none of the nineteenth-century reproductions that have nevertheless come to be called "Centennial" pieces. (These became popular in the 1880s, reflecting gradually emerging public interest in antiques.) In fact, the design of American furniture—old or new—was not highly regarded. Most Americans of the Centennial era looked to Europe for models. One critic expressed the consensus when he described most American furniture as not "fully equal, in point of elegance and artistic finish and design, to any of the English or even the French exhibits in the same line."[20]

Thus, the New England Kitchen at the Philadelphia exhibition was not intended to display American craft traditions. Part of the Women's Pavilion, it was conceived as a contrast to the adjacent modern kitchen, equipped with the latest labor-saving devices. Like its counterparts at the sanitary fairs, this New England Kitchen may have evoked for some viewers an apparently vanishing spiritual element in the American character. But it was intended primarily to point up material advances over the past one hundred years; and for most visitors, it was probably nothing more than a diversion.

The Centennial kitchen was an obvious derivative of its sanitary fair predecessors. With a big open fireplace as its focal point, it was attended by ladies dressed in colonial costume, and furnished with antiques and association items. Each object described in *Frank Leslie's Illustrated Historical Register Centennial Exposition 1876* was identified with a person or event of historical importance: for example, John Alden's desk; Governor Endicott's folding chair; a silver pitcher used by Lafayette; the cradle of the first child (Peregrine White) born on board the *Mayflower*. They combined, according to Leslie's publication, to convey "a pleasing view of life in New England a century ago."[21]

Large and interested crowds attended. But it was atmosphere, not accuracy,

The New England Kitchen in the Old Log Cabin at the Philadelphia Centennial, 1876.
Shown in Frank Leslie's Illustrated Newspaper, *June 10, 1876.*
(Winterthur Museum photograph)

that counted. The kitchen was furnished in that miscellaneous manner characteristic of the nineteenth, rather than the eighteenth, century. Bedroom, parlor, and true kitchen accessories were combined with heedless abandon. The purpose was not to give a correct impression of past life, but to gather objects around which stories could be built. This emphasis on the quaint and romantic aspect of antiques fits the contemporary standard for art. Referring to the Philadelphia fair, the art historian Oliver Larkin has described the consensus in 1876 that a work of art "must stab the eye with its novelty, enlist one's pity, or stir one's sexual curiosity. And whether it took the form of a picture or a chair, a statue or a stove, it must be a prevarication. . . ."[22]

The influence of the New England Kitchen as a catalyst for interest in antiques has been exaggerated. It was simply a very small part of a very large exhibition. Any nostalgic fondness evoked for antiques must have been overwhelmed by the relentless, gleaming machinery that dominated the Philadelphia fair. Writers and artists, the sanitary fair kitchens, and local Centennial celebrations were much more important in gradually broadening the appeal of American antiques.

Washington relics at the
Philadelphia Centennial.
Shown in Frank Leslie's
Illustrated Newspaper, *1876.*

Chapter 1

The First Collectors

Antiques as Relics

 EARLY AMERICAN ANTIQUARIES WERE A DIVERSE LOT. ONE OF THE FIRST known is the Reverend William Bentley (1759–1819), who collected a variety of things related to the history of Essex County, Massachusetts. Clergyman, scholar, historian, diarist, linguist, and naturalist, Dr. Bentley was one of the most important men of his day. He was an enthusiastic participant in most aspects of Salem's life from 1783 to 1819. Old furniture and other decorative-arts objects formed only one among the many categories of things accumulated, for "Bentley was an early collector with an unbelievably wide variety of interests. He gathered portraits, prints, books, manuscripts, furnishings, and coins, as well as all sorts of materials related to natural history, ethnology, and archaeology—some on a local, and others on a world-wide basis."[1]

He collected antiques both as association items and, far in advance of his time, as evidence of customs and craft methods that had almost disappeared. Bentley's famous diary contains frequent references to objects of great age, or with specific historical or genealogical associations. Among his treasures was a slat-back chair that had belonged to Mary and Philip English, accused of being witches in 1692. He had the chair painted green, with an inscription in memory of the Englishes on the slats. Today it stands in his former bedroom in the Essex Institute's restored Crowninshield-Bentley house.

"This day I was at a Vendue where I received from the family of Appleton a settle which was formerly in the family of Dr. Appleton," wrote Bentley on May 18, 1819. "I was not a little pleased with the possession & I found no rival claims. All were willing honourably to dispose of to a friend of the family what they feared to destroy & dared not disgrace"—but clearly did not want! As Huldah M. Smith has pointed out, "During the classical Federal period," when Bentley acquired the settee (or "settle"), it must "have been thought to be ugly, ornate, and outmoded."[2]

To Bentley, however, it was interesting and important as a part of Salem history, for his interest in antiques seems to have stemmed from his attraction to old things as a guide to the past. "I grieved to see the connection between the past and the present century so entirely lost," he wrote, upon visiting a seventeenth-century house in 1796. "There is something agreeable, if not great, in the primitive manners. So much pleasure and peace at home, while the great world is scarcely known. . . . From the Spoon to the broad platter, from the Shoe to the whole of the Wardrobe, from the chair to the bed. Everything in its own likeness, and away, far away from present fashion."[3]

Bentley's sentimental evocation of the former "pleasure and peace" of home

Turkeywork settee preserved by Dr. Bentley in 1819.
(Courtesy, Essex Institute, Salem, Massachusetts)

*The Reverend William
Bentley. Oil on canvas by
James Frothingham.
(Courtesy, Essex Institute,
Salem, Massachusetts)*

was inspired by an actual survival: a seventeenth-century house furnished more
or less in seventeenth-century style. He lamented that he could not "purchase
all the furniture of the house"[4] because he had no adequate place for it. His
motive for acquiring these things would have been to preserve them as visual
documentation of a particular time and place—documentation which, he realized, was vanishing irretrievably.

Like many collectors who came after him, Bentley stressed the associational
aspect of his antiques. But in recognizing the objects of an earlier time as a key
to attitudes and customs, Bentley was amazingly ahead of his contemporaries.

The antiquary John Fanning Watson (1779–1860) of Philadelphia shared Dr.
Bentley's enthusiasm for the American past. He, too, saw the importance of
preserving some record of the patterns of early American life. Watson's approach to the study of colonial customs in his area was imaginative. To obtain
material for his *Annals of Philadelphia, Being a Collection of Memoirs, Anecdotes, and Incidents of the City and its Inhabitants from the Days of the
Pilgrim Founders*, published in 1830,[5] he made up a list of thirty-seven questions to ask "aged Persons of Philada."

Along with compiling written information, Watson also collected objects as
evidence. But it was their associations, rather than their artistry, that interested
him, and he thought of the objects as relics. "Even though he was given a clock
from Stenton by Deborah Logan in May 1839," writes Frank Sommer, "the

John Fanning Watson, May 1860. (Courtesy, Henry Francis du Pont Winterthur Libraries)

magnificent furniture of that house fascinated him only because it (or some of it, at least) had been owned by James Logan."[6]

Although Watson devoted his regular working hours to business, his heart seems to have lain in the past. He journeyed to Pennsbury Manor to investigate the house, its contents, and its original owner, William Penn; and to Harrisburg to see and sit in the chair he believed John Hancock had occupied while signing the Declaration of Independence. The "Hancock" chair (dethroned in the twentieth century when it was assigned a date after the signing) so inspired Watson that he commissioned one similar in style. Meant to commemorate important historical events in Pennsylvania, Watson's chair was loaded with relics: mainly woods associated with Christopher Columbus, William Penn, Chief Justice Marshall, and with other people and things of historical interest. It may be seen today in Independence Hall.

Watson's chair was modeled after an older one, but most such "relic furniture" (made of old wood) was done in a contemporary style. The New York Crystal Palace Exhibition in 1851, for example, featured a chair made of wood from the castle of San Juan de Ulúa, which was captured during the Mexican-American War of 1846–48. Designed in the contemporary rococo-revival style, it was carved with war trophies and symbols of patriotism and peace. The themes of homage to American patriotism and to a specific historical triumph informed the viewer that this was no ordinary chair.

The Centennial celebration held in Philadelphia in 1876 inspired a number of pieces of relic furniture. Some, in Renaissance-revival and other contemporary styles, were of hickory wood from the grounds of Andrew Jackson's house in Nashville; one chair was made of wood from the elm in Cambridge, Massachusetts, under which Washington reportedly stood while accepting command of the Continental Army in 1775; and several objects were fashioned of wood from Hartford's Charter Oak, said to have been the hiding place for Connecticut's charter when it was in danger of being seized by the British in 1687.[7]

Left: *Commemorative armchair designed by Watson and made of relic woods in 1836 by William Snyder. (National Park Service)*

Right: *Armchair made from the "Washington Elm." (Smithsonian Institution; photograph courtesy of* The Magazine Antiques)

Chapter 2

Cummings Davis

and "The Whisperings of the Past"

NEW FURNITURE FROM OLD WOOD WAS ONE ASPECT OF THE INTEREST IN historical associations. Genuine old furniture, and other antiques related to a specific romanticized part of the American past, were another. Without realizing the lasting value of his efforts, Cummings Davis made an extraordinarily rich collection of the antiques of Concord, Massachusetts. It is now on display at the Concord Antiquarian Society's museum.

Cummings Elsthan Davis (1816–1896) was born in Brooklyn, New York, and arrived in Concord via Harvard, Massachusetts, where he had lived for a time. He was married twice, to Caroline Symonds (whose subsequent fate is unknown) in 1839, and to Mary Bull in 1841. For some reason, Mary Bull Davis preferred remaining in her pleasant Harvard house to joining her husband in Concord. Davis lived there alone with his antiques, which he began to acquire about 1849.[1]

By selling newspapers, soft drinks, candy, and other sundries in his Refreshment Depot Saloon; tailoring; and delivering newspapers to residents of Concord, Cummings Davis provided himself with a meager living. Huddled in an old shawl to protect himself in raw weather, he hurried on his newspaper rounds. "One man," according to a biographical note, "admits to having been in a gang of mischievous boys who would call 'Little Davis, change a penny?,' and then have to scatter and flee from the wrath they had aroused."[2]

The advantages of delivering newspapers outweighed the aggravations, however, for the route afforded Davis a wonderful opportunity to become acquainted with Concord's old houses, their contents, and their owners. He could learn that unwanted or unneeded old things were around, and let it be known that he would be only too happy to have them. In this way, he was able to acquire antiques as gifts or in exchange for services, or sometimes for small sums of money.

Davis didn't specialize. He made, said one writer, "no discrimination between mahogany and the simpler woods, glass, pewter, china, and even tin. As a result, his collection ranged from the seventeenth to the nineteenth century, from the kitchen to the bedrooms and the parlor."[3]

Descended from five generations of Concord residents, Davis perhaps began to collect partly as a way of establishing contact with his ancestor Dolor Davis, one of the town's original settlers. From his own ancestors, Davis moved on to an interest in all early Concord families, and in famous or dramatic historical figures. Although Davis's antiques most often related to Concord, they were occasionally associated with historical person

Cummings Davis in an eighteenth-century costume from his collection. (Concord Antiquarian Society)

such as Napoleon or Mary Queen of Scots.

Things that had descended in Concord's oldest families, like an im
seventeenth-century Stone family press cupboard, were especially attr
Davis. Or pieces by a Concord cabinetmaker, such as the serpentine-f
made some time between the years 1760 and 1780 by Joseph Hosmer
of a famous Concord literary figure, like those from Thoreau's cab
Pond and Dr. Ezra Ripley's writing-arm windsor, used later by
Hawthorne. All these Davis eagerly gathered and preserved, bu
of their associations rather than any intrinsic artistic merit.

In arranging his collection, Davis displayed the same
beauty. From the little photographic evidence that survives
no interest in displaying his antiques to best advantage,
Things were jumbled together, with no attention given
the next. The association—the story—of each piece wa

Writing-arm windsor, eighteenth century, used by Emerson and Hawthorne. (Concord Antiquarian Society)

Left: *Lantern said to have been used to signal Paul Revere in 1775. (Concord Antiquarian Society)*

Chest of oak, seventeenth century, said to have been made for Cummings's ancestor Dolor Davis of Concord. (Concord Antiquarian Society)

In *The Quest of the Colonial* (1907), Robert and Elizabeth Shackleton tell of meeting Cummings Davis:

> . . . an aged man who was custodian, in his own house, of the local museum. . . . His mind had begun to grow a little dim, but the passion for collecting, that had been his one passion since his youth, was still as strong as ever.
>
> In every part of his large house there was a massing of all varieties of household belongings. There were corner-cupboards, some made to stand detached, others which had been built into the walls of old houses. China filled the cupboards, and in one was what many consider the finest lot of Lowestoft in the United States.
>
> He did not, indeed, realize the full value of everything. . . . It was a town legend that, regarding this very Lowestoft, some one commented with a cry of surprise upon what it was. "What a lot of Lowestoft!"
>
> Whereupon he responded, with a look of high displeasure, that it was not "low stuff"; it had been Mrs. So-and-so's very best china![4]

Mr. and Mrs. Shackleton probably visited Davis in the late 1880s or early 1890s. By 1870, people had begun to take his collection seriously enough to pay to see it. Davis and his objects were the subject of a local newspaper story in August of that year:

> Here lives an antiquary, Mr. Cummings E. Davis, a small erect, lithe man, who, with spirited and cavernous eyes, seems a fit object to flit about among ruins. What wonder that in this old town, with its 5 burial grounds, and its elms grown till their girths are 16 feet or more, a man should be given to dreams and the whisperings of the past. His collection of antiques is worth several thousand dollars, and consists mostly of furniture, glassware, paintings, Indian relics, &c. But the man is more than the collection. His pursuit holds him with the fascination of an invisible power. Rust and age have a weird influence over his heart. "Whatever belongs to the remote past," he says, "has an unspeakable charm for me." Here is the secret that sweetens his toil. He is held, he is led on.[5]

Davis had first installed his antiques in the old Concord courthouse, where he received visitors in eighteenth-century costume, complete with knee breeches and long white stockings. The fit was poor, but the effect was achieved. Davis pointed up the quaintness and age of the objects on view. When the collection grew too large for its courthouse quarters, he apparently moved some of it to a commodious eighteenth-century dwelling, the Reuben Brown house, filling the rooms rather haphazardly. It was here that Davis received the Shackletons, who reported that "he freely offered us the privilege of sleeping in a room that was so crowded with antiques that there was scarcely space to move, and of sleeping there in a Jacobean four-poster which he believed had come over in one of the trips of the Mayflower . . . but the room and the bed were of so extraordinary a mustiness that we declined the privilege."[6]

Davis's friend and fellow antiquary, George S. Tolman, was a charter member of the Concord Antiquarian Society, which was organized in 1886 expressly to provide for Davis and his collection. Tolman wrote of this in the catalogue he later prepared for the society, saying that Davis was afraid that after his death the collection would be broken up and sold. Davis desired especially, said Tolman, that his antiques "should remain together, and in Concord, where the collection should be his best monument, and should secure to his name some share of immortality among those who have made the fame of the old town."[7]

Negotiation with some of the town's leading—and commendably foresighted—citizens produced an agreement to provide a place for the collection's permanent custody and preservation, and to allow Davis to keep whatever fees he took in for showing it. If these were not enough for him to live on, the society promised to contribute the balance. In theory, this was a fair and workable arrangement. But Davis was either unable or unwilling to give up the collection. "He had been in the open road too long to understand the new and narrow rut in which he found himself," wrote one society member. Not only was Davis selling and trading pieces from what now belonged to the society— one chair he had sold was seized in transit to Ohio and returned—but he refused to cooperate in other ways. He would not admit a committee sent to report on the condition of the collection. When the inspection was finally achieved, "The collection was found . . . to be in such a state of neglect that the only solution seemed to be to remove Davis from his custodian's responsibilities and appoint the secretary as custodian pro-tem to clean the house and put it in good order." In 1893, George Tolman became custodian.[8]

Shortly thereafter, Davis went mad and was committed to the Danvers Asylum, where he died in 1896. He must have been sad and bewildered in his last years, but his work has transcended the unhappiness and confusion of that time. Not only has his "best monument" survived but it is regarded as one of the most remarkable collections of its kind. Divided by date and style and installed in a series of chronologically arranged period rooms, the antiques and relics Davis loved for their associative values are now on view in a Georgian-style building completed by the Concord Antiquarian Society in 1930. By preserving what others were discarding, Cummings Davis provided a rare and permanent insight into the tastes and customs of one small town over a period of three centuries.

Chapter 3

Ben: Perley Poore
Antiques as Old-time Atmosphere

Ben: PERLEY POORE (1820–1887) WAS MOTIVATED BY ATTITUDES AND INTER-
ests similar to those of Cummings Davis, but he operated on a much grander
scale. Though he spent a good deal of his adult life in Washington, D.C., Poore
was a New Englander by birth, having descended from an old family of West
Newbury, Massachusetts. His fascination with heroes like Napoleon, figures and
events in American political history, and local Essex County families set the
tone of Poore's collection. Unlike Davis, Poore used his objects together to
create a romantic old-time atmosphere, but he too made no effort to arrange
them according to period and style. Photographs of Poore's antiques-filled interiors indicate his majestic disregard of consistency.[1]

Poore's house was known as Indian Hill. In the front hall, furniture of
Jacobean, William and Mary, Chippendale, and Empire periods was surrounded by stained glass, heavy dark paneling, a suit of armor, a stag's head,
and a gallery of "ancient portraits." From the hall "other rooms in seemingly
endless chain opened out, all filled with a truly fabulous collection of antiques
and relics."[2]

As a boy, Poore had traveled with his father to Europe. He is said to have
visited Abbotsford, the imposing turreted castle conceived and built by Sir

Walter Scott. "I have been busied all this season in finishing a sort of a Romance of a house here, built in imitation of an old Scottish manor house," wrote Scott in 1822, "and I think I have attained not unsuccessfully the scrambling style of these venerable edifices."[3] While entertaining the Poores among his antiques, Scott is reported to have encouraged their enthusiasm for his romantic antiquarianism and to have urged Ben: to create an American version of Abbotsford when he grew up.

Whether this is fact or family folklore, the romantic approach to history expressed in the "stone and earth" of Abbotsford became equally apparent at Indian Hill. About 1850 Ben: began expanding his family home, making it considerably less austere than Abbotsford, but extremely picturesque. Gables and turreted towers were blended in a rambling vine-covered stone mansion whose general effect was—to the Victorian eye—romantic and medieval. Leonard Woodman Smith, who had visited Indian Hill as a boy, wrote in 1920 that "I never shall forget my first sight of the impressive stone house with its red roofs gleaming in the sun. It was the first time I had seen such an unusual house, and its round stone towers, its diamond paned windows swinging outward filled my eyes with admiration."[4]

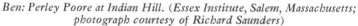

Ben: Perley Poore at Indian Hill. (Essex Institute, Salem, Massachusetts; photograph courtesy of Richard Saunders)

Poore's house grew with his collection. By 1887, the Exeter *News-Letter* reported, it was filled with "ancient looking halls, old fashioned stairways, broad fireplaces, medieval galleries, chambers full of suggestion and all kinds of peepholes in the shape of windows, and of sally ports in the shape of doors. The place is a veritable museum of antiquities."[5] Poore's interest in collecting apparently had begun early, for among the antiquities was a group of objects from Egypt and the Holy Land acquired in his travels as a young man.

Poore was attracted by old things of all kinds—furniture, china, pewter, tools, books, paintings and prints, firearms, and Indian artifacts. His interest extended to old houses. When a historic one was being remodeled or demolished, he would buy paneling, stairs, and mantels to incorporate into his own residence. This is among the earliest instances in America of what was to become an extremely popular practice among collectors. The transplantation of architectural elements from a well-known building is clearly related to the use of wood from a famous source to make relic furniture and other commemorative objects. Poore and his contemporaries undoubtedly felt that the addition of parts of famous old houses added immensely to Indian Hill's interest.

Indian Hill contained paneling from the Old Province House, Boston, which had been remodeled in 1851; paneling from the elegant John Hancock House, Boston, demolished in spite of a great outcry in 1863; fluted pillars from Boston's Old Brattle Street Church; stairs from the Tracy house in Newburyport, where Washington, Lafayette, and other notables reputedly were entertained; and a mantel from the Stuyvesant house, New York. An inventory now in the files of the Society for the Preservation of New England Antiquities shows the Stuyvesant mantel as having been taken to Indian Hill about 1830 when Ben: was only ten years old, and before the trip to Abbotsford. This document, along with several other references in the Indian Hill inventory, indicates that Poore's father had bought antique furnishings and fragments of old houses in the 1820s and 1830s—remarkably early dates for such collecting.

"Indian Hill must have been a delightful place when the Poores were in residence," wrote Josephine Driver in 1953. "From the tallest of the elaborate chimneys to the smallest flower in the perennial border, the place radiated order, beauty and an easy, informal hospitality. . . . The house was generally full of guests, frequently very distinguished ones. . . ."[6]

It was his own distinguished career as a writer, editor, and *bon vivant* that brought Poore into contact with many of the eminent men of his day. He wrote a very popular syndicated column as Washington correspondent for the Boston *Journal*. He was also editor of the *Congressional Directory* (1865) and clerk of the Senate committee on printing public records. Poore was thus in a position to meet powerful men. An obituary described him as having known "everybody of consequence in the capital for 30 years or more . . . a living storehouse of anecdotes, a popular diner-out."[7] He entertained widely both in

Right: *The parlor at Indian Hill, furnished with antiques and incorporating paneling and pilasters from the Province House, Boston. (Society for the Preservation of New England Antiquities)*

Below: *The Fourth of July at Indian Hill, West Newbury, Massachusetts. (Society for the Preservation of New England Antiquities)*

Left: *The colonial kitchen at Indian Hill. (Society for the Preservation of New England Antiquities)*

Washington and at Indian Hill: "And what entertainments, festivals and con-ferences were provided at Indian Hill each summer! The ploughing contests . . . the agricultural meetings . . . the great Fourth of July celebrations, featured by a dance in the spacious barn cleared for the occasion and by fireworks on the hill. . . ."[8]

One report describes the Fourth of July festivities held in 1875. A rifle battalion set up tents and camped on Poore's front lawn; there were appear-ances by a brass band, a choir, and a speaker, which were followed by a collation and then a sham fight by the battalion. Three thousand people at-tended the celebration, which, says a contemporary account, "passed off to the delight of all present."[9]

Ben: Perley Poore had married Virginia Dodge in 1849. She was from a wealthy Southern family, and Southern customs were in evidence at Indian Hill (and at the Poores' establishment in Washington). A guest remembered that "when one drove into the grounds, one colored servant would come out and hold the horse or horses, another one at the door to take one's card and the whole place was conducted on the line of southern hospitality."[10]

Once settled in, guests were entertained much as they would have been at an English country house. There was

> a walk about the garden and to the top of the hill to enjoy the view; an inspection of the barn and livestock and of the particular experiment that the Major [Poore] was interested in at the time; a drive about the country and especially a tour of the house conducted by the host himself, to show and explain his collections. . . . The replica of an old printing-office was also shown, where the principle [sic] object was a primeval printing-press once used by Ben Franklin himself. Nor would the Indian room be forgotten with its unrivalled showing of arrowheads, weapons and cooking and planting implements, some of which had been picked up in the West Newbury fields.
>
> The old Colonial kitchen, the rare china pieces and the shelves of valu-able books in the owner's library all were proudly exhibited. This tour of the house might take one hour or several, depending on whether the guest's interest was merely politely perfunctory or genuinely enthusiastic.[11]

Poore lived at Indian Hill only in the summer, for his job required spending most of the year in the capital. He was as diligent and successful in newspaper work as in collecting. Many years after his death, a reporter for *The Christian Science Monitor* paid Poore this tribute: "His ability and reliability were of such unprecedented character . . . that his work is still emulated by Washing-ton correspondents. These count it a notable honor to be invited to the mem-bership of 50 in the Gridiron Club which Mr. Poore founded and of which he was the first president."[12] Poore's influence continues to be felt, for an invita-tion to join the Gridiron Club remains an honor among journalists today.

Poore's interests were wide. Besides his newspaper work and his collecting, there were farming and forestry experiments always in progress at Indian Hill. He also had a sense of humor. Unfortunately, he could not be present to witness the plight of President Taft, who visited Indian Hill after Poore's death. Some of the passages between rooms were so narrow that the portly Taft became wedged in one in an embarrassing manner.

Poore bet a friend that Millard Fillmore would carry Massachusetts in the presidential election of 1856. The agreement was that the loser would wheel a barrel of apples from his home to the State House in Boston. When he lost the bet, Poore honored his pledge. It took two-and-a-half days for him to walk the thirty-six miles, but he finally arrived, wheeling his barrow amid "at least 30,000 enthusiastic spectators."[13]

Ben: Perley Poore's interest in his furnishings sprang from a fascination with their history and associations, and from the desire to create a romantic atmosphere. As he is reputed to have been a great raconteur, he must have taken pleasure in pointing out to guests such items as the magnificent mahogany sleigh bed with a gilded eagle on each corner that had once belonged to Napoleon; the paneling from the Province House; and the piece of carpet on which Lincoln supposedly stood to give his second inaugural address. He also possessed cast-off White House furniture and china. According to one writer, "The White House in Washington is usually refurnished when a new president comes in and many of the old pieces were given to the Major so that the Indian Hill house has some pieces of furniture, and some pieces of china from almost all the different administrations." Two of the four adjoining parlors at Indian Hill were furnished with "furniture from Mt. Vernon, Major Poore bought them before the Mt. Vernon association purchased the real estate. The association would give any price to get these two parlor sets."[14]

One writer reports Poore as having once told a friend that he spent all his spare funds on collecting. Another says that he actively pursued his hobby both at Indian Hill and in the South. Yet a third recounts the story of an aunt's sale of an old Essex County family cradle to Major Poore one afternoon when the rest of the family were out. Having resolved to make use of their absence to rid the house of some "trash," this misguided aunt "stood on her door-step bargaining with the purchaser." Major Poore passed by and immediately asked, " 'How much will you take for the cradle?' . . . She named a price. 'Done' he agreed and drove off with his prize while the dealer stood open-mouthed."[15]

The decisiveness that characterized him in this transaction is apparent in another story. Poore was reported to buy "outright entire rooms-full of furniture or other articles that attracted his interest, moving it all to Indian Hill and having a room built to house it."[16] In doing this, Poore was a bellwether in the collecting movement. Fifty years later, super-collectors like Henry Ford and Francis Garvan would become famous for buying entire collections of American antiques, as J. P. Morgan had done with the art and antiques of Europe. Poore was the earliest, so far as we know, to collect American antiques in this grand manner.

Although Poore died in 1887, Indian Hill survived into the twentieth century. In 1939, the family donated the property to the Society for the Preservation of New England Antiquities. Much of it burned down in the late 1960s, making it necessary to rely on undated photographs in the society's files for an idea of how Indian Hill looked in Poore's day.

Poore is important not just as one of our first major collectors of American antiques but as an influence on subsequent collecting. From Henry Sleeper's magnificently atmospheric Beauport, begun about 1907, to Henry du Pont's equally romantic Winterthur, begun in the 1920s, the influence of Poore's perception of antiques as elements of a romantic and/or inspiring interior is evident.

Poore's basic motive for gathering antiques, however, was his fascination with their historical and political associations. He took great pride and pleasure in telling stories about them, and saw no inconsistency in displaying unrelated objects together. What was important was for each piece to have its own tale, and to enhance the overall romantic atmosphere of Indian Hill.

Poore's exhibition table at Indian Hill.
(Society for the Preservation of New England Antiquities)

Chapter 4

Edward Lamson Henry

Artist and Antiquary

IN BOTH HIS PAINTING AND HIS COLLECTING, E. L. HENRY (1841–1919) EXPRESSED nostalgia for the old, homogeneous America that was being transformed by immigrants and industry. Born in Charleston, South Carolina, Henry studied art in New York, Philadelphia, Paris, and Rome. By 1862, he was established in a studio in New York. The subject of his paintings was often some quaint or picturesque aspect of rural life in the past. They suited the taste of his contemporaries perfectly, and by 1869 Henry had become a member of the National Academy of Design.

Many of his paintings show antiques and old houses. The antiques seem to be American, including some presumably from his own collection. Henry's correspondence, however, indicates that he bought foreign things as well. As with Davis, Poore, and the sanitary fair exhibits, a primary goal was to collect curiosities, or objects related to a famous person or event. A photograph of an arrangement of things that Henry lent to an exhibition in 1872[1] reveals their miscellaneous nature. It includes several portraits of George Washington, a Philadelphia Chippendale chair, a spinning wheel, an exotic epergne, an imported clock, and a set of dishes. Henry's skill and experience in composition are apparent in the thoughtful arrangement of varying shapes and sizes, but the

E. L. Henry. Photograph by Jessie Tarbox Beal. (New York State Museum Division of Historical Services)

objects have no consistent style, period, material, or use. Except for the group of Washington likenesses, each seems chosen for a different associational reason.

This impression is confirmed by Mrs. Henry's description of her husband's collecting. Henry was "very fond of collecting not only everything that would be useful in his work," she wrote, "but an old mahogany table, chair, desk, clock, even old china, not only had value to him for its age and beauty of workmanship, but he would draw some story or some allegory from it." Mrs. Henry told of her husband's great fondness for an old tall clock; he often reflected on the parallels between the clock's life and the course of human existence.[2]

The catalogue to the auction of Henry's "Paintings, rare old engravings, colonial furniture, bric-a-brac" held in 1887 included glass, ceramics, clocks, mirrors, and textiles as well.[3] These things were undoubtedly the contents of Henry's New York City residence, which he gave up that year.

Entries in the catalogue point up the importance attached to associations. Number 77, an "egg-shell cup and saucer," was described as one of six presented by the Mikado to President Lincoln and given by him in turn to Charles Sumner, the famous abolitionist senator from Massachusetts. Rather as an afterthought, the catalogue added that this was "supposed to be the finest example of the rare egg-shell ever seen out of the Imperial Palace." Number 132, a "Very fine mahogany cabinet ball feet," had come from the collection of Henry's friend and fellow antiquary William Kulp. The compiler of the catalogue obviously considered the history of the object more important than a detailed description: "This piece, when found, was in such bad order that it was rebuilt by Mr. Kulp, & the drawers were made from wood taken from Mr. Penn's house, which was being demolished."[4]

The basic motive for Henry's collecting is reflected in the way he used antiques for his paintings. On canvas, the specific associations of antiques necessarily gave way to the general feeling that they helped to create, of harmonious peace in an idealized past. His painting of a couple examining old china, taking each piece carefully from its place in an eighteenth-century corner cupboard, conveys the sense of quiet pleasure in a cultivated pursuit. In the atmospheric painting *The Widower*, an old gentleman sits in a delicate Hepplewhite side chair with his back turned, his elbow resting on a table set for tea with old silver and china. An early portrait hangs on the wall between a Queen Anne

The Old Clock on the Stairs, *by E. L. Henry. Painted in the hall of the home of William Kulp, Henry's friend and fellow antiquary. (New York State Museum, Division of Historical Services)*

side chair and a wing chair (the model for the latter can be seen in a photograph of the artist's New York studio). *The Widower* suggests refinement, tranquillity, and order.

Photographs have survived of both of Henry's studios. One was at 3 North Washington Square in New York City, the other in the house he designed and built at Cragsmoor, a small Catskill community he helped transform into an art colony. Like Ben: Perley Poore, Henry incorporated old woodwork into his interiors. Mantelpieces, a carved staircase, columns, and other architectural elements from old houses gave his rooms character and interest. Elizabeth McClausland, author of the definitive catalogue of Henry's life and work, believes he bought them from "the Second Avenue wreckers" in New York.[5] Henry's Cragsmoor house was described by a contemporary in 1885: "Mr. Henry, in building a studio, found great difficulty in impressing his ideas of architecture on the local carpenters. 'If you have the rafters show like that,' they complained, 'and stick the roof all over with little gables, you'll make your studio look like one of them old Dutch manor-houses at Kingston.' "[6]

The serenity of the "old Dutch manor-houses" and of his paintings is missing from Henry's own rooms, which were cluttered in the Victorian manner. Paintings covered the walls of the New York studio solidly, interrupted only by a delicate neoclassical mantel crowded with vases and urns and surmounted by an Empire looking glass. The paintings proceeded unhindered to the corner, where they paused briefly to make room for a cupboard overflowing with old china. Furniture, both antique and colonial-revival, competed for attention with Oriental carpets.

It is probable that Henry no longer actively collected antiques after 1887; his Cragsmoor house was full, and he may have wanted to concentrate on his costumes and carriages. They were described in a memorial after his death by the Century Association:

Henry's antiques-filled studio on Washington Square, New York City. (New York State Museum, Division of Historical Services)

Mr. Henry's house at Cragsmoor was a museum of curios after his own heart and in line with his peculiar genius. A collector of actual stage coaches and postchaises of a century ago stands in a class by himself; and when these unusual relics were supplemented by the actual costumes, the arms, even the

tools of that distant period, it is easy to understand how the atmosphere of his mountain retreat, was the atmosphere of his paintings.[7]

As the memorial suggests, both costumes and carriages from Henry's collection appeared in his work. Elizabeth McClausland says that Henry's costume collection was famous. He and Mrs. Henry often donned antique clothes for charades, and Henry had the reputation of having a costume for "every period, every age, child, man and woman." These he used on his models when he was painting period pictures.[8]

In 1870, Henry wrote the sculptor Edward Valentine:

I never thought to write you before that my great reputation, my stock in trade is that of an antiquary. I know and have illustrated nearly all the old houses and churches in Philadelphia, New York, Newport, and other places where there is anything worth looking up and, not least of all, the James River. I have painted some of the gorgeous old manors on the James River.[9]

As early as 1859, Henry was drawing pictures of colonial buildings. While serving with the Union troops in the Civil War, he drew the famous Virginia

Mr. and Mrs. Henry at Cragsmoor, wearing colonial costumes from Henry's collection. (Photograph courtesy of Kaycee Thompson)

mansion Westover. His depiction of the John Hancock House in Boston preserves an image of that elegant Georgian structure—perhaps the handsomest in America before it was, in Henry's words, "taken down for common modern houses about 1863."[10]

Henry's concern for historic buildings extended beyond setting them down on canvas and paper. "There is much evidence in the Henry Collection [at the New York State Museum] that Henry fought to mobilize public opinion to preserve historic landmarks," comments Elizabeth McClausland. She cites a letter from William Kulp about saving old houses in Newport. Mrs. Henry wrote of her husband that he was "greatly interested in keeping the old landmarks of the city [of New York] for coming generations." With Kulp, he restored Independence Hall in Philadelphia.[11]

The effectiveness of Henry's efforts at historic preservation is not known. His paintings and drawings, however, are important pictorial records of buildings since destroyed. Furthermore, his collecting of antiques and actual architectural elements was active preservation on a different scale. He extended this work beyond his own desires by acting as agent for his friends. Henry engaged in still another kind of preservation by painting genre and historical subjects. Although he may have oversentimentalized, he captured aspects of a way of life that was disappearing from America.

Henry's goal was to take a dramatic or sentimental situation and paint it affectingly. The resulting works range from panoramic scenes such as *A Presentation of Colors to the First Colored Regiment of New York . . .* (1869) to rural genre subjects like *A Quiet Corner in the Door* (1873), in which a grandfather, a child, a dog, and a Queen Anne chair are grouped in the open doorway of an old house. His paintings became very popular in his own day, and reproductions were being published by 1887. His following diminished, however, from the turn of the century until his death in 1919. According to an obituary in *The New York Evening Post,*

> Without claiming for Mr. Henry a dominant place, there are few American artists who have better served their country in preserving for the future the quaint and provincial aspects of a life which has all but disappeared since we have become the melting pot of other races than our own.[12]

II

Antiques as Symbols of Taste and Background

After the Civil War, "men were divided not by their regions
or their roots, but by objects and notions that
might be anywhere and could be everywhere. Americans
lived now not merely in a half-explored continent of mountains
and rivers and mines, but in a continent of categories."
Daniel Boorstin, *The Americans,* 1965

A GENERATION OF SERIOUS COLLECTORS AROSE IN THE DECADE CONTAINING THE Centennial of American independence. They were going full tilt by the 1880s, when Cummings Davis and Ben: Perley Poore had reached the final stages of their collecting careers. The new generation was influenced, like its predecessors, by specific patriotic and historical associations. It also shared the belief that had found expression in the New England kitchens at the sanitary fairs and the Philadelphia Centennial celebration: antiques symbolized the high quality of home life in early America.

The interest of these newer collectors was more serious and thorough, however. They began, in the words of Dr. Irving W. Lyon of Hartford, "a somewhat systematic study" of their antiques, with more stress on classification.[1] What they gathered might still range widely in material, date, form, and place of origin; but their collections were usually more cohesive than the earlier ones. They were seeking not only the relics of famous men and events—which were still, and remain today, premium items—but also forms that would express the spirit, and shed light on the daily habits, of their forefathers.

Who, they asked, were these Pilgrims and Puritans and Revolutionary heroes? What were they like? What objects did they use daily, and how did they regard them? This new generation believed that American antiques deserved recognition for more than their associational value. In fact, they were engaged in a pioneering effort at what Holger Cahill has called "a kind of archeology."[2]

The new collectors also turned to American antiques because they believed that much of what machines produced was shoddy and poorly designed. The new methods for manufacture of furniture, silver, glass, and ceramics had initiated the decline of hand craftsmanship as early as the 1830s. From then on, objects were produced in vast quantities, but often of inferior materials. As a result, English arts-and-crafts reformers like Henry Cole, John Ruskin, and William Morris began, in their different ways, to campaign vigorously against bad taste and poor design.

It was the Englishman Charles Locke Eastlake, however, who made the most American converts to the arts-and-crafts point of view. His book *Hints on Household Taste* went through eight American editions, beginning in 1872. In 1878 an American advocate, Clarence Cook, published *The House Beautiful*, in which he adapted the English reformers' ideas to American needs.

Despite the interest generated by Eastlake and Cook, it was still a relatively small minority of Americans who devoted thoughtful attention to questions like these. The new collectors were among them. Beauty and taste were crucial in shaping character, according to the arts-and-crafts view, and the general public was being degraded by the tasteless, graceless assembly-line products in their homes. The collectors felt that American antiques, on the other hand, embodied the superior values and virtues of seventeenth- and eighteenth-century craftsmen, and of home life in the society they had served. Antiques could therefore not only represent the spirit of those earlier times but also transmit it; with their fine workmanship, high-quality materials, and good design, they could inspire those who came in daily contact with them.

Besides, good *new* furnishings of the kind that satisfied criteria recommended by Eastlake and the others were expensive. The rising generation of collectors were mainly middle-class professionals: doctors, lawyers, teachers, and businessmen. American antiques, which were not then in great demand, were within their financial reach. By becoming collectors, these men and women gained both an engrossing hobby and furnishings that were attractive.

The growing arts-and-crafts interest in home furnishings—antique or otherwise—of spiritual merit and good taste, and the continuing love of antiques for their quaintness and storytelling value, were equally apparent at the Albany Bicentennial Loan Exhibition of 1886. The official program explained the purpose of the exhibition:

. . . We have here collected into one pleasing museum the treasures of our homes, to exemplify our perception of taste, our artistic culture, our veneration for the past. . . . And there is much that comes to us redolent with sweet suggestions of the past; with richness of design or material more or less perhaps, or possibly with no especial artistic beauty at all, except the quaintness which in such matters is often beauty's hand-maiden, yet none the less of priceless value to us, since each piece whispers some story of the past.[3]

Earlier, at the Centennial exhibitions and the sanitary fairs, antiques had been regarded generally as curiosities. Here, they are described as treasures—but not, as yet, true works of art.

This represented a major development in point of view, even though many of the earlier attitudes persisted. Furthermore, the Albany display was more selective. Although it had the crowded, unsorted look so typical of both domestic interiors and public exhibitions of the period, its organizers must have exercised considerable restraint in turning down objects for display. Twenty years earlier, nearly anything had been accepted at the sanitary fairs, and historical-association items like a tablecloth labeled as having come over on the *Mayflower* were shown as relics whose importance was about equal to that of "a petrified cactus" and "the tongue of a fish from the Amazon." The Albany

Exhibition of "Old Furniture, Ancient Dress and General Relics" at Albany's Bicentennial Loan Exhibition, 1886. (Collection, Albany Institute of History and Art)

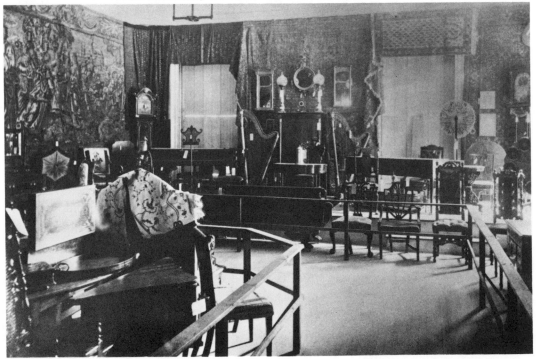

Bicentennial Loan Exhibition, on the other hand, was fairly well confined to furniture and other objects with a local or patriotic history—things either made or used in America. Unbridled enthusiasm for all kinds of curiosities waned slowly, however, and the "Dress of a Bedouin Sheik of to-day" crept in, along with a few other exotic imports.[4]

A more rigorous attempt to adhere to a specific theme, and to exhibit antiques and paintings logically, characterized the exhibition held in New York during the centennial celebration of Washington's inauguration. A strong patriotic and sentimental motive was combined with the desire to select and exhibit systematically. Now largely forgotten, the observance of Washington's inauguration was a major event in the year 1889. It was, according to *The History of the Centennial Celebration of the Inauguration of George Washington as First President of the United States*, "more grandly and sacredly observed" throughout the United States "than the celebration of any other event in the history of the country." The commemoration included, in New York's Metropolitan Opera House, one of the best-organized exhibitions of American antiques, or "relics," held up to that time. The theme was clearly stated. The scope of the display of

> Portraits and Relics was to be confined to those relating to Washington, his Cabinet, members of the First Congress, members of the Constitutional Convention, and others connected with the inauguration of Washington, together with pictures of scenes and localities pertaining to the period. It is the purpose of the committee, therefore, to exclude . . . such pictures or relics as properly belong to the Revolutionary period only, in order to avoid a repetition of certain features of the exhibitions held in connection with the Centennial Celebration at Philadelphia in 1876.[5]

This was possibly the first exhibition to set such a specific goal and to define its limits so carefully. The committee had succeeded in gathering a group of objects so impressive, according to *The History*, as to be "pronounced on all sides . . . the most complete and interesting collection of portraits and memorials of Washington and the men and women of his time ever brought together. . . . Such an opportunity for study and comparison in this field may . . . never be afforded again."[6] Here is evidence of a new seriousness—up to that time, only the furniture display at Salem's Plummer Hall in 1875 had attempted to sort and classify antiques logically. But the exhibition made an excellent beginning at standards that have come to be important in comparable modern events. There was a theme, so that the visitor started out with a point of view beyond mere diffuse curiosity. One single period was selected, and the ceramics, furniture, and metalwares of that period were displayed so that the viewer could focus both on their design and decoration and on the spirit that pervaded them.

Exhibition of silver and other antiques, held at the
Metropolitan Opera House, New York City, during the
celebration of the Centennial of the Inauguration of George
Washington. (Courtesy of the New-York Historical Society,
New York City)

The sentimental and anecdotal attitude toward American antiques that had prevailed earlier remained very much in evidence. The inauguration centennial exhibition was conceived as an adjunct to a patriotic event, and its contents were meant to inspire viewers in patriotic and moralistic ways.

Another significant aspect of this event was that it included one exhibition within another. The leading silver authority of the day, John H. Buck, an Englishman who had worked for the Gorham Company and served as curator of metalwork at the Metropolitan Museum, volunteered to organize a display of silver of the inauguration period. There were 352 pieces, including heirlooms from such distinguished dynasties as the Schuylers, Cadwaladers, Livingstons, and De Peysters. This was an impressive start at gathering silver that had come down in American families— although the exhibition was by no means confined to objects by American silversmiths. An attempt was made to identify each piece by place of origin, maker, and date.

Although *Harper's Weekly* for April 27, 1889, reported that "the silver exhibit is by far the finest ever brought together in the United States," the writer qualified his enthusiasm by adding, "Early American plate has bullion value, is curious, but has little artistic merit." His stress on the associational and inspirational aspects illustrates the persistence of this attitude toward antiques along with the newer, more serious one. The *Harper's Weekly* article concluded:

We treasure the relics of illustrious men. We are so constituted that though conscious that our welfare, peace, and happiness have depended on their acts, these seem less tangible than the material objects they have left behind them. In this hard matter-of-fact world, it is well that one should idealize something, be it the sword a hero has worn or the spurs he drove into his horse's flanks when he urged on his steed fighting for a just cause. The shreds of cloth worked with gold, though stained and tarnished, are more

than mere shoulder straps. They are the real live pictures, the active illustrations, of a national drama. They are part and parcel of history.[7]

Land had been the source of status and stability among the forebears of many in the new collecting generation; but with the Industrial Revolution and the urbanization of the East, those families had moved off the land and into the cities. The collectors had thus become interested in antiques partly as a replacement for the lost land—a symbol of their descent in old and respectable (though usually not aristocratic) American families. Because they could no longer define themselves in terms of farm ownership, they turned to a more abstract concept: the American past, and the enterprise of the men who had

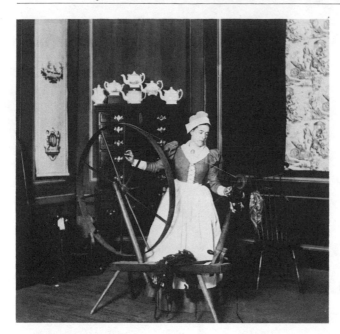

The Colonial Revival created increased interest in antique objects and old-time occupations. View of the corner of the tea room at the Loan Collection of the Massachusetts Society, Daughters of the American Revolution. This photograph taken in Salem on April 19, 1897. (Courtesy, Essex Institute, Salem, Massachusetts)

built and defended the nation. By searching out and living with the objects made and used by such men, the collectors forged a spiritual alliance with them. That approach met a serious psychological need, but it helped to perpetuate a frequently over-romantic picture of the American past.

By the 1890s, then, American antiques had become—in a limited way and among a limited group—status symbols. If acquired by inheritance, they represented social background, for a family in which they descended had been in America since colonial or early Federal times. The serious collectors of the 1890s reflected this attitude, as well as concern for the good taste demanded by arts-and-crafts reformers. In their eyes, American antiques provided evidence of both background and taste.

Collectors in the seventies had emphasized the courage and vision of the Puritan forefathers; collectors of the nineties focused also on American taste and refinement, as displayed in the eighteenth and early nineteenth centuries. Serious collectors now concentrated more heavily on Queen Anne, Chippendale, and early Federal objects; their lighter lines and urbane ornament represented a delicacy not present in seventeenth-century pieces, although the latter were still often sought.

Early American home life was increasingly thought to have been refined, rather than simple, honest, and virtuous. Instead of envisioning early American homes as sturdy, unpretentious Puritan dwellings, collectors in the nineties were much more likely to conjure up tastefully furnished Georgian manor houses.

As early as 1875, Eliza Greatorex, E. L. Henry's friend and fellow artist, had foreshadowed the new romanticized version of life in pre-Revolutionary America. In the text accompanying her book of etchings of eighteenth-century New York houses, *Old New York from the Battery to Bloomingdale*, Mrs. Greatorex said of those former days:

> Social life was cultivated and enjoyed, and the distinctions of class were observed and acquiesced in, apparently without any loss of self-respect or happiness to those who acknowledged the refined, the wealthy, and the intellectual superiority of others. . . . Many are questioning today whether, in exchanging this condition of society for a more levelling democracy, we have made any true progress in the higher life.[8]

Reaction against the recent immigrants from Europe, though not generally explicit, underlay to some extent the work of Henry and Greatorex, the writings of Cook, and the activity of the collectors. Over the period from 1820 to 1870, five million English, Irish, and German immigrants entered America. Between 1870 and 1900, many millions more Europeans poured in. "Around 1900," as the historians Nevins and Commager have put it, "there developed a widespread feeling that it was time to call a halt on unrestricted immigration. Labor resented the competition; 'old-stock' Americans feared that the racial strain was being debased by so many Slavic and Mediterranean newcomers; the average man thought that the United States had people and problems enough without inviting more."[9]

Furthermore, the educated classes feared that their native America would disappear beneath the cultures of the immigrants. One reaction to that specter was to reject the newcomers altogether, and to try to impede their progress up the ladder of security and success. Another—possible only for the very rich— was physical isolation in a large house situated far from the tenements. A more feasible solution for most was to create psychological distance from recent immigrants by emphasis on a family's presence in America for generations. Organizations like the Daughters of the American Revolution, the Sons of the American Revolution, and the Colonial Dames served this purpose; and for the small group of serious collectors, so did possession of American antiques.

Not everybody shared the collectors' perceptions. They were well ahead of most of their nineteenth-century contemporaries in appreciating the soundness and beauty of American antiques. European culture went back so much further that many Americans unquestioningly considered European antiques more valuable. The very rich lived "among foreign furnishings and foreign works of art, in as great a variety and profusion as could be managed."[10] Therefore, wrote Clarence Cook, "It is to be hoped that no one will let himself be laughed out of his fancy for a good piece of 'old American furniture,' to the extent of letting it slip out of his hands. . . ."[11]

Collectors thus felt a need to prove, both to other Americans and to the rest of the world, that colonial craftsmen had produced fine furniture and silver. One of the major revelations of Dr. Irving Lyon's book on New England furniture was that the fine pieces he illustrated had been made in New England, and not imported from abroad. And in an article entitled "Old Silver," published by *Harper's* in 1896, Dr. Theodore S. Woolsey argued that Americans would derive more enjoyment from collecting and studying their own silver than from European wares.[12]

The colonial revival, which became visible in both furniture and architecture in the 1880s (and which has been with us ever since), included and affected the attitudes described above. It was an important part of the milieu in which the collectors of the 1880s and 1890s lived, and it helps explain the gradual growth of enthusiasm for American antiques among Americans at large. It encompassed far more, however, than the exhibitions of antiques and relics, the writings of Clarence Cook, and the paintings of E. L. Henry. Any manifestation of "colonial" design—genuine or ersatz, good or bad—was included in the colonial revival.

One ironic aspect was the factory-made "colonial" furniture that appeared in the 1880s. Since arts-and-crafts reformers had often held up the handcraft traditions of earlier periods, including the colonial, as an example to contemporary cabinetmakers, many people began to think that things in an antique *style* would do just as well as the genuine article. But colonial-revival furniture often incorporated everything the reformers were protesting against: poor design and workmanship, low-grade wood, and lack of understanding of the style (or mixture of styles) being copied.

Many Americans were drawn to the colonial-revival movement by nostalgia, by a need to associate themselves with old, established families, or by eagerness to establish their good taste; most, however, didn't really care about design and construction. This lack of discrimination was less in evidence among tastemakers and designers who thought along arts-and-crafts lines. And it was rare among serious collectors, to whom genuineness was essential.

The variation in degrees of insistence on genuine colonial work during the 1880s and 1890s is clearly illustrated in the order books of the cabinetmaker Ernest Hagen (now at the New-York Historical Society). Covering the years 1880 to 1886 at Hagen's firm, Meier & Hagen, these books provide a fascinating insight into upper- and upper-middle-class furnishing fashions in New York.

Tucked in among orders for chic new overstuffed chairs and divans are others related to a wide variety of furniture, including antiques. Some entries make it clear that besides procuring and restoring antique furniture, Meier & Hagen sometimes destroyed it. When antiques were not actually taken apart to

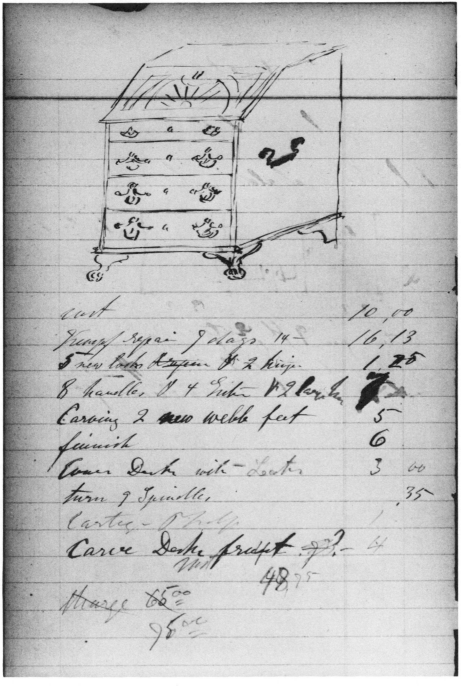

Slant-front Chippendale desk with colonial-revival embellishments,
as sketched in the order book of New York cabinetmaker Ernest Hagen, 1884.
(Courtesy of the New-York Historical Society)

provide old wood for new furniture, they were often repaired, recarved, or refinished past recognition.

The tendency during the late nineteenth century to lump together all hand-made, pre-industrial age furniture has often been noted. The adjective "colonial" was used freely to embrace furniture made from the seventeenth century down to the first third of the nineteenth. In Hagen's order books, it apparently referred to colonial-revival pieces as well. The famous glassmaker and interior designer Louis Comfort Tiffany placed an order on May 7, 1885, for "10 Maple Colonial Dining chairs." The accompanying sketches show ladder-back chairs with a high arched crest—definitely a colonial-revival design rather than a colonial one.

Both Hagen's and Tiffany's customers were people of taste and means. Their use of antiques and antique-style furniture indicates that by the 1880s antiques had come to be not only acceptable but fashionable. Yet these people were different from the true collectors, for in their interiors, antiques and colonial-revival pieces were mixed with furnishings of other kinds to create "tasteful" settings.

The colonial revival was apparent at the next American world's fair after Philadelphia. A number of state buildings at the Columbian Exposition of 1893 were either copies of specific colonial structures or in the colonial style. Those interiors furnished with antiques were meant to look less like exhibits (as the

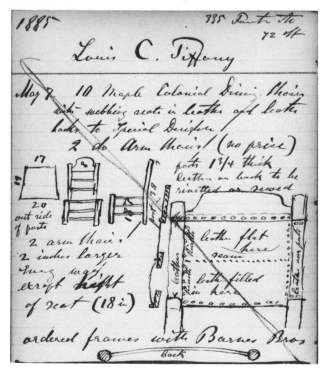

Louis Comfort Tiffany's design for "colonial" chairs, as sketched in Ernest Hagen's order book, 1885. (Courtesy of the New-York Historical Society)

New England kitchens had done) than genteel reception rooms in private houses. In their expanding role as symbols of taste and background, antiques had moved from the kitchen to the parlor. Owners of houses furnished with American antiques were more concerned with elegance than with anecdotal qualities.

Antiques were by no means a major theme at the exposition. However, the office of Mrs. Potter Palmer, president of the exposition's Board of Lady Managers, provided a dramatic example of their rise in social status. Mrs. Palmer's own enormous turreted castle on Lake Michigan was eclectically furnished in the fashionable Moorish, Renaissance, and Louis XVI modes; but American chairs and tables of the Queen Anne, Chippendale, and Empire periods occupied her exposition office. The antiques, gathered by the women of New Jersey, radiated refinement—as they stood upon a vivid Victorian carpet beneath a ceiling festooned with fishnets.

The Pennsylvania building, described as "practically a reproduction of Independence Hall, Philadelphia,"[13] contained the Liberty Bell. Speaking of its symbolism upon its arrival at the fair, ex-President Benjamin Harrison reminded his countrymen that the absorption of immigrants was part of the American tradition:

> This old bell was made in England, but it had to be re-cast in America before it was attuned to proclaim the right of self-government and the equal rights of men, and therein it was a type of what our institutions have been doing for that great teeming throng of immigrants from all lands who heard its voice over the great waters, and came here subjects to be re-cast into free American citizens.[14]

At the end of the nineteenth century, however, collectors and devotees of American antiques were seeking not to educate immigrants but to establish their own social superiority over the newer arrivals. In his novel *Our Mutual Friend*, published in 1865, Charles Dickens had reflected this attitude toward antiques as it existed in England. He described the Veneerings, a couple possessed of immense but new riches:

> . . . in the Veneering establishment, from the hall-chairs with the new coat of arms to the grand pianoforte with the new action, and upstairs again to the new fire-escape, all things were in a state of high varnish and polish. And what was observable in the furniture, was observable in the Veneerings—the surface smelt a little too much of the workshop and was a trifle sticky.[15]

Chapter 5

Clarence Cook

Antiques in The House Beautiful

Among the most persuasive advocates of good taste in American homes was Clarence Chatham Cook (1828–1900). The "miracles of ugliness" he and his fellow critics protested were described by the novelist William Dean Howells in *A Modern Instance* (1882). Referring to a house in Boston's West End, Howells wrote:

> As for the interior of the house, it had been furnished, once for all, in the worst style of that most tasteless period of household art, which prevailed from 1840 to 1870; and it would be impossible to say which were most hideous, the carpets or the chandeliers, the curtains or the chairs and sofas; crude colors, lumpish and meaningless forms, abounded in a rich and horrible discord.[1]

Clarence Cook's most successful book, *The House Beautiful* (1878), was a collection of articles that guided his readers away from "lumpish and meaningless forms" toward simple, graceful ones. In the articles, which had originally appeared in *Scribner's Monthly Magazine* during the years 1875 to 1877, Cook adapted English arts-and-crafts ideas to American needs, American design, and American sources of supply. He had assimilated Ruskin's romantic notion that the Gothic spirit encompassed the individualism, freedom, and richness of expression which machines had erased, and that the products of the Gothic age embodied its spirit. Cook invested the artifacts of colonial America with similarly romantic, but somewhat different, intangible attributes. He combined the arts-and-crafts appreciation of antiques' exemplary designs and craftsmanship with a respect for their value as symbols of descent in old American families. American antiques were, he felt, the "outcome of a refined and cultured time."[2]

Clarence Cook was born in Dorchester, Massachusetts (the home of pioneer collector H. Eugene Bolles), of parents with deep American roots. In the 1870s Cook's nephew, the colonial-revival architect Arthur Little, wrote to Henry F. Waters of Salem, asking whether he could bring "my uncle Mr. Cook and his wife to see your collection . . . Mr. Cook has written some articles on Furniture in the Scribner's and so is very much interested."[3] Cook's association with

Illustrated grouping of seventeenth-century New England furniture.
From Clarence Cook's The House Beautiful, *1878.*

enthusiastic New England collectors is reflected in his frequent recommendation of antiques as tasteful furnishings.

Although he achieved recognition as an art critic in New York, Cook retained his New Englander's belief in the importance of family tradition and heirlooms, and of the status they conferred:

> In the rage that has sprung up of late for "grandfathers" and "grandmothers,"—a kind of thing till very lately ignored if not despised, in the bumptious arrogance of our social youthfulness,—it adds inestimably to the value of sideboards, andirons, and old china, if they have come to us by descent, and haven't had to be hunted up in a chaise. But everybody can't have a grandfather, nor things that came over in the "Mayflower," and those of us who have not drawn these prizes in life's lottery must do the best we can under the circumstances.[4]

Taste, however, and not merely antiques or family background, was Cook's central concern. He advocated well-designed contemporary goods, as well, in his campaign to encourage people of all levels of wealth to furnish their houses attractively. For, he said, "when people are spending money in furnishing their houses, they will find it costs no more to get pretty things, things that are in good taste."[5] However, he warned that the reader must supply the taste himself, for the author could only guide him. Cook believed that since many of his readers could not afford the best modern furnishings, antiques might be the answer, although he did say that antiques were becoming more expensive.

The general usefulness of most antiques appealed to Cook, too. "In making this furniture," he wrote, "our ancestors were aiming at lightness of form, economy of space and delicacy of execution. All the best pieces are finished with extreme care, and they are so well put together—so skillfully and so conscientiously—as in many cases to have defied the wear and tear of nearly a century. . . ."[6]

Cook thus urged his readers to buy antiques and create surroundings that reflected their own good sense and taste. He advised patronizing dealers and scouring the countryside to find old furnishings—blue-and-white "India China," as well as oak, walnut, and mahogany furniture. The result, he said, would be many satisfying hours spent "picking up" old things to blend in interesting and tasteful interiors.

The fact that people were actually beginning to buy antiques struck Cook as "one of the best signs of returning good taste in a community that has long been the victim to the whims and impositions of foreign fashions."[7] In this, he echoed the thinking of an earlier American tastemaker, the horticulturalist and landscape architect Andrew Jackson Downing.

After his graduation from Harvard in 1849, Cook had studied with Downing and his assistant Calvert Vaux at Downing's country estate on the Hudson at Newburgh, New York. His work with these two men was invaluable in training his eye in line and proportion, but he chose to teach and write rather than emulate his mentors in designing houses and landscapes. Although Downing was killed in a steamboat accident in 1852, his influence is apparent in Cook's appreciation of harmonious and natural arrangements, and in his ability to adapt foreign ideas to American needs.

Downing must also have fostered Cook's concern with developing a national taste, for Downing was among the first Americans to urge, as the English reformers had done, that attractive surroundings were a civilizing force. "So long as men are forced to dwell in log huts and follow a hunter's life," wrote Downing, "we must not be surprised at lynch law and the use of the bowie knife. But, when smiling lawns and tasteful cottages begin to embellish a country, we know that order and culture are established."[8] This belief in the power of environment is one that appears again and again in the collecting saga. It is particularly prominent in the writings of the china collectors, who deplored the thick plain white crockery that furnished so many American tables, and in other early collectors' belief in the value of re-creating early American home

A Rhode Island blockfront chest of drawers and a Chippendale looking glass. From Cook's The House Beautiful, *1878.*

life. Cook's *The House Beautiful* was the result of his own similar conviction.

Clarence Cook's attention to his countrymen's taste in home furnishings was one aspect of his concern with art in general. He made his reputation as a critic with a series of caustic articles on the paintings exhibited at the New York Sanitary Fair of 1864. "His spirited art column in the *New York Tribune*, 1863–69," wrote a biographer, "was read by everyone, but so scathing, almost brutal, were his attacks on contemporary work that a delegation of his victims visited Horace Greeley to protest (to that editor's amusement), and Cook was feared rather than loved, by American artists."[9]

Although he was an acerbic critic, Cook exemplified in his own person the cultivation he had described appreciatively in *The House Beautiful*. A biographer wrote:

> Clarence Cook ranks as a brilliant pioneer in the professional criticism of art in America. If his pen was dipped in gall, it may have been his reaction to the undiscriminating praise then in vogue. He was among the first in America to appreciate the Impressionists. His style was lucid and when he was not on the war-path it was also graceful and urbane. He was much in demand as a drawing-room lecturer. Personally, he was charming. All who knew him recall his pleasant voice and manner, his gentleness and culture, the atmosphere, altogether gracious and graceful, that enveloped him.[10]

In arguing that colonial furniture was not only preferable to all but the most expensive contemporary pieces in workmanship and design, but was also valuable because it embodied an important aspect of the American cultural tradition, Cook was one of the earliest and most influential supporters of American antiques. Such other tastemakers as H. Hudson Holly, who wrote for *Harper's*, noted the virtues of antiques in passing, but didn't urge their appreciation and use so consistently and thoughtfully as Cook. Passages like the following, reflecting Cook's belief in the intrinsic value of American antiques, almost certainly helped shape the vision of collectors like Lyon, Bolles, Erving, and Seymour:

> There is . . . the pleasant knowledge that this furniture, if not all of it made in America, was all of it made for Americans, or bought by them; and there is a feeling that in going back to its use, in collecting it, and saving it from dishonor, and putting it in safe-keeping, we are bringing ourselves a little nearer in spirit to the old time.[11]

Chapter 6

Old China
History and Art, Hearth and Home

COLLECTORS HAVE ALWAYS BEEN FASCINATED BY POTTERY AND PORCELAIN. New or old, plain or fancy, the colors, shapes, and romance of old china have appealed to many people in many times and places. The Hartford collector Henry Wood Erving described his own feelings:

> There are many more interesting bits of china to be found in out of the way places than good furniture; and old china is fascinating stuff, and one's imagination can create all sorts of histories and romances connected with it. The old glazes and enamels are ofttimes more satisfying to one than meat and raiment.[1]

Erving's attitude was shared by many in the 1870s, when he began to collect. His contemporary Alice Morse Earle (1851–1911) was another passionate collector of antique china, and author of many books on colonial life and artifacts. Her *China Collecting in America*, published in 1892,[2] combines seriousness and sentimentality in a way that was representative of her generation.

Mrs. Earle's serious interest in identifying and studying the different kinds of ceramics found in America is manifest in her book, along with her unmis-

*High chest with steps for
the display of old china.
Illustrated in Alice Morse
Earle's* China Collecting
in America, *first published
in 1892. (Courtesy of the
New-York Historical
Society)*

takably sentimental, patriotic, and historical enthusiasms. She summed up her arguments for china collecting as a worthwhile hobby in one rather extended sentence:

> Insight into human nature, love of my native country, knowledge of her natural beauties, acquaintance with her old landmarks and historical localities, familiarity with her history, admiration of her noble military and naval heroes, and study of the ancient manners, customs, and traditions of her early inhabitants have all been fostered, strengthened, and indeed almost brought into existence by the search after the study of old china.[3]

A major difference between the ceramics of early America and its furniture and silver is that nearly all the ceramics had been imported from England and the Orient, whereas most of the furniture and silver were eventually shown to have been made locally. One kind of pottery that was made specifically for Americans was the blue-and-white ware of Staffordshire, England. Pictures of American landmarks, vistas, and heroes had actually been transfer-printed onto dishes made for the American market by Staffordshire potters from about 1820 onward, capturing pre-industrial America on the eve of its disappearance. By the 1870s, when china collecting began in earnest, these blue-and-white wares had become in some cases the only surviving pictorial record of a vanished scene or building, and therefore of great interest to collectors. Mrs. Earle's comment reflects this unique aspect.

Alice Morse Earle combined her patriotic and scholarly enthusiasm for early imported china with an equally strong distaste for contemporary American ceramics. Her attitude was shared by others interested, as a result of the arts-and-crafts movement, in good design, materials, and workmanship.

In America, the course of china collecting followed that of other antiques: ceramics were valued largely because of their histories or associations until about the time of the Philadelphia Centennial Exposition. Then taste became a factor. European displays of ceramics at the Centennial, especially those which imitated old Spanish and Italian majolica, inspired artistically oriented Americans to replace their thick factory-made dishes with more delicate European products, or with thinner, gayer antique wares.

Pottery and Porcelain of All Times and All Nations, the first comprehensive and factual American book on ceramics, was published in 1878. Its author, William Cowper Prime, deplored the decline of taste: "The farmers' wives of New England and New York fifty years ago had, as a class, more good taste in table furniture than many persons in our cities now have," he wrote, "and any one who can procure a few of those old crockery plates may be proud to serve a course at dinner on them, and will win praise from all guests who have correct appreciation."[4]

Prime, and others influenced by arts-and-crafts thinking, felt that drab, ugly home furnishings produced a drab, ugly soul. Beautifully shaped and decorated objects, on the other hand, had a civilizing influence on the user. Thus, the use of lovely old crockery at mealtimes would contribute to a finer, more cheerful society. Speaking of old pottery and porcelain as elements of interior decoration—on walls and mantels as well as on the table—Prime said:

> Families brought up with such articles around them feel their civilizing and refining influences. Children grow up among them with knowledge, appreciation, and love of beauty. The table furnished with tasteful ware is bright, and ceases to be a mere feeding place. Its memories become important possessions to the members of the family who go away. The dearest associations of old age with childhood are connected with the home table, whether its furniture was the rarest porcelain of China, or the simple and always beautiful blue-and-white crockery of Staffordshire. The lover of ceramic art and the collector of its treasures of beauty can afford to pity those who are unable to enter into the enjoyment which he is happy in possessing.[5]

This almost religious view of the value of old ceramics affected to some degree early collectors of all American antiques.

The members of the China Hunters Club, formed in Worcester, Massachusetts, just after the Philadelphia Centennial, expressed the same faith in the spiritual power of old china. The family fireside as a stabilizing force in modern society, and the importance of antiques in creating a welcoming home atmosphere, are themes that had been suggested by the New England kitchens in the 1860s and 1870s. These themes were developed by the China Hunters specifically in terms of ceramics:

> . . . The country home had almost always bright and beautiful table furniture, and the family must have enjoyed it and lingered around it. Probably, on that account, domestic influences, home thoughts, and family thoughts, had more influence on men in those days. There cannot be any force exerted on a man's or a woman's mind by a lot of white crockery set out to eat from. But a woman may be expected to retain and increase the womanly characteristics of gentleness, kindness, and all kinds of loveliness, who has a pretty tea-service to preside over every day, however cheap and homely it may seem to the more wealthy. And men under the influence of such women, and such cheerful home associations, are always better citizens.[6]

These were the thoughts of a small group of educated, upper-middle-class women, who had the leisure to ponder questions of taste and the civilizing powers of old china. The average American was much more likely, as Charles Eastlake pointed out in *Hints on Household Taste*, to prefer the garish new to the genteel old:

> Indeed, there is no branch of art-manufacture exposed to greater dangers, in point of taste, than that of ceramic design. . . . The tendency of the uneducated eye is, in most cases, to admire the smart and showy but effeminate hues of the day rather than the subtle and refined combinations of colour which distinguish ancient pottery and porcelain. Extravagance of form is preferred to a sober grace of contour, and neatness of execution to the spirit of artistic design.[7]

The permanent disappearance of the old ways and the old landscapes beneath a tide of industrial development was frightening to many Americans. But at the same time the coming of machines meant an easier, more luxurious life for most. As for ceramics, the mechanization of the industry meant that nearly everybody could drink his morning coffee from a ceramic mug and eat his dinner from a ceramic plate. A century earlier, pottery and porcelain had been available only to the well-to-do. "Smart and showy" ceramics, or the simpler thick white cups and plates rejected by arts-and-crafts advocates, represented real luxury for many people. New china *must* be better, because until the Industrial Revolution new things had represented a step up. Inferior materials, workmanship, and design had never before been major problems; the majority of Americans certainly did not recognize them as problems now. It was for this reason that china hunters were as successful as they were.

The Centennial decade was a good time for people to get interested in old china. The Industrial Revolution, which had produced new ceramics that were cheap but usually neither pretty nor graceful, had also created a leisure class. People were freer than ever before to pursue hobbies. Good roads and railroads made travel easier, and china collectors were able to get around both city and countryside looking for old plates and pots. Then, too, china was light and portable—suitable for ladies to collect and carry home. And, as Henry Erving pointed out, it was easier to find "interesting bits of china . . . in out of the way places" than it was to find furniture of comparable charm. It was the field of collecting, especially in the area of "Old Blue," which most easily allowed the collector to indulge patriotic, artistic, and historical interests simultaneously.

A beaufet or corner cupboard filled with "Old Blue," illustrated in Alice Morse Earle's China Collecting in America. (Courtesy of the New-York Historical Society)

For all these reasons, during the last quarter of the nineteenth century old china was probably the most widely collected of the antiques that had been made or used in America. Although many American collectors pursued their pastime in Europe also, the majority of specimens in early collections had been imported to colonial or early Federal America, and had come down in American families. New England was full of English and China Trade ceramics, which therefore formed the backbone of most New England collections.

Early writers like Alice Morse Earle and N. Hudson Moore (*The Old China Book*, 1903) gave the beginning collector helpful advice and friendly warnings. Mrs. Moore made it clear that the true victim of "china mania" could not preserve an absolutely clear conscience. Some people, she said, are born with a gift for collecting: they have a knack for knowing where to look and how to go about gaining possession of the piece they covet. But she added: "That the ways of the collector are devious everyone knows. The simon-pure collector has got rid of every rag of conscience, and in return has his collection, a fair exchange many of us think."[8]

One way of finding good pieces was to let it be known in your community that you were a collector. Mrs. Moore told of a man whose appearance "showed that he held close communion with the soil," and who turned up one day at the door of a known collector. The caller clutched a bundle done up in ragged newspaper which, when unwrapped, was found to contain three perfect "Old Blue" plates. After a period of dickering, a bargain was struck, and the collector asked his caller where he had obtained the plates. " 'Oh, I got them in our town,' " was the reply. "What the town lost," remarked Mrs. Moore, "no doubt it never knew, what the collector gained he feels tingling through his veins every time he regards his plates."[9]

The art of overlooking the dubious provenance of a coveted piece went hand in hand with the ability to wheedle a desired plate or tureen from its reluctant owner. These early china hunters were masters of the art of selecting the most effective phrase, of giving the wrong impression with just the right degree of ingenuousness. Mrs. Earle gave some examples:

> I have been on the trail with a Yankee china dealer, and his unique method of management was delightful. He worked upon the most secretive, the most furtive plan. . . . his way of carrying on his business of china buying deserves to be told as a matter of interest and instruction to amateur china hunters, for he was a professional, a star. He never, by any chance, told the truth about himself, and above all never gave his correct name and place of residence, nor drove away from the house in the way he really intended to go. He represented himself as an adopted son, this seeming to be more mysterious than ordinary family conditions, never gave twice alike the name of his adopted father, but had a series of noble parents, the most prominent and influential men in the country around. . . . He was at one farmhouse a tender-hearted, indulgent husband, whose delicate invalid of a wife had expressed a wish for a set of old china and he was willing to spend days of search in order to satisfy her whim. It is needless to add that he was a bachelor.[10]

In spite of such wiles, early china hunters fairly often met with refusal to sell. Some owners were simply stubborn or sentimental, and preferred to keep their old crockery because of family tradition: this pitcher had always held molasses; that bowl was always used for applesauce. Some, like one Indiana farm wife, knew more than city folks expected, as a traveler to the Midwest found to her distress. In 1878, *Scribner's Monthly Magazine* published in its September issue an article by Maurice Thompson entitled "Glimpses of Western Farm Life." Mr. Thompson described a trip he and his wife had recently taken through "a rather uncouth and primitive looking part of Indiana." About noon one day a sudden storm blew up, and the Thompsons sought shelter in a farmhouse. They were asked to stay for the noon meal, and were served a delicious roastbeef dinner on wonderful old Staffordshire china. Mrs. Thompson (who, her husband said, had "keramomania") offered to buy the whole set, and was entirely unprepared for her hostess's response:

> . . . she found the old woman quite well informed as to the value of her relics. . . . "I happened to be a-readin' in a paper what come round some goods John bought. . . . Well, in that 'ere paper what come round the goods I read all about how valuable old-fashioned cupboard things had got to be. So I went right and examined mine, an' lo an' behold! there was all them choice makers' marks and names on 'em! I tell you I was proud as I could be! No, mum, these is hard times, but I can't sell my collection of china."[11]

In spite of such setbacks, American china collectors achieved the extensive success described by Alice Morse Earle in 1892:

> Many rich private collections exist. Vast stores of old colonial treasures are preserved in private houses in our Eastern States. . . . In Hartford the col-

Wood and glass case containing part of Dr. Horace S. Fuller's collection of antique ceramics at the Wadsworth Atheneum, 1905. (Courtesy of Wadsworth Atheneum, Hartford)

lections of Mr. Trumbull, of Dr. Lyon, would make envious any English china-buyer. In Albany, in Philadelphia, in Worcester and Providence, in New Haven and Washington, in New York and Brooklyn, many a closet and room full of well-preserved colonial china show the good taste and careful judgment of loving owners.[12]

Gurdon Trumbull (1841–1903), brother of china collectors Annie Trumbull Slosson and Mrs. William C. Prime, was an artist who specialized in painting fish. His friend Henry Erving described him as "one of the very earliest real collectors of old china." He began hunting specimens in the Connecticut countryside in 1877, and in 1878 went abroad for two years to study and collect in Europe. Erving wrote that Trumbull "was most particular . . . and has told me that he weeded out specimens until his real collection . . . is comparatively limited in number, but consists only of pieces of superb quality."[13]

Like Dr. Lyon's special friends, Stephen Terry and Dr. Horace S. Fuller, Trumbull kept a notebook in which he recorded each new ceramic purchase. Descriptions, comments, and sometimes notes on the seller were included. The notebooks eventually accompanied the collections of all three to the Wadsworth Atheneum in Hartford.

Although Mrs. Earle named several other prominent private collectors, she commented that "There is but one public collection in America which I have seen that is of positive and unfailing worth . . . the Trumbull Prime Collection," started by Gurdon Trumbull's sister.[14]

Mrs. William Cowper Prime was described by Henry Erving as "probably the first person in this country certainly the first woman, to collect china systematically. At her death, Dr. Prime carried on the collection under the name of the Trumbull-Prime Collection which eventually became the best collection of china in the United States." Prime's leaving the collection to Princeton University, his alma mater, was, said Erving, "at that time a most unwise decision, because there was no one in Princeton to appreciate it or value it. They actually sold some of the pieces and bought, with the proceeds, a stained glass window."[15]

Although the Primes lived in New York City, perhaps the major center of china collecting was Hartford. Among those who specialized in ceramics, many were keenly interested in furniture as well. In fact, Hartford was a focal point for the collecting of American decorative arts in general during the latter part of the nineteenth century. And the central figure on the scene was Dr. Irving W. Lyon.

Chapter 7

Irving W. Lyon
The Hartford Patriarch

O F THE MANY COLLECTORS WHO BEGAN TO GATHER AND STUDY AMERICAN furniture and other antiques in the Hartford area during the late nineteenth century, Dr. Irving W. Lyon (1840–1896) is probably the best known. He eventually set down the fruits of his extensive research in *The Colonial Furniture of New England*, first published in 1891.[1] Dr. Lyon's sphere of influence increased with the years, as he studied colonial New England home furnishings. He eventually knew, or knew of, most of the serious collectors in Massachusetts, Rhode Island, and Connecticut. It is evident from the illustrations in his book that he had examined the collections of antiquaries from Northampton, in northwestern Massachusetts, to Salem, on the state's far eastern perimeter. In his own city of Hartford, Dr. Lyon had considerable influence, despite his shyness. He was devoted to his family, a few good friends, his medical practice, and his study of antiques.

Dr. Lyon's zeal as a collector stemmed from an interest in his own ancestors, particularly those of his mother's family, the Phillipses of the prestigious Phillips Andover and Phillips Exeter Academies of New England. Lyon's pride in his New England forebears extended naturally to a generalized interest in the life and culture of the times in which they had lived. With an intentness and thor-

Dr. Irving W. Lyon on his fiftieth birthday. (Photograph courtesy of Mrs. Stephen T. Keiley)

oughness that characterized all his endeavors, Lyon began to study colonial New England ceramics and furniture. This broadening of a fascination with his own ancestors to an interest in colonial New England life is similar to the path taken by Cummings Davis. The analogy ends there, however, for Lyon's interest in the past was much more analytical and less sentimental than Davis's.

Lyon's conclusions about the homes of the forefathers have held up startlingly well. *The Colonial Furniture of New England* was so carefully researched and thoughtfully crafted that it remains a standard reference today—an extraordinary accomplishment, considering the sophisticated research and the technological aids available to the modern student of furniture. No other early furniture scholar's work has the same continuing validity. Dr. Lyon once told an acquaintance that in his medical practice his goal was always to get back to first causes. He took a comparable approach to his furniture studies, with excellent results.

The second of eleven children, Irving W. Lyon was born in 1840 on the family farm in Bedford, New York. He went from Lawrenceville Academy to Vermont Medical College, and then to Bellevue Hospital in New York. In 1866 he moved to Hartford and set up a private practice. He became, as well, chief medical examiner for the Hartford Life and Annuity Insurance Company.

The Centennial year, with its attendant local and national celebrations, patriotic fervor, and historical reminiscing, apparently gave impetus to Lyon's collecting career. He attended the Centennial Exposition in Philadelphia in 1876, and according to family tradition the expedition marked the beginning of his collecting. In fact, Lyon himself stated that early the next year he and a few others began to collect old furniture in the Hartford area. During these first years of collecting, however, he and his friends focused more on ceramics than on furniture.[2]

Because of his interest in ceramics, Dr. Lyon went to England in 1879 to establish just what he had in his own collection—how the British designated similar pieces, and how they regarded them. He and his friends had gathered their ceramics in New England, and since so much of what they found was English—though Dutch Delft and China Trade pieces turned up too—they assumed that comparable wares would be even more plentiful in England. Dr. Lyon was fascinated to discover that this was by no means entirely true. He wrote home that "I know about as much about English Pottery as they do here—they know more about porcelain, though my trip has wonderfully posted & confirmed me in ceramics already."[3]

Lyon studied English ceramics in museums and private collections. He wrote in particular of one trip to the Jermyn Street Museum. The keepers opened a case to show him some ceramics, and alas, "I . . . was so unfortunate as to break a dish (saucer). I offered at once to pay for it, but they were exceedingly kind and courteous and would take no pay and made me feel very comfortable over it."[4]

There were many people scouring the New England countryside for old china as early as 1879. A. R. Crittenden of Middletown, Connecticut, tracked down old china for a few collectors as a diversion from his hardware manufacturing business. During the years 1878 to 1881, he sent a series of letters to Dr. Lyon concerning the ceramics Crittenden was scouting for him while traveling through New England. In September of 1878, Crittenden wrote Lyon the sad story of his own thwarted collecting career: "I gave up making a

Antique ceramics from the collection of Dr. Irving W. Lyon.
(Photograph courtesy of Mrs. Stephen T. Keiley)

collection for myself over a year ago. . . . Mrs. Crittenden does not care a straw for old ceramics, and does not like me to have a house full of them, and for her sake I decided to give up making a collection."[5]

By the time of his next trip abroad, 1881, Lyon was devoting most of his time to furniture and having a family genealogy compiled. He was still very interested in ceramics, however; he visited a leading English collector, Lady Charlotte Schreiber, and offered to buy ceramics for his collecting friends Stephen Terry and Dr. Horace Fuller, if they would remit the money immediately. He had spent his own on research, and for copies of Chippendale's and Sheraton's design books.[6]

Lyon's interest in collecting ceramics seems to have diminished as the 1880s went along, and by 1884 he was already engrossed in the project of writing a book about native New England furniture. In his search for the facts about such furniture, as well as for actual pieces, Lyon traveled about in Connecticut, Massachusetts, and Rhode Island. He visited many dealers in Boston and on the north shore—inspecting their stocks, making notes on what was on hand, and trying to gather information about European antecedents and prototypes. He also talked his way into private collections that the dealers told him about.[7]

Lyon was particularly anxious to see the collection of the Salem genealogist and collector Henry Waters. He recorded his visit to Waters's house in his journal:

> I went to the house of Mr. Henry F. Waters on Pleasant St. Salem to see his furniture which Mr. Moulton spoke so highly about. He is in Europe in London. . . . Mr. Whittredge did not like to let me in to see the furniture; & I had to almost beg to get in the house, where he finally showed me the most of the things I judge. He had from three to six chairs like Walter Hosmers best ones—& Mr. Whittredge said they could trace them to their beginning. . . . He had a beautiful oaken cabinet—Gothic carving. . . . He also owned another oaken cupboard . . . very fine & old—But some of his other oaken pieces—chests & notably a cupboard had been spoiled in doing over—scooped or planed down so as to look fresh as new oak—& I think other liberties had been taken with feet & possibly moldings—
>
> At Mr. Whittredge's Sister's house, near by, to which he took me I saw the two storied oaken cupboard & also the little table which are illustrated in Clarence Cook's book—these had also been planed down & freshened & modernized so as to be painfully noticed.[8]

The reference to the cupboard and chairs illustrated by Clarence Cook shows that Lyon was aware of Cook's advocacy of the desirability of antiques over cheap home furnishings.

The planing and refinishing that Lyon deplored was the fate of a good deal of the early American furniture rediscovered in the 1870s and 1880s. The

*Oak chest, 1640–1680, bought in Windsor, Connecticut by Dr. Irving W. Lyon
and illustrated as Figure 1 in* The Colonial Furniture of New England.
(Yale University Art Gallery, Mabel Brady Garvan Collection)

reason was probably partly that so much of it was in terrible condition when it was found—sometimes outdoors, often in the barn or henhouse. The preference of the general public was, in any case, for new finishes. Dr. Lyon noted in his journal for 1883 that in the antiques shop of Perkins of Salem, not just finishes but whole pieces were new. "His Oaken chests were most all reproductions, newly carved brand new, & he so told me. The price was always about $75. & he said his customers bought these tight new pieces in preference to the old, & Mr. Moulton said the same thing—Moulton had two new chests, as I thought, but he would not admit that they were new." Noting also that the feet of many of the genuinely old oak pieces might be new, Lyon concluded, "Oaken pieces—good & genuine, would seem to be very scarce about Eastern Mass." Captain Samuel Brown, a dealer in Newburyport, made a similar statement when Lyon paid him a call on October 30, 1883.[9]

Lyon had visited Europe in 1881, and he went again in 1886, to sort out what furniture was actually made in America and what had been imported for American use at an early date. Lyon was a genealogist of the family tree of furniture. He was interested in antecedents—in tracing to their sources the forms, the names, and the uses. He then made his tree, showing how each of several furniture forms had evolved: where it had started, how it had developed, where it had ended up.

On his trip of 1881, Lyon went to see antiques in France. He wrote home in June: "I went to the Cluny Museum & spent the day and *such* a day. Such old furniture I never hit on before—I was perfectly happy & just feasted & reveled in the riches and abundance." Nevertheless, his staid New England soul was offended by French food, religion, and morals, and he was very glad to get back to England. On a trip to Haddon Hall, he reflected that it had stood "so for nearly six hundred years," and that "England has had a superior race upon its soil during these past centuries."[10]

The next time abroad, in May and June of 1886, Lyon went to the English museum that is now the Victoria and Albert and wrote his daughter:

> Tell Uncle Stephen [Terry] & Mr. Simons & Mr. Hosmer that the Jones Collection of furniture in the South Kensington Museum is elegant & rich & valuable beyond description. I had no idea that it was so large and so fine.
>
> The whole collection is a set of gems, the most elegant furniture, piece after piece belonging to French Kings and Queens, the best that the best French cabinetmakers could make. . . . It covers a period (18th century) hitherto not well represented . . . one could spend a year there & see new things all the time.[11]

Lyon then went to work in "the Libraries of the British Museum searching old newspapers from 1666 to 1757 having two assistants for eight days. The result is very satisfactory and will enable me to write my proposed book . . . with more freedom and knowledge." Lyon noted that he expected to examine other material—prints, directories, and dictionaries—"that may give me accurate knowledge of the furniture used in the seventeenth century." He also consulted British furniture scholars, and visited the editor of the New English Dictionary to check on nomenclature.[12]

In America, Lyon pursued the same sort of intensive research. He studied newspapers, wills, and inventories in the Northeast, paying particular attention to those of Hartford County and Boston. He combined this material with detailed examination of several pieces for each form considered, and further consultation with experts in the United States and abroad. In particular, his debt to the Hartford cabinetmakers Hosmer and Simons is very clear.

In 1891, these efforts culminated in the book that, according to a contemporary comment, "illuminated as few books have ever done many of the features of the comparatively obscure story of home-life one and two centuries ago." *The Colonial Furniture of New England* was joyfully received by collectors and inheritors of old furniture, because there had been no previous reference for "verification, identification, and, in numerous instances, for the distinct name itself." The book's great revelation was that "far the greater part of the old oaken chests and cupboards found in New England are of New England manufacture. All collectors of these articles are aware that their origin is generally declared to be foreign, customarily English." The author's pioneering research had confounded the conventional wisdom.[13]

Dr. Lyon recorded in his notebook for 1883 that he paid the dealer James Moulton of Lynn, Massachusetts, $30 for a six-legged high chest— perhaps this one, which appears as Figure 28 in Dr. Lyon's book. (Yale University Art Gallery, Mabel Brady Garvan Collection)

In spite of the fact that the book was so sorely needed, Lyon was several years in finding a publisher. He apparently had a manuscript as early as 1888, when he asked Henry Waters to write Harper's attesting to his qualifications. Neither Harper's nor Putnam's—both in New York—was interested, however, and it was the Boston firm of Houghton, Mifflin that finally decided to accept the book. During this early period, there was very little collecting of American antiques in New York; even in New England the practice was distinctly limited. Interest in collecting was to broaden markedly, however, in the next generation.[14]

Lyon was very apprehensive about the success of his book. He wrote to his son Irving, then at Yale, that he had taken a copy to the Reverend Dr. Walker of Hartford for review and had been anxious about the reaction. He was thus delighted to hear Walker describe it as "a most delectable book . . . an admirable piece of work, exceedingly well written, &c &c. . . ." Dr. Lyon concluded from this enthusiasm that the written review would be highly favorable. "So

I have had one of my best days today," he wrote, "& feel that the book will meet with a very flattering introduction to the Hartford people, at least."[15]

His book did more than that; it met with a flattering reception everywhere, as reviews preserved by Lyon in a scrapbook (now at Winterthur with his other papers) indicate. *The Atlantic Monthly* described it as "the first thoroughly scientific examination of one interesting corner of this field." Lyon was basically very pleased, calling the writer "one of the most penetrating in his analysis; except," he added, "when he said I had touched only a *little corner* of the subject." The review in *The Nation* was positive as well, and Charles Dana, editor of *The New York Sun*, wrote to ask whether he might publish an article making liberal use of quotes and photographs from the book. Furthermore, Lyon received many letters from collectors and others interested in American antique furniture, which he neatly pasted into his scrapbook.[16]

Lyon was a man of enormous energy, in desperate need of a serious and consuming hobby. Despite the success of his book, therefore, he embarked immediately on another, this one on the houses of colonial New England. In a letter published after Lyon's death, the Reverend Dr. George Leon Walker wrote:

> In the studies contributory to the projected volume on old houses he spared no time which could be snatched from the exacting demands of his profession, and no expense. It was an exhilarating delight to him to run on, if but for a fraction of a day, to Boston or Salem, or Plymouth or Providence, or to some town of lesser note, to verify some fact of construction in some antique edifice; or to trace the development of some feature of the house-building habits on these new shores. . . . The work, if completed, would be a storehouse of information concerning early New England life, resources, and the attempts to adjust old world habitudes to new world conditions, of exceeding interest and value.[17]

By 1892, Lyon was deep in his work on old houses. He wrote to his son Irving: "Am getting ahold of something new almost every day—found a house built 1750 with cedar clapboards, the original ones, yet on. I knew of cedar shingles before—but not of cedar clapboards. Also found a case of very early cut nails. . . . Keep quiet about my cedar clapboards." This conspiratorial admonition was characteristic of Dr. Lyon. He had asked the same caution of Henry Waters when he requested the latter to do a little furniture research in London. He wanted to surprise the public with his discoveries.[18]

He urged his son Irving to make a number of observations for the projected book when the younger Lyon went to Europe in 1895. Study, young Irving was told, "all you possibly can the old houses that you see, especially in the country, so as to bring me all the points that you can." And Lyon confided that his architectural research was a great satisfaction: "I am knuckling right down to my old house work, & am bound to push it right along now & when I can do such work it tends to make me feel cheerful."[19]

The next year, however, Dr. Lyon died of pneumonia at the age of fifty-six. The manuscript for his cherished project remains as he left it. Norman Isham, who became one of the most thorough and learned students of early New England houses, went as a young man to see Lyon in his office at the Hartford Life and Annuity Insurance Company. Years afterward, Isham described the visit: "I found a bearded and spectacled gentleman seated in a little glazed cubby-hole, with a sort of lap robe over his knees." Lyon received him cordially, and they got to talking about their respective studies of architecture, at first cautiously, then animatedly. After Lyon died, Isham offered to finish the book, but the Lyon family turned him down.[20]

The doctor's antiques were divided up among his three children: Irving P. Lyon, Charles Woolsey Lyon, and Mary Lyon Albree. Irving had already begun to collect, along with his roommate C. Sanford Bull, while he was at Yale in the late 1880s and early 1890s. An article on Mr. and Mrs. Bull's collection published in *The Magazine Antiques* more than fifty years later describes the students' activities:

> Doctor Irving P. Lyon's father, Irving W. Lyon . . . furnished the boys' room with old pieces. Mr. Bull decided to contribute a desk to the cause. To the amusement of their classmates, the Lyon and the Bull scoured the Connecticut countryside for early furniture. Mr. Bull found a cherry desk for $20, but felt that was too much to pay. The elder Doctor Lyon eventually bought it for $17. Another time the two boys found a Carver chair for $1.50, and a Windsor side chair for $.05. Mr. Bull says . . . "The day we found the Carver chair, we walked altogether 30 miles, carrying the chair between us. When we were tired, we would stop and take turns resting in our new purchase."[21]

Another time, as the younger Lyon related in a letter, he was equally lucky:

> This chair I (personally) discovered in an old farmhouse in Harwinton, Ct., about 1890. It was a roost for hens. The owners, two old ladies, said it had come down in their family. They sold it to me for thirty cents. It had evidently never been restored. It was in a filthy condition. My father had it taken apart, cleaned and reconstructed in all of its details as it was, without change, addition or subtraction (except of dirt). There is not a new piece of wood or nail in it now.[22]

As a doctor just beginning to practice in Buffalo, New York, Irving P. Lyon kept up his interest in old furniture. Every summer, he and his young family went to the Massachusetts shore, and he went antiquing with his Aunt Clarissa. Later he published articles in *The Magazine Antiques*, presenting the kind of thoroughly reasoned, well-documented argument for which his father had been noted.

Irving Lyon kept his one-third of his father's collection—which included all of the ceramics, six cases filled with over six hundred specimens—until the mid-twenties. He then sold the ceramics to a Mrs. Blair from New York, and much of the best furniture to Francis Patrick Garvan, a Hartford native who was then in the process of amassing one of the great collections of American antiques. Many of Dr. Lyon's choicest pieces of furniture are thus now part of the Garvan Collection in the Yale University Art Gallery.

Mary Lyon Albree used her own and her father's antiques to furnish her house near Pittsburgh; some have remained in the family, and some are now at Yale. Charles Woolsey Lyon was the black sheep. Old Dr. Lyon seems to have worried about him a great deal, to judge from references to "Charley" in letters to his other son. On June 23, 1895, Dr. Lyon wrote: "Charley . . . is punctual, & seems for once to be working hard. . . ." And later, "Charley keeps on correctly at work—goes to bed & gets up now on time. Has been sent to Boston three times with a superior to do some office work there over Sunday. He talks and acts better than ever before, so this is encouraging."[23]

Charles Woolsey Lyon apparently didn't like office work, however, as he went into the antiques business with his share of his father's collection. Old Dr. Lyon had not approved of dealing in antiques—he considered a little genteel trading among friends all right, but not outright *selling*—and he probably would have seen Charley's choice of profession as just another wrong step.

Charles set up shop in Albany, New York, the place where he found and sold many of his finest pieces. Later he moved to New York City, and established himself during the 1920s as one of the leading dealers in American antiques. The firm declined with the onset of the Depression, however, and never regained its former prominence.

Irving W. Lyon's son Dr. Irving P. Lyon and fellow collector C. Sanford Bull, pictured in the thirty-fifth reunion history of the Yale Class of 1893. (Yale University Library)

Lyon and Bull stopped for a brief visit on their way through.

Chapter 8

Henry Wood Erving

Collecting in and about Hartford

PERHAPS MORE THAN ANY OTHER FIGURE, HENRY WOOD ERVING (1851–1941) represents the attitudes prevalent among the generation of collectors that arose toward the end of the nineteenth century. Like several others in the Hartford group, he collected both china and furniture. His very personal attachment to all his American antiques stemmed, according to his friend Henry Watson Kent, from his patriotism, and from his great interest in the craftsmen and craft methods of colonial times. "If I had been going to speak of only one of Erving's qualities," wrote Kent,

> I think I should have dwelt upon his loyalty. It was his allegiance to his friends, people, and country, present and past, that stood out above the others. And it was this that made him the unique collector. It was loyalty that was at the bottom of his belief in the goodness of American things. It was for him, one of the first to collect examples of our early American craftsmanship, jealously to maintain their virtues. He was their champion, with pride and love for everything old. Behind his beautiful chests, chairs and tables he saw the men of the times who made them. He delighted in the skill of these craftsmen, and in their invention; and, even when a piece

Henry Wood Erving, in a photograph probably taken in 1926, when Trinity College awarded him an honorary M.A. (Photograph courtesy of The Connecticut Historical Society)

was "of no great shakes," as he would say, he found joy in it and its maker's simple efforts. Every piece had the place of a familiar friend, and spoke to him in a language he understood.[1]

Erving combined the romanticism of his predecessors Davis and Poore with a serious interest in the actual lives, houses, domestic habits, and craft traditions of his forebears.

Hartford was a crossroads in which an extraordinary number of early collectors and students of American furniture lived, studied, or at least spent some time. Erving indicated one reason for the growth of Hartford as an early antiques-collecting center: "It is because of . . . New England thrift, that we are now able to find, and occasionally possess, many treasures," he wrote. "In the early days of New England nothing was thrown away, and little wantonly destroyed. When an article of household furnishing had served its day and generation, it was set aside, removed to the attic or barn, but seldom demolished." Thrift also characterized the collectors, who recognized antiques as well-made and well-designed furnishings at reasonable prices.[2]

Another reason for early interest in antiques in the Hartford area was probably the persistence there of the cabinetmaking tradition. Although much

knowledge of the old ways of woodworking had been lost, some had survived.
Erving wrote of the 1870s:

> There were two old craftsmen at that time employed by the long estab-
> lished house of Robbins and Winship—then Robbins Bros.—who had been
> in business in Hartford since early in the century. It was like shaking hands
> with a man who had met Washington. . . . Mr. Edwin Simons, the veteran
> cabinetmaker, together with Walter Hosmer, knew more of Eliphalet
> Chapin [the cabinetmaker] of South Windsor, for instance, than any other
> then living, and their gossip and reminiscences were mightily interesting
> to me.[3]

It is easy to imagine Erving and some of his collecting cronies sitting and
watching Hosmer and Simons at work; their shop may have been the hub of
that part of the New England collecting universe. (Both cabinetmakers formed
notable collections of old furniture themselves, and some of Hosmer's eventually found its way into the Metropolitan Museum.) Erving wrote that he
learned all that he could about manufacturing and repairing furniture. His constant research into old craft methods was one way to achieve kinship with the
American colonists who had made and used his antiques.

Born in Westfield, Massachusetts, in 1851, Erving was educated in schools
in Hartford and Suffield, Connecticut. He is one of the major collectors for
whom we have some indication of Dr. Irving W. Lyon's influence. Erving had
begun working in 1870, earning $100 during his first year with the Charter
Oak National Bank. This position was worthwhile in promoting his collecting
career, for Erving wrote that "Dr. Lyon was a frequent caller at our bank, as
were several of the earliest china collectors—Trumbull, the artist, Dr. Fuller,
and Attorney Stephen Terry, who were all among my early and valued
friends, and from whom I learned much."[4]

Of the early days of his collecting, Erving recalled:

> At that period there were many in country homes who considered things
> ancient as rubbish, but the trouble was to locate such; and when found, the
> owner's estimate was often justified. It is also true that once in a while
> desirable objects were discovered in the most unlikely places. Many a fine
> old home might not contain, from pantry to attic, a single article which
> would appeal to a collector, and again a bit of early oak might be discov-
> ered—usually by accident—in a cellar or chicken coop. We really found a
> chest, large but very good, essentially Connecticut I think, in a cellar and
> holding potatoes. This, the lid missing it is true, we secured and brought
> away. My little son, who accompanied us, found no room on the return
> save inside the chest.
>
> . . . It required a lot of nerve, or rather cheek, and a peculiar talent, to

"The Connecticut chest."
From Erving's Random
Notes on Colonial
Furniture, *1931.*

call at a house and ask the self-respecting mistress who answered the knock
if she had any old furniture or china which she would dispose of, and—
believe it or not—this I did not possess to a sufficient degree to be entirely
successful. . . . I don't recall that I was ever rebuffed; on the contrary, I met
many charming people in homes where it was pleasant, subsequently, to call.[5]

Erving's methods were probably typical of those of his fellow collectors in the
nineteenth century. He began by making forays into the countryside with a
horse and buggy, stopping, as he said, at likely-looking farmhouses to inquire
for old things. He kept a sharp eye on the orchard and barnyard, as well. "I
recall," he wrote, "rescuing a very decent slat back chair from a woodpile, and
a butter-fly table from a garden where it had stood for so long—used for
potting plants—that the feet were rotted off and had to be replaced. . . . I had
no real adventures," he lamented, ". . . but many tiresome drives and much
labor and many disappointments. What couldn't have then been accomplished
with an automobile?" In the end, he felt that becoming known to the dealers
and pickers, and having them bring him their discoveries, was a much more
satisfactory—and possibly even cheaper—method of collecting.[6]

As more people became interested in acquiring antiques, Erving said, "the
oncoming dealers" began to "discover the stuff and secure it." One of the most
enterprising of this new breed was Old Prior of Cromwell, Connecticut, a
town about fifteen miles south of Hartford. Prior's activities contributed to the
progress, if not the reputation, of the Hartford collecting fraternity. Erving
wrote most entertainingly and informatively about Old Prior:

He had a pleasant voice, and the face of a bishop—valuable qualities possessed by certain men in high quarters, and to their great advantage even at

the present day. He had a queer little trick of gaining a second or so to think, by swallowing—knowing, probably, he was making a statement his auditor wouldn't be able to swallow. I recall that on one occasion when he was giving me a bad one, he looked me squarely in the eye, declaring, "Why, you know, Mr. Erving, that it's of no use for a *liar* to lie!" He habitually carried in his wallet a fifty-dollar bill which, with his plunder all on his wagon, he would tender the owner to change, which, of course, was usually found impossible. He would then remark that he would be passing again in the course of a week and would have smaller bills and settle, and then would give that locality a wide berth for months. . . .

"A Block-front Scrutoir."
From Erving, Random
Notes . . .

Once I noticed on a veranda in South Windsor several excellent Windsor chairs. I remarked to a scout who received many goods from Virginia and the Carolinas through agents whom he paid, that it seemed to me unwise to leave such good articles exposed all night so publicly. "Well," he replied, "if *they* don't take them in, Old Prior will."[7]

Prior, said Erving, "loved danger with his sport." He would try to get away with almost anything, and often did, but when "confronted . . . by the irate owner and a sheriff, Prior would crumple and pay handsomely to avoid prosecution." In spite of his unscrupulousness, or perhaps because of it, Prior "probably brought more high-class stuff into Hartford than any other two men."[8]

Prior was equally pertinacious in selling anything. Occasionally he seemed to insist upon selling to a particular individual. He appeared in the office one day and asked me to look at a case of bottles in his wagon. They were these square high-shouldered, short-necked Dutch Schnapps bottles of dark green glass, each holding over a quart, twelve all perfect, but the case rather dilapidate. "It's fifteen dollars to you—they're worth twenty-five." "Don't interest me." "Well, you *would* like them at ten?" "No, I don't want them." "Well, say five, a mere nothing." "No, I don't *want* them, Mr. Prior." "What would you give?" "Don't want them, but I'll give you a dollar." "They're yours," and he brought them in.[9]

Obviously, Erving loved to tell stories of his early collecting adventures. This led to his writing down some of his choicest anecdotes and reminiscences, which are a legacy almost more precious than his collection. Taken together, his writings form a record, compiled from his own memory and presented in his own well-chosen words, of collecting in the Connecticut River Valley in the early days. Erving's account of how the Hadley chest acquired its name exemplifies his ability to combine the facts with the flavor of collecting:

The first chest we ever found was in Old Hadley, in 1883. Someone at a distance had told us that

"A Thrifty Attic." From Erving, Random Notes . . .

such a person owned an old chest with the front "all wrought." The owner, a lady, said she had been approached by others but would never consider selling. She told me that just at that time she wished for a sum of money for some special purpose and would be glad to dispose of the old piece, which had belonged to her grandmother, deceased in 1824. It had never been touched by a repairer, and faith! I've sometimes thought that it might never have been moved from its original position at the end of the hall in the second story of that very old homestead, easily of the early 18th century. We had but a light buggy, and do you know, I drove ten miles down to South Hadley Falls and then, with a light wagon and a fresh horse, went back the

ten miles to Old Hadley in the evening and took away the chest, driving back again to South Hadley; and my friend there was amazed, the next day, at my care in boxing and packing with hay such an old grain box to ship by freight to Hartford. Subsequently we found two others all by ourselves, Connecticut pieces both, and in talking with friends I always spoke of the first as my "Hadley Chest," a designation others took up—hence its accepted name.[10]

Erving's book, *Random Notes on Colonial Furniture*, was published in 1931, and it was as unpretentious a source of interesting facts and observations as the author himself. He felt that there were enough books outlining the history of furniture and describing periods and styles; he proposed, therefore, to deal with "the minor and perhaps unessential but none the less interesting details of construction and domestic environment." He offered a very personal discussion of those aspects of furniture and furniture making that interested him. Erving's talent for description, and for conveying his own love of the things he collected, is apparent in this charming paragraph about mahogany veneer:

Do you remember how, while waiting to be served in Gray's Inn Coffee House after his return from abroad, David Copperfield brooding at his table, saw himself "reflected in unruffled depths of old mahogany?" Never was a better description of beautiful old wood. Ancient crotch grain mahogany in a way resembles malachite, in that one can apparently see into it,—far below the surface.[11]

Henry Kent spoke of Erving's gifts in a memorial written on the occasion of his death:

Erving had the love of companionship, and he had what is essential to such fellowship, the art of conversation. His was good talk, wideranging, full of interest, wit and anecdote, to which he added felicitous quotation—that all but lost art—especially from his favorite author, Dickens. He might be marked out for his fine bearing when he entered a room, but he was remembered for his talk when he left it.[12]

Erving's vitality did not desert him in old age. An article published in *American Collector*, when he was eighty-four, reported that he was no "aged recluse childishly gloating over the fine things he had gathered. Instead, a spare man with a keen face, youthful mind, and positive opinions greets the visitor. His speech is tinged with New England idioms and intonations. 'Gosh' is his favorite exclamation."[13]

His enthusiasm and ability carried him as far in the world of business as it had in the world of collecting. Leaving the Charter Oak National Bank on January 1, 1887, he went to the Connecticut River Banking Company. He moved up in that institution until, on April 1, 1930, after sixty years as a banker, he was elected chairman of the board of directors.

This must have meant a great deal to him. Nine years later, at the age of eighty-eight, he wrote to a friend that "I was very sick last winter, insomuch that I *saw things*." Nevertheless, he said, "I come down to the office now every morning and go home about one o'clock. Saturdays I don't come down at all."[14]

Erving's collections grew to such an extent that he eventually wrote: "I've been conscious at times that my home was cluttered, but that's entirely the fault of the house and not what is in it. But, I am conscious, too, that the contemplation of the silly stuff has lengthened my life and greatly increased my happiness." The statement indicates that he, like many other collectors of his generation, was not interested in arranging his antiques by any particular system. His joy came from the possession and contemplation of his treasures, not from their orderly classification. He sat in the midst of choice old oak, cherry, and mahogany furniture in "a somewhat ungainly modern upholstered armchair, 'clumsy but comfortable.' "[15]

Here, in Erving's double living room, were pieces of American furniture ranging in date and style from the seventeenth century to the nineteenth. A sampling includes a seventeenth-century Connecticut oak cupboard, a mahogany block-front secretary, a mahogany Chippendale daybed, Hepplewhite and Sheraton tables, and "a dozen or more 18th-century gilt mirrors." Among these things, Erving mused, "he best enjoys his valued pieces, who can see reflected in his mirrors the faces of former possessors, and can recreate the people of olden time sitting in his chairs, at his desks, and before his andirons."[16]

From his first two-week antiquing trip, taken in 1879 with a horse and light wagon, to the end of his life, said Erving, "I have disposed of perhaps half a dozen pieces." Even so,

> while I never regretted a purchase even at the sacrifice of other things which might then have been properly considered necessities, I have always been sorry that I ever sold anything. In time one seems to get to love the foolish stuff—an evidence of mental debility, I dare say. But observing the tasteful designs and the careful, skillful workmanship, one takes off one's hat to certain of these unknown old craftsmen and admits that they were the better men. In the quiet of an evening, with an open fire for sole company and surrounded by bits of antiquity, it requires no undue amount of sentiment for one to find it possible to develop an atmosphere enjoyed by the ladies and gentlemen of former times. One lacking imagination should never undertake collecting.[17]

Chapter 9

George Dudley Seymour

and the Hale of Fame

WHEN *The Colonial Furniture of New England* WAS PUBLISHED IN 1891, George Dudley Seymour (1859–1945) wrote to Dr. Irving W. Lyon: "The book is not only intrinsically valuable to me but also splendidly justifies me before my friends in my passion for the furniture of the old time. I am also greatly pleased to find that the chest of drawers that I bought during the Summer of Simons and Co. appeared among the illustrations."[1] Seymour added that he had hardly had a chance to study the book himself, because it had been out on loan so much.

His acquaintance with Dr. Lyon had developed in 1878, when he was an out-of-town student at the Hartford High School. According to a friend, Seymour "frequently called upon Dr. Lyon during that period."[2] Like Cummings Davis before them, both men were originally motivated to collect by an interest in their own ancestors, which broadened into a reverence for the culture, customs, and patriots of colonial New England. But Seymour's orientation as a collector was never so scholarly as Lyon's. He loved to find pieces that had come down in some branch of his own family—particularly the Seymours and Churchills, who had been among the earliest settlers of Hartford County. If an antique lacked that distinction, but had been made in Connecticut or bore evidence of Yankee ingenuity, Seymour also found it of special interest.

Of his fascination with his own family, Seymour wrote:

> The author's passion for genealogy goes back to his earliest years, when as a small boy he stood by his maternal grandmother's chair and listened, entranced, to stories of her "background with figures"—the background being her grandfather's fine farm in the outskirts of Newington, and the figures her grandfather and grandmother Wells and their large household. Born Laura Wells, she was doubly descended from Gov. Thomas Wells of Connecticut, a connection that brought in the Wolcotts and Appletons, of which she was also proud. The author's first desire as a collector was sometime to acquire the gold loop earrings shown in her portrait, and ultimately he did acquire them, but only by acquiring the canvas itself, a primitive, if you please, but greatly admired by no less a judge than the late John La Farge.[3]

George Dudley Seymour standing in the doorway of the Hale Homestead. (The Connecticut Historical Society)

Like many other members of this early generation, Seymour had a very large collection. The range of his antiquarian interests was wide: it extended from antique furniture to silver, printed material, houses, cornerstones (often repositories of relics and documents), songs, social customs, nailhead coffins, and cast-iron stoves. The coffins and the stoves reflected Seymour's interest in the vaunted Yankee ingenuity, which he considered an important part of his Connecticut heritage.

Seymour was born in Bristol, Connecticut, in 1859. After graduating from Columbian (now George Washington) University with a degree in law in 1880, he spent the next three years in Washington as a specialist in patent cases. In 1883 he moved to New Haven, where the firm of Seymour, Earle, and Nichols capitalized on Yankee ingenuity in their role as patent lawyers. His home in New Haven was the Casa Bianca, at the corner of Bradley and Lincoln Streets, "that snug and trim little house with its 'spattered' floors and staircases, its white walls and red china closets, the great blue-and-white platters placed upstairs, safely centered, like babies, on soft white covered four-poster beds."[4]

Seymour was also very much concerned with the present and the future. He was active in civic improvement projects, such as setting up parks, and was a member of the zoning commission and the committee for building the public library in New Haven. At home in the Casa Bianca, however, he lived according to the old traditions, "among his books and pamphlets, ancestral portraits, Colonial silver and Franklin stoves with their glistening brasses, plus the Whistlerian touch of blue-and-white Nankin china and Japanese prints."[5]

His house, said a friend, "was orderly as only a bachelor's can be, and kept immaculate by old Alice with the Dutch-cut hair—an excellent cook, grave Alice, and one who appreciated ceremony as keenly as did her master. The silver basin and white cloth passed around after the main course was but a mediaeval survival in Colonial Connecticut."[6]

Seymour entertained people of all kinds, old, young, and occasionally famous, like President Taft. He had an active sense of humor, and was even able to muster considerable amusement at the headline announcing his involvement in an automobile accident in 1925: "G. D. Seymour/ Hit by Auto/ Is Improved." Sometimes, Seymour would divert his friends with songs: "With but scant persuasion our host would sit at his clavichord and sing 'Listen to the Mocking Bird' and, were the evening well worn and the Burgundy of especial merit, the 'Sword of Bunker's Hill' would be more shouted than sung with the greatest fervor and gusto."[7]

Fervor and gusto led, as well, to Seymour's collecting so many antiques that they eventually filled three houses, with the overflow on loan to the Wadsworth Atheneum. Although the family genealogy commissioned by Seymour states that it was his aim to secure only pieces of Connecticut origin, many things from other parts of New England found their way into his collection. Seventeenth- and early eighteenth-century furniture interested him most, as it did so many of his contemporaries.

Seymour's furniture is now at the Connecticut Historical Society. With great foresight, he left both money and his own personal notes so that a catalogue could be published. The notes make fascinating reading because of what they reveal about hunting and repairing antiques, and in general about the flavor of collecting in New England one hundred years ago.

There are many references to furniture found in very bad repair—a sunflower chest with "the lid and both drawers" gone, for example, and a dignified seventeenth-century press cupboard encased "in an enamel of yellow paint." Although considerable restoration of antique furniture was required in this early period, Seymour made no bones about his dissatisfaction with the Hartford cabinetmakers' work. Nevertheless, he continued to regard Hartford as the only place to have antiques restored. All through his collecting career, he sent newly acquired pieces there to be "put in order" by Edwin Simons, Patrick Stevens, or Morris Schwartz. Seymour's complaint—exactly that of curators and collectors who acquire such restored pieces today—was usually that too much, rather than too little, repair work had been done.[8]

Dr. Lyon and Henry Erving were much more satisfied with the work of these same cabinetmakers, and spoke of them with respect and affection. In fact, Lyon wrote in the preface to *Colonial Furniture* that Edwin Simons "has had the rare intelligence to leave pieces that have fallen into his hands for repair just as they were originally made." The difference in attitude must have resulted from Seymour's living in New Haven, which precluded his checking on the progress of the work every day or so. He once stated that had he been on the scene to discuss each step with the cabinetmaker, he might have prevented much that he considered bad restoration. For example, in the case of a table whose top was removed in restoration and replaced by another of a different wood and shape, Seymour wrote:

> I was told that the top was not original, and it was removed. . . . This was the tragedy of the table. I am satisfied that the old top was the original top and that it should have been retained. I do

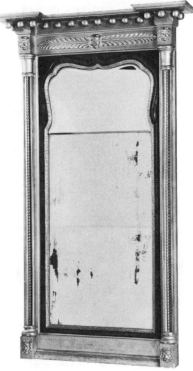

Looking glass which came down in Seymour's family. The original Queen Anne glass was given a new Empire frame at the time of Seymour's grandmother's marriage. (The Connecticut Historical Society)

Press cupboard, oak, seventeenth century, which Seymour found encased in several coats of yellow enamel. (The Connecticut Historical Society)

not charge bad faith, but if the old top was removed and reserved by the
man on the job for use on some other job on account of its age and quality,
that would not be the first time in the history of Antique Furniture Repara-
tions that such a thing had happened—that the unsuspecting owner had been
so imposed upon, for be it known that those who repair old furniture are
always in quest of fine pieces of old wood, which are hard to come upon.
. . . The wise collector personally superintends the repair of his pieces, in-
spects them daily during the progress of the work, and has profound con-
ferences with his cabinetmakers. I learned these lessons too late in my long
career as a collector to save some of my best pieces from being too much
"restored" and to prevent their deprivation of much precious patina. The
Life of Man is Vanity and the Way of the Collector is Hard.[9]

In a calmer vein, Seymour told of a Connecticut chest that he found and
rescued:

In the eighties, I should say, I went to Berlin to spend a Sunday with my
Cousin Leonard Churchill Hubbard, whose mother, then a very old woman,
was Nancy, eldest daughter of my great-great uncle, Solomon Churchill.
She frowned on any references to old furniture on the Lord's Day, but
Cousin Leonard smuggled me into the woodshed, to show me this chest, set
up on end and used as a repository for harnesses. At length and at last I re-
duced it to possession . . . the family Court Cup-Board, having been carried
off upstairs, so blocked the narrow hallway that it was ejected from the house
(a desperate woman must have inspired the act) and carried out into the
back yard, where, before it could find sanctuary in the barn, it was espied
by those all-seeing "Cromwell Thieves" (the two Priors), who stole it and
carried it off to Hartford and sold it.
    . . . I am lucky to have secured the drawerless "Connecticut" chest be-
fore it was discarded.[10]

Here again is the wily Old Prior, this time joining with a relative to thwart
Seymour. Still another collector wryly described this ubiquitous dealer as "not
entirely without guile."[11]

Although Seymour was obviously devoted to the decorative arts, the interest nearest his heart was the Connecticut patriot Nathan Hale. Seymour's
"adoration" of Hale, as one writer described it, had its roots in the same
fervent patriotism that—combined with an admiration of early American families and culture—made him an avid collector. Hale, of course, was caught and
hanged by the British at the outset of the American Revolution while on a
secret mission to secure information and documents. This heroism captured
Seymour's imagination, and he spent many years bringing Hale to national
attention.

The Hale Homestead, Coventry, Connecticut. Bought, restored, and furnished by Seymour in honor of Nathan Hale. (Antiquarian and Landmarks Society)

In 1914, Seymour bought the neglected and abandoned Hale house in Coventry, Connecticut. It is described in the Seymour genealogy as "a stately farmhouse built in 1776 by Nathan's father, Deacon Richard Hale, who incorporated in it a fragment of the actual birth house built by him on substantially the same site in 1746. . . . Mr. Seymour reconditioned the mansion with knowledge and taste, gathered furnishings of Connecticut origin for it, including some pieces of immediate Hale interest, such as Hale's army trunk."[12]

Seymour always referred to the Hale homestead as the "Birthplace." His will, which has been called a "veritable antiquarian item," described the Birthplace as

> a memorial to Captain Nathan Hale—the Nation's youthful hero and supreme symbol of patriotism, next to the flag. . . . The farm was Nathan's only *home* from the time of his birth, in 1755, until he was hanged by the British in 1776. Deacon Hale, his father, lived in the present house from its building until his death in 1802. It is said that Nathan's name was never spoken in the house after he was hanged until after his father's death, in 1802—so stricken was that household by the calamity that befell it.[13]

On Hale's birthday, Seymour flew the flag. One day "an English exchange student passing the house noticed that one of the flags had twisted round the staff over the porch, and volunteered to scramble up and untangle it. Mr. Seymour told him that it was flying in honor of Nathan Hale's birthday, and added, 'Of course, you don't know who he was.' 'Oh, yes sir,' answered the Cambridge lad, 'he was that spy we hanged!' "[14]

To protect the Birthplace, Seymour bought the farmhouse across the road. Built in 1720, it had been the home of Hale's "good grandmother Strong." Seymour refurbished and furnished this house, which was his country home for many years. Here, as well as at the Birthplace and his New Haven house, he installed New England antiques of mainly Connecticut origin. At the Birthplace he also kept a "considerable collection of early Connecticut folk-pottery (made in New London and Norwich), and a collection of the painted basketry of the Mohegan Indians." Seymour left the Hale homestead to the Connecticut Antiquarian and Landmarks Society; today, it is open to the public.[15]

In 1913, a sixteen-year effort by Seymour had borne fruit when a statue of Nathan Hale was erected on the old campus of Yale College, Hale's alma mater. The statue was designed by Bela Lyon Pratt, who was later responsible for the portrait of Nathan Hale that was used on the 1½¢ stamp from 1925 to 1938. The Hale stamp was of course also Seymour's idea, and he took considerable trouble over many years to see that it was issued. Seymour later described his campaign:

> The author cannot refrain from telling the story of the stamp. . . . The idea came to him like a flash during a sleepless night on a Pullman sleeper. . . . Forthwith he wrote to President Harding, from whom he received a patriotic but noncommittal reply. Later on, at the suggestion of Mr. Taft [a close friend of Seymour] he wrote to President Coolidge, whose reply equally patriotic but not more helpful suggested that the matter might be taken up with the Postmaster-General. Undaunted, the author made a personal appeal to the Postmaster-General who was sympathetic but hardly encouraging; it apparently was a new thing to receive a suppliant who did not want a postmastership, but the favor of a Federal stamp for a national hero.[16]

The stamp was finally issued in 1925, and nearly three billion were printed before Benjamin Franklin replaced Hale as the 1½¢ incumbent in 1938.

It seems fair to conclude that without these zealous promotions Nathan Hale would not be a household word today. However, Seymour had many other interests. He published innumerable papers and pamphlets on historical and antiquarian subjects. For example, his great interest in Yale resulted in a number of writings related to that institution. But Hale remained paramount, and provided the focus for publications such as *The Familiar Hale*; *Hale's Last Words Derived from Addison's 'Cato'*; *Hale and Wyllys—A Digressive History*; and Seymour's crowning literary achievement, *A Documentary Life of Nathan Hale*. The last work was published at the end of Seymour's own life, when he was bedridden and, as a result of a stroke, unable to speak. "He lay propped up in his bed with an elaborate apparatus of beams, pulleys and ropes above it, laboriously but always cheerfully, tapping out words and making sentences from a child's alphabet mounted on a cardboard."[17]

Seymour died in January 1945, at the age of eighty-five. With him died many of the old rituals, old songs, and old loyalties. He was among the last of a great collecting generation—that group of New Englanders who were first to appreciate, study, and "piously preserve" the artifacts and customs of an earlier America.

Chapter 10

Horace Eugene Bolles
and
Charles Hitchcock Tyler

Two Early Boston Collectors

O N DAYS WHEN IT WAS POSSIBLE TO SNATCH A FEW HOURS FROM HIS BOSTON law practice, Eugene Bolles (1838–1910) would set off in pursuit of an old chair or table reportedly for sale. In the early 1880s, when it was still possible to find early American antiques by traveling through the countryside, Bolles began to amass a collection that grew to exceed six hundred pieces. It became the largest and finest of its kind; purchased by the Metropolitan Museum in 1909, it eventually formed the nucleus of the museum's American Wing. The acquisition was a critical step toward widespread recognition of the importance of American antiques.

That is certainly the way Bolles himself regarded it. "I sincerely hope," he wrote shortly after the sale,

> that it will be the basis of a much larger and complete collection, and inspire a genuine and abiding interest in that range of things from the simple and quaint to the really beautiful, which are commonly called colonial. It is a line of collecting which has hitherto been wholly neglected, to my great surprise, by our large museums, although among the people of New England and their descendants throughout the United States, I think there is hardly

Horace Eugene Bolles.
(Walpole Society Note
Book, *1952)*

any kind of collection which appeals so directly to their hearts or gives them so much simple reminiscent pleasure. This is wholly in addition to the quasi historic interest they have from their association with the customs, surroundings and life of our provincial and colonial history and the character, in a sense classic, which they must have from their association with the early beginnings of a great nation.[1]

Nostalgia for the good old days, interest in early American home life, and patriotism are the motives for collecting reflected in this passage.

There is no indication here, or elsewhere, that Bolles set out to form a comprehensive collection that would be especially appropriate for museum purposes. (However, George Palmer, Bolles's cousin and collecting companion, wrote to Henry Watson Kent at the Metropolitan that he and Bolles had consciously formed complementary collections which they hoped would eventually be displayed together at a museum.) Bolles's collection went to the museum at a time when American antiques had just begun to be catalogued and classified. But after its purchase it was described by Kent, the museum's secretary, as follows:

> It would be difficult to overestimate the value of this collection to the Museum, not only because of the beauty and importance of many of the individual pieces, but because the collection as a whole is a unit, the dominant idea being to portray the history of the development of form and ornament in furniture during a period of more than two centuries.[2]

The earliest furniture forms made and used in New England were Eugene Bolles's specialty. He bought English things as well, obtaining them on both sides of the Atlantic. In 1909, when he was evaluating his antiques in order to insure them for their trip to the Hudson-Fulton Exhibition, it was these seventeenth- and eighteenth-century pieces that he considered the most valuable:[3]

American court cupboard, carved with doors below	$2,000
English court cupboard, open below	$1,000
highboy, 6 turned legs	$ 800
lowboy, 4 turned legs, mate to above	$ 400
table chair which belonged to Peregrine White	$2,500
table board, "the oldest American table known"	$ 750

In December of 1910 another of Bolles's cousins and his law partner, Charles Tyler, wrote a memorial tribute, characterizing him as "an unusual and extraordinary combination of the collector of furniture and the practical tryer of law cases—the former naturally and because all his instincts and tastes led him necessarily into collecting; the latter unwillingly, and, as he used often to say, by force of circumstance. That he should have been equally successful as collector and lawyer but proves the exceptional and versatile character of the man."[4] According to Tyler, Bolles had had an extraordinary feeling for the furniture of New England, combining instinct and analytical ability just as he did in the practice of law. Tyler wrote of his cousin's collecting:

> Each piece of this collection was thoroughly studied before it was bought, and was then taken into the house of its purchaser to be lived with, while the original study made before purchase was completed by searching and daily analysis, which sometimes, but not often, resulted in an elimination of a doubtful piece. The fairmindedness and honesty of the man, the catholicism of his examinations, and the correctness of his determination to eliminate when reached, were remarkable, and insured beyond all peradventure the character of the pieces he finally kept.[5]

Eugene Bolles used every possible method of securing objects for his collection. He scoured the countryside in a horse-drawn buggy; he bought from dealers, to whom he was known and who probably looked out for things that would interest him; and he attended auctions. Bolles's willingness to endure inconvenience, discomfort, and delay comes through in his account of a search for "a large, square, old four legged early New England table with heavy stretchers."

> After going by steam and electric cars and on foot through the snow to an old farmhouse I found that the table had been stored by its owner in Newburyport. My trip that day was in vain. About two weeks ago I went down to Newburyport to see it, but as the one who showed it had to take the next

Chair table, white oak with pine top, c. 1675, which Bolles listed as having belonged to Peregrine White, who was born aboard the Mayflower *in 1620. It was one of Bolles's chief treasures. (The Metropolitan Museum of Art; gift of Mrs. Russell Sage, 1909)*

train back I only had fifteen minutes with him, and really want to look at it again. . . . I think I shall get it. . . .[6]

Bolles's pilgrimages extended much farther afield than Newburyport, however. When Henry Erving's friend William Hurlburt of Cromwell, Connecticut, died in 1904, Bolles was on the scene to buy the best things from his collection. Kent wrote that Bolles had obtained furniture from Dr. Lyon's collection upon that gentleman's death in 1896. But Bolles's greatest coup had come in 1894 when he and his cousin George Palmer bought the distinguished furniture collected by Walter Hosmer of Hartford.

In the notes that accompanied his furniture to the Metropolitan Museum, Bolles gave what he knew of the provenance of each piece and provided, as well, information as to restorations and repairs. The notes are evidence of Bolles's sincere desire to know how his antiques had looked when new, and to restore them accordingly. Sometimes sentimental, he was nevertheless seriously interested in proper restoration and finishes. Of a press cupboard dated 1699, Bolles wrote that he had bought the piece from Hosmer "in the rough and defective in 1894." It was missing the door, columns, top boards, and many moldings, and Bolles had no doubt that it should be restored. He had Hartford's Patrick Stevens do the work.[7]

Bolles's approach as a collector was described vividly by Dwight Blaney:

> My first meeting with a real student and collector was with Eugene Bolles. . . . I met him first prowling around some Boston shops—and later my wife and I exchanged calls with Mr. and Mrs. Bolles. He lived somewhere near Boston and I had a grand experience seeing his early American oak. I was horrified at his repainting his pieces in heavy oil paint, but of course did not criticize. He was so enthusiastic, it seemed unkind to destroy or interfere in his work. He had tables piled with "Bible boxes" so called—and drawers in his highboys filled with trays of sets of lovely genuine brasses for bureaus, etc. A point which I observed, and I still have boxes of brasses myself, which, alas, I shall never use.[8]

This candid impression of one early collector by another is precious because it is so rare, but it is also misleading. Expressing his horror at Bolles's repainting of furniture, Blaney implied that Bolles had too little concern for its original condition. A sampling of Bolles's notes suggests otherwise. In writing of the Oliver Putnam secretary purchased in Boston, Bolles said: "To save the old color which was rich under the scale of dirt, I had the old finish rubbed down by hand nearly to the surface of the wood instead of having it scraped." And of a small Hepplewhite table, "bought by me 10 or 12 years ago from a dealer in Boston named Jacobs," Bolles said he stopped the dealer's restoration immediately upon purchase and had the "old dirty finish scraped off with much care, so as not to destroy the color of the old inlay. The difference can be seen in the inlay of the oval in the top and in the other leaf."[9]

Receiving an inquiry from Henry Kent about restoring some of his pieces after they had gone to the Metropolitan, Bolles replied immediately:

> You speak of Mr. De Forest having under consideration the matter of re-storing the pieces. I hope you will feel as I do, that a piece in its unrestored condition is much more interesting and attractive than after restoration, and that restoration should be limited to those pieces which physically require it for their preservation, or which have been so painted or otherwise dealt with that it is necessary to restore them to give an adequate idea of what they originally were. It is true that one can restore a piece at any time so there need be no hurry. He can never unrestore it, and an error in this direction is final.[10]

Thus, Bolles seems to have had a much greater attachment to old colors and finishes than either Blaney or many of today's students have realized. He was apparently motivated partly by the romantic view—still held by many—that an old piece should look old, that a certain amount of wear and tear enhances it. Of the proposed restoration of a japanned highboy, Bolles said: "When placed in a proper light I think it looks faded, interesting and museum-like just as it is. . . . You see I am naturally very conservative."[11]

Yet he had confidence in the rightness of restoration when parts were missing or destroyed—an attitude not shared by everyone today, when some students feel that showing a fragment is more appropriate than creating new pieces to make the fragment whole. Bolles wrote of an American court cup-board: "It is apparently in its original condition as to color, except where the color is largely worn off. This cupboard should be restored. Before this is done, each moulding and part should be studied to see which was black, and which red, and sample drawings made and colored, so that when the old finish is taken off they can be restored properly. Probably the two lower columns were exactly the same size and style as the two upper ones."[12]

His collection appears to have overflowed every room in his house. A room-by-room inventory at the time of sale to the Metropolitan furnishes evidence that Bolles's parlor, no matter how large, must have been jammed. The parlor list includes five Bible boxes, three chests, two court cupboards, a highboy, a lowboy, a desk, three tables of various sizes and shapes, four armchairs, a roundabout chair, three Chippendale chairs, eight mirrors, a Hepplewhite dressing case, a bodice with embroidered front, and smaller objects of pewter and other metals, wood, bone, and glass. What Bolles couldn't fit into the main house, he put into his storeroom.[13]

The inventory suggests that Bolles, like other collectors of the 1870s and 1880s, felt perfectly comfortable in rooms crowded with antiques of all periods and styles. He lived in Dorchester, first in an eighteenth-century house on Willow Court where, according to a friend,

> Mr. Bolles, from the beautiful interior surroundings became interested in the study and collection of antique furniture, at first a pleasant hobby, which in later years brought him fame not only for his wonderful collection, now

Above: *Eighteenth-century pieces from the Bolles collection, on view at the Metropolitan Museum in 1913. (The Metropolitan Museum of Art)*

Left: *Japanned high chest, made in Boston, 1725–1750, from the Bolles collection. Bolles wrote of one of his japanned chests that "when placed in a proper light I think it looks faded, interesting and museum-like." (The Metropolitan Museum of Art; gift of Mrs. Russell Sage, 1909)*

largely in the Metropolitan Museum in New York, but as a connoisseur of the first rank. Into this pursuit Mrs. Bolles also entered, and through extended foreign travel together, became only second to her husband as an authority on antiques.

About 1886 Mr. Bolles bought the Chickering house at 401 Quincy Street and here they created a delightful home, crowded with priceless furnishings which were enjoyed by innumerable travellers and friends who always found the most gracious hospitality. It was always their pleasure to show and explain.[14]

The few written descriptions we have of Eugene Bolles do not present him as vivid or magnetic. According to Kent, he was a "serious, sober, worried person." It is easy to infer also that collecting gave Bolles relief from heavy burdens, real or perceived, that he bore. In 1910, he wrote to Kent: "I am at my office on Sunday and expect to be here all day and have been at the office several evenings this past week . . . I have not yet been able to retire *very far* away from the troublesome practice of law, but am hoping. If nature had only been as generous to us in all things as she has in the amount of hope she gave us, life would surely be worth living." Before very long, Bolles was dead. Charles Hitchcock Tyler wrote in a memorial tribute: ". . . it was not Eugene Bolles the collector or lawyer that we loved the most—it was Eugene Bolles the man and dear friend . . . he was alike in time of happiness or in time of trouble always the truest and best of friends."[15]

The size and range of the Bolles collection are apparent in this view of the study room at the Metropolitan, 1917. (The Metropolitan Museum of Art)

Charles Hitchcock Tyler.
(Harvard University)

Bolles had been Tyler's mentor in collecting. In describing Bolles's and Palmer's purchase of the Hosmer collection, Henry Erving commented:

> Afterwards, anything that Bolles didn't want, that had merit, he passed along to Charlie Tyler and that was about the beginning of Tyler's collecting. Bolles was the incentive and really the outside man who met the dealers and others, and I think that Tyler left many things in the early days entirely to Eugene Bolles's judgment. Tyler soon became entirely able to take care of himself and his buying, which he continued long after Bolles' untimely death, as did Palmer also.[16]

Charles Tyler was twenty-five years Bolles's junior, and they had very different personalities. Henry Kent described Tyler as collecting "grandly, through dealers," while Bolles "began in a buggy, going from house to house in the New England country on his vacations." In the end, Tyler's collection rivaled Bolles's and was even broader in scope. As Bolles's collection formed the nucleus of the Metropolitan Museum's American antiques, so Tyler's became the "virtual keystone of the [Boston Museum of Fine Arts'] holdings. The Tyler collection contained many of the most famous early examples, such as the 'Mary Pease' Hadley chest, as well as having unusual strength in depth with, for instance, five versions of court or press cupboards."[17]

Charles Tyler (1863–1931) was born in Cambridge, Massachusetts, and grew up in Winchester where, according to the family genealogy, his father was one of the town's most prominent and respected citizens. Tyler graduated from Harvard in 1886, and for many years thereafter made his home with his mother, who lived to be nearly one hundred. Toward the end of her life, Tyler refused to lend to exhibitions or to have anything in the house moved, because his mother was blind and knew her way around by touch.

Tyler, wrote a friend, was "one of Boston's foremost lawyers . . . his office was littered with antique furniture, bronzes, engravings, etc." He was also a trustee of the Museum of Fine Arts, a prominent member of the select group of Boston collectors of Americana known as The Trestle Board, and a lecturer at Boston University Law School. He had three houses—one in Boston, one in Beverly, on Boston's North Shore, and one in Sanbornton, New Hampshire—all filled with antiques. In New Hampshire, Tyler bred hunting dogs, blooded cattle, and prize fowl.[18]

In his collecting, Tyler was probably influenced by the same motives as his cousin Bolles. He seems, like Squire Hardcastle in Goldsmith's *She Stoops to*

Conquer, simply to have loved "everything that's old." He amazed his friends with his interest in so many different areas of the past. Tyler was far ahead of his time in collecting the arts of the nineteenth century, which have not until quite recently achieved acceptance among serious collectors. When his antiques went to the Museum of Fine Arts upon his death in 1931, most of the Victorian pieces were sent to auction. There are those at the museum today who wish very much they could somehow retrieve those pieces.

"Of his mania for collecting," wrote a friend,

> most of which we could appreciate and which amounted almost to an obsession with him, we still found it difficult to understand why he had extended himself in so many fields. There was hardly a line of Americana in which he did not possess splendid examples, while in some of them he simply stunned one by the completeness of his coverage. . . . Probably no one has ever seen all of his collections, for, besides his three houses, which

Above: *Great chair, oak, c, 1680–1700, southwestern Massachusetts. From Charles Tyler's collection. (Courtesy Museum of Fine Arts, Boston)*

Left: *Hadley chest, oak, seventeenth century. From Tyler's collection. (Courtesy Museum of Fine Arts, Boston)*

were "crammed to the guards," he had storerooms full of treasures. It is doubtful if even he could remember all that he had.[19]

In the field of furniture, Tyler's collections extended from the seventeenth century to the nineteenth. His selection of Bennington wares, luster, and various other ceramics was vast; there were bronzes, engravings and paintings, and American silver with an emphasis on New England makers. Among the latter were two particularly remarkable pieces: a standing salt by Jeremiah Dummer and a sweetmeat box by John Coney, both monumental and beautiful examples of seventeenth-century American silver. When the Walpole Society gathered at Tyler's house on one of their visits to Boston, Tyler "placed on the table a sweetmeat box and standing salt which took our breath away"—quite a feat in that distinguished group of collectors. The admiration of knowledgeable fellow Walpoleans must have delighted Tyler, for he

> derived great pleasure in his collecting, and received much satisfaction in showing his treasures to appreciative friends. His unselfish nature craved companions to share with him the delights of his hobby.
>
> With a life filled with activity, it was hard to give up to his last illness. Unable to go to his office, yet mentally just as keen as ever, he kept in touch with all his interests so far as his strength permitted. . . . Unable to visit antique shops dealers brought pieces to his home, for he continued his love for collecting to the end. On the day he died he planned to see a dealer from Boston, who had some prints and paintings, which he thought might be of interest to him.[20]

"When I last visited him, ill in his bed," wrote Kent of Tyler, "he was collecting the sculptured animals and birds that our mid-Victorian grandparents loved to stand on their mantel pieces and marble-topped tables." All this went to the Museum of Fine Arts, and an auction was held almost immediately to reduce the collection to manageable proportions. One staff member remembers going into Tyler's Boston house beforehand. The walls were covered solidly with prints, and every stair tread held a piece of pottery. During the auction, the curator overheard two shrewd dealers discussing a Bohemian-glass chamber pot that had just been put on the block. "You know, dearie," said one, "you just take the handle off, and it makes a lovely rose bowl."[21]

Chapter 11

Dwight Blaney

and the Craft of Collecting

"Common natures do not suffice me," said Charles Lamb. "Good people, as they are called, won't serve. I want individuals."[1] He would have been delighted with Dwight Blaney (1865–1944)—collector, naturalist, perfectionist, lover of good wines and old songs, and valued friend.

In a letter addressed to the Walpole Society on the occasion of its twenty-fifth anniversary meeting, Blaney wrote that he had always been a collector. Eugene Bolles was the first person he had known who truly shared this interest; when the Walpole Society was founded he met others, "and life began to carry on." In 1945 Henry Kent recalled:

> When Eugene Bolles, Luke Lockwood and I, sitting at luncheon in Boston's Union Club, way back in 1910, listing the names of the men we thought might be interested to join our proposed club of collectors of early American things of one sort or another—men with antiquarian propensities— the very first name that came to the mind of each of us was that of Dwight Blaney. . . . He was full of surprises and delights. He was possessed of real knowledge of our early crafts and craftsmen . . . and, being a craftsman himself, he had a fellow feeling for other workmen; but he was possessed, also,

of what was even more important, the spirit of the times when such works of craftsmanship as those he collected were made and used.[2]

This vital interest in the crafts of early America set Blaney apart from his contemporaries, and even—in its intensity—from some of his fellow collectors. He liked to do woodworking himself, a pleasure he shared with two other early Boston collectors, the brothers James and David Little. "He just didn't care for the Victorian but had an artist's eye as well as interest in Yankee ingenuity and feeling for the simple early pieces."[3]

From boyhood, Blaney had loved to sketch. His first job was in a tombstone maker's shop, where he eventually became chief designer. Then "one day, while sketching on the marshes, a stranger looking at his work over his shoulder, and impressed by it, proposed a new job for him, that of draftsman in the office of a Boston firm of architects, Peabody and Stearns." After six years with the firm, Blaney retired and "gave himself up to painting, in water colors and oil-colors, to etching and to collecting."[4] John Singer Sargent, one of Blaney's friends, felt that his watercolors were his best efforts, and recommended that he concentrate on that medium. Blaney's work was exhibited at the Carnegie Institute, the Cincinnati Art Museum, and the Pennsylvania Academy of the Fine Arts.

Serpentine-front mahogany chest of drawers, 1805–1815. Labeled by Thomas Needham; from Blaney's collection. (Photograph by Richard Cheek)

For Blaney, as for many of his contemporary collectors, American antiques were only one aspect of an appreciation that encompassed a wide range of objects. His collection of Japanese prints and ivories, and of paintings and prints from many sources and centuries, reflected the informed taste of his time. Blaney's love of antiques was always enhanced by an American origin, however. Like others of his generation, he was drawn to colonial New England, and fascinated by Revolutionary heroes. He shared with George Dudley Seymour an enthusiasm for old New England songs and customs, and the two men are occasionally mentioned in the Walpole Society chronicles as having rendered old favorites with great gusto.

Dwight Blaney.
(Photograph by Richard
Cheek)

Although Blaney was himself an artist of some accomplishment, he apparently (like most collectors of his time) did not regard American antiques as true art of the highest caliber. He began collecting furniture as a way of furnishing his house when he was married, for he found eighteenth-century pieces more pleasing than those of the 1890s. "He had exhilaration" in his purchases, wrote Kent, "and so, true to form, he went on with them and became before he knew it, the Collector."[5]

Three pieces from the dealer Stickney of Salem were among Blaney's first purchases. He wrote his wife-to-be about them in 1893:

I hope we will be able to go to Salem tomorrow . . . and I want you to see the furniture at Stickneys', which I asked him to reserve. He said he would make a discount, if we bought anything and said he would sell the $50 chest of drawers, the $50 Chippendale sofa and the $25 mirror for $100 which was quite an offer, I think. The chest of drawers and the mirror are first class pieces. The sofa six feet long perhaps, so so.[6]

The future Mrs. Blaney approved, and the so-so sofa became part of a budding collection, along with the mirror and the serpentine-front chest of drawers— which, because it bore the label of Salem cabinetmaker Thomas Needham, turned out to be very important.

The Blaney collection grew to be formidable. (In fact, after Blaney died and his four surviving children had all taken what they wanted, it took three days to auction off what remained.) Fortunately, Blaney had the means not only to purchase but also to accommodate his antiques, which filled three houses to overflowing. His wife was an heiress, the daughter of the owner of the Eastern Steamship Company. Her sister had married the yachtsman

C. H. W. Foster, in whose contemptuous opinion Blaney's beloved furniture was merely second-hand—not an uncommon attitude in the nineties, even though the number of collectors was increasing.

Blaney had, eventually, a double house on Beacon Hill in Boston, an early farmhouse in Weston, Massachusetts, and a Greek-revival farmhouse on Ironbound, an island off the coast of Maine. (There was a fishing blind on Cape Cod, too, but even Blaney could not devise a way to furnish that with antiques.) The Blaneys left Boston for Ironbound every spring, taking food and other provisions not available on the island, along with the regiment of maids necessary to keep the house and the little Blaneys in good working order. They traveled on a steamship, for it was much easier to make the entire trip by sea in those days. Once there, they settled in for several months' stay. Friends from Boston, artists, and naturalists came to visit and to work. A bronze bas-relief of Blaney by the sculptor Bela Pratt has in the background the spruces and rocky coast of Ironbound; and John Singer Sargent, a frequent visitor to the island, painted a portrait of Blaney there.

Blaney's best things, naturally enough, were in the Mount Vernon Street house on Beacon Hill. His furniture ranged from the seventeenth century to the nineteenth, but his dislike of fussiness is apparent in the simplicity of each piece, early or late. And he preferred the early things. His favorite was a small maple trestle table, with drop leaves that could be raised and supported by

A selection of punch and toddy ladles of silver and whalebone. From Blaney's collection.
(Photograph by Richard Cheek)

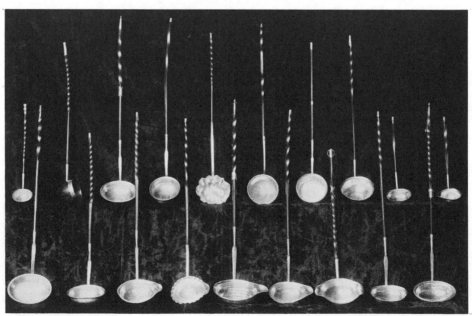

butterfly-shaped wings. The combination of butterfly supports and trestle base fascinated Blaney, for he had never seen another table like it. His own individualism probably predisposed him toward this and other examples of unusual and imaginative craftsmanship.

Blaney's early American silver was notable, too (much of it is now at the De Young Museum in San Francisco). It was used in the Mount Vernon Street house, where it was kept in the pantry under lock and key. Besides hollow ware—tankards, cans, porringers, bowls—Blaney took a special interest in spoons and ladles, and his collection of punch and toddy ladles with twisted whalebone handles was large.

There were also ceramics of English, Continental, Oriental, and American origin; pewter, brass, iron, and other metal objects; enameled patch boxes; glass; the little carved-ivory Japanese objects called netsukes; and hundreds of prints and paintings. Blaney devoted himself to all these, and more. He knew a great deal about each type of object he collected, and his eye for line, proportion, color, and simplicity of ornament always prevailed. "This was not an aggregation," said a fellow Walpole Society member, "but a collection of which each piece was known and loved."[7]

Blaney must have become well known among the Boston dealers. In a letter to Israel Sack, one of the earliest, canniest, and eventually most prestigious of dealers in American antiques, Blaney said that he was looking forward to Sack's proposed book: "After all your busy years at collecting and helping the rest of us 'Old boys' gather our Antiques you should have a great deal to say of thirty years ago in Boston. Mr. Eugene Bolles was my first collecting friend and [I] remember he went about with you in search of some of his wonderful pieces. Certainly the many beautiful pieces I obtained through your help have been a great joy to me."[8] Mr. Sack returned the compliment in a letter to Blaney's daughter many years later. ". . . I am ever grateful to him," wrote Sack, "for the love of Americana he imbued in me."[9]

Blaney never felt the need to buy matching sets. His houses were filled to the brim with antiques; they had continuity because they met his standards, not because one form echoed another or because all were of the same period. Nor did he arrange them conventionally. "I seem to remember," wrote a friend, "that in the long parlors of the two houses, one walked not across and freely around and about the rooms, but in symmetrically laid out aisles between arrangements of furniture of the finest character."[10] There were so many pieces to be accommodated that Blaney's favorite butterfly table with the trestle base, in the living room of the Mount Vernon Street house, was under a larger Duncan Phyfe table covered, in turn, by a Turkish carpet. Topping everything off was a fine tin-enameled dish. It was enough, apparently, that Blaney knew the trestle-base table was there, even if invisible. When he wanted to show it off, no doubt he simply moved things around a bit. His daughter remembers that he thought nothing of bringing a group of dinner guests into her room long after she'd gone to sleep, because of an old print or piece of furniture there that he wanted to show.

Blaney's things may have looked jumbled to the uninitiated, but the maids knew better. "DO NOT TOUCH anything on or in this desk," was the sign that protected the familiar disarray of his effects. Not only were the rooms crammed with antiques, but the walls were covered solidly with books and pictures. One day Blaney's son decided to count the pictures actually hung—as opposed to leaning against the walls—in the Mount Vernon Street house. Starting at the bottom level, he went all through the house, and found six hundred pictures (prints and paintings) hanging. They were old and new, etchings, drawings, engravings, and oils, by his friends—John Singer Sargent and Childe Hassam among them—and by artists he admired. His Monet, part of the Haystack series, was one of the earliest French Impressionist paintings to be brought to America.

Blaney was very careful of his furniture. He would never allow a piece to be sent out for repair because it might be returned minus some of its original parts. (A not uncommon approach, which Seymour suspected the Hartford cabinetmakers of applying to his furniture, was to remove old parts and replace them with new, leaving the hapless collector with a considerably less valuable piece.) All Blaney's antiques were therefore repaired in his home, under his watchful eye.

Blaney's rule of never letting an antique out of the house was violated only once. When 250 guests were expected at the Mount Vernon Street house for his youngest daughter's wedding reception, it seemed imperative to move all the furniture temporarily out of the first floor into a hired van. Blaney was not consulted. He stayed upstairs in his library during the festivities, and if he realized that some of his precious antiques were sitting outside in a van, he never let on.

Just as the Mount Vernon Street house was filled with Blaney's finest things, in keeping with the formality of Boston, the Weston house was furnished with simpler pieces. "On Mt. Vernon Street life was lived according to polite conventions," wrote Kent, "with art, music, friends, and a distinguished cuisine; at Weston, according to the conventions of the XVIII-Century, more or less; but on Ironbound, life was spent according to natural laws from sunrise to sunset, painting and fishing."[11]

Blaney was an ardent fisherman. Another of his chief occupations on Ironbound was exploring the waters of Frenchman's Bay. He published the results of his investigations in *The Nautilus*. Kent wrote that because of Blaney's serious interest in this aspect of natural history, "naturalists and scientists came to visit him, among them the Prince of Monaco; and the learned, in recognition of his contributions to the knowledge of prehistoric things of the sea, named a

Blaney's study in the Mount Vernon Street house overflowed with antiques, books, prints, and paintings. (Photograph by Richard Cheek)

new-found species of chiton—found by him in his dredging in 20 fathoms, off Ironbound—'Tonicella Blaneyi.' "[12]

After the day's activities at Ironbound, everyone gathered for dinner at an impeccable white-linened table, where Blaney and his friends sang sea chanties between courses. "You remember," wrote Kent, "his knowledge of the music, of the songs of the early days—folk songs, I suppose you would call them—and how lustily he used to sing them for our delight?"[13] Good fellowship prevailed wherever Blaney was in charge. John Cotton Dana, in a lightly satirical report of the second Walpole Society meeting, held in Boston in 1910, described a visit to Blaney's Mount Vernon Street house:

> Mr. Blaney gave us lunch in his home at 82 Mount Vernon Street. It is not well to attempt here to suggest the atmosphere of lunch. The discussion of mugs, cups, beakers and goblets shifted at times from dates and makers and names to the mere matter of contents. The Secretary and Mr. Canfield have prepared a special report on the pie.[14]

Pottery, glass, and tools in Blaney's Weston farmhouse. (Photograph by Richard Cheek)

Chapter 12

Canfield, Perry, and Pendleton

The Gambling Collectors

Once when Richard Canfield was "returning incognito from an art-buying trip abroad, he was faced with filling in, on his customs declarations, the space after the word 'business.' He found it no problem. 'Gentleman,' he wrote."[1]

Such a reaction is hardly conceivable from Lyon, Erving, Bolles, and the other great, but sedate, New England collectors. That they were gentlemen was taken for granted—their business was something separate and also eminently respectable. But the backgrounds of collectors Canfield, Marsden Perry, and Charles Pendleton precluded their being automatically considered gentlemen. Probably to compensate for their unconventional lives, all three set out to create impeccably refined home environments.

The three men are said to have been boyhood friends in Providence, Rhode Island. Canfield was a professional gambler, whose gaming houses were elegant, exclusive, and lucrative. Pendleton, also a professional gambler, studied law but seems to have given it up early; he dealt in antiques, apparently as a result of his addiction to both gambling and collecting, and gathered his own notable collection of high-style English and American furniture. Perry left home at

Richard A. Canfield, Esq.
*Painted by James Abbott
McNeill Whistler, c. 1902.*
(Photograph courtesy of
the Photographic Archives
of the National Gallery
of Art)

age twelve, made a fortune, and filled his house with rare objects and books; he also enjoyed playing cards for high stakes.

Unlike the other collectors of their time, they looked to antiques not to enhance social status but to provide it. Also, instead of identifying with respectable early New England householders, as Lyon, Erving, and the others did, they emulated wealthy eighteenth-century connoisseurs. In very high-style American and English furniture and silver, Oriental porcelains and carpets, and European and American paintings, they saw evidence of the taste and artistry that are hallmarks of a cultivated society. These qualities attracted them strongly, for they aspired to be gentlemen in the explicit and formal English sense. Collecting books and paintings, furniture and silver, were unmistakably gentlemanly pursuits. It was more important to Canfield, Perry, and Pendleton to be recognized for their educated taste than to be associated with old American families and the virtues of the Founding Fathers.

They achieved their goal. Although Pendleton died before the exclusive Walpole Society was founded, Canfield and Perry were among its proudest members. And Pendleton's collection achieved such renown that the Rhode Island School of Design, in accepting it as a gift shortly before his death in 1904, met his condition that a fireproof Georgian house be built to display it.

Richard Albert Canfield (1855–1914) was born in New Bedford, Massachusetts. His father was a printer, and Canfield aspired to a more elevated station. When he graduated from grammar school in 1868, he was one of five children chosen to deliver a speech. He gave Josiah Quincy's "Our Obligations to the Fathers of New England," learning it so thoroughly that "forty years later, in an upstairs room at Delmonico's in New York, he repeated it verbatim for the edification of a champagne supper which he had given for members of the Four Hundred."[2]

Canfield's interpretation of his own "Obligations to the Fathers" seems to have been remarkably liberal for his day, for not too long after delivering the speech he began what was to be a lifelong career in gambling. After an apprenticeship in Rhode Island, Boston, and New York, he set off to observe European methods. Returning in 1879, he set up his own faro house in Providence. When it was raided six years later, he was sent to jail for six months. He always maintained that this period was the making of him: "Jail," he said, "was my Harvard." Studying history, literature, and art, he emerged from prison feeling considerably less apologetic about his lack of education and background. He later said that if he had his life to live over, he would be a professor of literature.[3]

As it was, he seems to have enjoyed life very much. His Saratoga establishment, the Club House, was legendary. There he introduced amenities that gave gambling the same kind of glamour he created for himself with his clothes, cuisine, and collections. Even if he was unemployed, "his suits, jewelry and cigars were the best money could borrow, if not buy, and his suave manners, studied courtesy and remarkable ability to remember names won him not only respect but also jobs."[4]

Canfield's gaming houses were run very much like English gentlemen's clubs. Evening dress was required, credit was given without question—to customers admitted only after careful scrutiny—and the appointments and refreshments were faultless. Canfield kept a high-salaried French chef on duty at the Club House during the short season, and paid him to travel about Europe developing new recipes during the rest of the year. The restaurant, therefore, lost money, but Canfield felt the attraction was worth the loss. One of the restaurant's special features was a pool with live fish from which diners were asked to pick their prospective dinners. The patron saw his choice removed from the pool and sent to the kitchen in a basket. The trick was that upon arriving in the kitchen, the fish was immediately thrust into a pipe and returned to the pool. The cooked fish placed before the unwitting diner was considerably less fresh than he thought. Canfield asserted that such deception was not practiced in the gaming rooms, however, and the actor Monty Woolley, the son of one of Canfield's oldest friends, remarked that "If there is such a thing as an honest gambler, Canfield was that man."[5]

Richard Canfield had homes in Providence and New York. Both were filled with rare furniture, paintings, books, ceramics, and other *objets d'art*. "Although he was away from Providence much of the time in the early years, supervising his gambling establishments in New York and Saratoga, his family always lived in Providence," wrote a fellow Walpole Society member. He paid dutiful visits to Rhode Island once a month.[6]

Canfield's collections were of great importance to him, and he is said to have maintained that love of art was his only weakness. He cherished his friendships with artists, collectors, and others active in the artistic professions. His regard was returned, but there is an apologetic tinge to Henry Kent's tribute in the Walpole Society *Note Book*: "He liked us, and we liked him, and we all liked the same things . . . and we never left off talking about them whenever we met; we did not have time to talk about anything else."[7] There is an implication that talk of other things might have proved uncomfortable.

Philadelphia dressing table. From the Canfield collection. (Photograph from Luke Vincent Lockwood's Colonial Furniture in America, *Vol. I)*

When he died in 1914 after a fall in a New York subway station, *The New York Times* published a front-page article:

> Canfield acquired a wide reputation as an art connoisseur, his judgment in ceramics and paintings being recognized everywhere. His collection of ancient vases, bas-reliefs, and pottery of all kinds attracted attention wherever it was exhibited. He made the second largest collection of Whistler paintings in America. It was sold to M. Knoedler & Co. last March for a price in the neighborhood of $300,000.[8]

Canfield was a close friend of James McNeill Whistler, who painted the only known portrait of the gambler. The painting, which the artist called "His Reverence," shows the portly Canfield somberly clad in a dark robe—a strangely ecclesiastical pose for "the best known and wealthiest individual gambler in the world."[9]

The continuing relative obscurity of furniture collecting is evident in the absence of any mention by the *Times* of Canfield's furniture. Yet it was notable. Many pieces were illustrated by Luke Vincent Lockwood, Canfield's lawyer, in his book *Colonial Furniture in America* (1901). Elaborate English Chippendale pieces were interspersed with high-style American forms in the Canfield collection, bought by his friend Marsden Perry when he died. "Perry then possessed such a quantity of furniture, that he sold much of it at an American Art auction in January, 1916, and included in the sale were many items from the Canfield estate." George S. Palmer bought some of the Canfield pieces at this auction, and he in turn sold some to the Metropolitan Museum in 1918. "There are few, perhaps," wrote a friend of Perry,

Marsden Jasiel Perry.
(National Cyclopedia of
American Biography)

> who join me in a memory of [the Canfield furniture], carrying out the purpose for which it had been created through daily use in library, drawing room, and dining room in Mr. Perry's noble house in Providence, the house which in 1786 John Brown built on the slope of the Hill, now the home of the Rhode Island Historical Society. Canfield had been dead ten years when I saw his eighteenth-century furniture in that house of the same period, the whole presenting a harmony seldom attained. . . . No one will see the Canfield collection again as a whole.[10]

Marsden Jasiel Perry (1850–1935) preferred elegant English furniture and Oriental porcelains to American antiques. But he had some very high-style American furniture, including Canfield's, and he restored and lived in one of the great colonial American houses. Perry was another member whom the Walpole Society received graciously but with some reservations. "Unhampered by the traditions of childhood," wrote his memorialist in the Walpole Society *Note Book*, "he was free to develop his own taste and to find out for himself what was best."[11] The writer goes on to praise the Perry collection for meeting the very highest standards; but the impression remains that Perry's childhood was less genteel than was desirable, despite his descent from Richard Perry, one of the grantees of the Massachusetts Bay Colony.

Perry left school at the age of twelve, devoting himself thereafter to building a fortune in public utilities, railroads, and banking. He used the proceeds to buy his collections. Not only did he share Canfield's and Pendleton's predilection for high-style furniture of the Chippendale era, Oriental porcelains and carpets, and fine old silver; he was also a bibliophile. A member of the Grolier Club, he was a serious collector of Shakespeareana, and his was the finest private collection in the country until it was surpassed by the Folger. His chief desire, according to a friend, was to secure the Devonshire quartos. Although he was unable to buy them, he never gave up hope until he was told they had been bought for the Huntington Collection. "My collection can never now achieve top rank," said Perry, "and I think that it's time to sell it." Soon thereafter, the Philadelphia dealer A. S. W. Rosenbach bought the Perry collection.[12]

In 1901, Perry purchased the John Brown house in Providence, called by John Quincy Adams "the most magnificent and elegant private mansion that I have ever seen on this continent." In restoring the house and filling it with his collections, Perry was motivated, according to one memorialist,

> by the desire as he became financially more and more secure, to better his style of living and improve the character of the things with which he lived— his house, his books, his furniture, and his accessories of many sorts. He was astonishingly successful in his creation of an artistic entity through the pursuit of this purpose. Perhaps he should be thought of as creative artist rather than as collector.[13]

This "harmony of house and contents" delighted all who visited Perry until his death in 1935. It was described at that time in terms that would surely have pleased its creator: "Everything in it, almost, had been made in the first place to live with, and these things fitted into a home where people lived as gentlefolk. This essentially livable home was like a dream of the abode of a cultured eighteenth-century gentleman."[14]

Charles Leonard Pendleton (1849–1904) apparently liked to give the impression that he had graduated from both Yale College and Yale Law School, for that information has been reprinted a number of times over the years. The class book for the year 1869, when Pendleton would have graduated, proves otherwise: "Charles Leonard Pendleton left the class second term Freshman. Studied law in Providence, Rhode Island; practiced in Westerly, Rhode Island; then returned to Providence, where he now is. We advise future historians not to trouble themselves to learn further details concerning him."[15]

This stern advice was taken, and the fascinated reader never solves the mystery of his fall from grace. The only apparent solution is his gambling—and possibly his dealing in antiques. Whatever the reason, Pendleton's name was eventually expunged from the roster of the class of 1869.

He made his mark elsewhere. His collection was probably the most famous of his day, and his giving it to the Rhode Island School of Design ensured its enduring fame. The collection included "130 pieces of English and American furniture, English and Continental pottery and porcelain, Chinese porcelain and export ware, glassware, and rugs." The fireproof Georgian structure built for it by the school was modeled mainly on his own eighteenth-century residence, but included elements copied from other fine old Providence houses. Pendleton House was opened in 1906. The Providence *Sunday Tribune* wrote:

Providence will rejoice in finding itself pre-
eminent in its possession. . . . The place is unique
in that the house and furniture are in perfect harmony, giving not the impression of a museum and
collection, but of a house of a gentleman of refined taste and discrimination who lived in the
eighteenth century and furnished his house with
the best examples of noted cabinetmakers of that
period, Chippendale, Sheraton, and Hepplewhite,
which he could find.[16]

Charles Leonard Pendle-
ton. (Photograph courtesy
of Richard Saunders)

Pendleton's specification that his antiques should be
displayed in a building like a private house, so that
the public could see them as he believed they had
originally been used in the eighteenth century, was
unusual for his day. It has been pointed out that "In
Europe, particularly in England where Pendleton
often traveled, there were notable private collections housed in their own
buildings, but nothing of the kind had been attempted in America." The Concord Antiquarian Society had bought the pre-Revolutionary Reuben Brown
house for the display of Cummings Davis's collection in the 1890s, but the idea
of providing eighteenth-century-style interiors for eighteenth-century furnishings was still unusual in America in the early 1900s. Although Pendleton's
reasons for providing sympathetic settings for his antiques were aesthetic and
associational, he may have influenced the more scientific period rooms that
George Francis Dow created in Salem, and that Kent planned for the Metropolitan. In 1910, Kent wrote in the museum's *Bulletin* that Pendleton House
was among the very first museum installations in America "to accord the art of
our own country the proper display."[17] Pendleton's own goal, however, was
probably to have the collection and its setting impress with their tastefulness
and refinement. He wanted to live like a gentleman, and to be remembered as
one.

Richard Saunders has uncovered some interesting evidence of Pendleton's
dealing in antiques. Saunders cites a receipt of 1901 that documents Pendleton's
sale of "one base to block front high case of drawers" to the Providence
cabinetmaker-antiques dealer Rudolph Breitenstein. The printed heading reads:
"Bought of C. L. Pendleton/Fine Antique Furniture, Rare Old Porcelain,
Oriental Rugs, and Decorative Works of Art." Saunders also reports that
Breitenstein's grandson told of his grandfather's taking "a horse and wagon on
buying trips once or twice a year as far as Philadelphia, sometimes into the
south, and on his return would sell the great pieces to Pendleton." Pendleton
kept for himself the finest high-style pieces, but probably sold others. Some of

New York card table, 1755–1790, which Pendleton bought from the Wendover family of Kinderhook, New York. (Museum of Art, Rhode Island School of Design)

his elaborate Chippendale-style pieces, however, have turned out to be fakes, and have been removed from the collection.[18]

What remains are a number of Chippendale chairs, secretaries, tables, and other forms of the highest quality from England, and also from Boston, Portsmouth, Newport, New York, and Philadelphia. According to the catalogue, the collection was strong in American pieces because Pendleton's primary goal in forming it had been to secure "the best American specimens extant. He has succeeded in his object to an extent not approached by any other collection."[19]

It was furniture of this quality that Canfield and Perry also collected, sometimes with Pendleton's help. Hedy B. Landman has pointed out that, "as a collector and gentleman-dealer, Pendleton undoubtedly bought and sold numerous pieces from and to Canfield and Perry. Canfield, in fact, often served as his scout and buyer on trips to England."[20]

Lockwood was the lawyer for Pendleton as well as Canfield, and the recognized furniture authority of the day. He wrote a sumptuous illustrated catalogue to the Pendleton collection, issued in 1904. But today the value of Lockwood's catalogue, according to Hedy Landman, lies not so much in its scholarship as in the fact that "it recorded the individual objects along with views of interiors in Pendleton's house showing the furniture as he arranged it. . . ."[21]

Like his friends Canfield and Perry, Pendleton sought to create an atmosphere of taste and culture to compensate for any lack of those attributes that might be perceived in his life away from home.

Bombé chest of drawers, probably Boston, 1755–1790, which Pendleton bought from the Dexter family of Providence for $55. (Museum of Art, Rhode Island School of Design)

III

American Antiques
as Art

It is not the objects placed in a museum that constitute its value,
so much as the method in which they are displayed and
the use made of them for the purpose of instruction. There must be
nothing like the miscellaneous collection of all kinds of
"curiosities" thrown indiscriminately together which constitute
the old-fashioned country museum.

William Henry Flower, 1895

At the time of the Hudson-Fulton celebration in 1909 . . . I said to
Mr. de Forest, who was then Secretary of the Metropolitan
Museum, that it seemed to me a museum which showed Greek, Roman,
Egyptian, Chinese, and other Eastern things surely ought to
show to its public the things America had accomplished.

Henry Watson Kent, 1949

THE IDEA THAT AMERICAN ANTIQUES REPRESENTED GOOD TASTE, WHICH HAD ARISEN late in the nineteenth century, was extended in the 1890s and early 1900s to the belief that they were sometimes examples of genuine "art"—a category from which they had previously been excluded. There was still a great deal of patronizing talk about the inferiority of American antiques to those of Europe. This attitude, however, co-existed with real admiration—sometimes, incongruous as it may seem, in the same person. And despite some continuing condescension, or even outright rejection, the appreciation of American antiques grew steadily.

They remained popular as upper-middle-class symbols of background and of their owners' cultural and social distinction. During this period, however, a related but more positive and democratic trend took root. Consistent with their heightened importance, American antiques were to be employed as educational and inspirational tools, to lessen the distance between old native stock and the new arrivals. They seemed appropriate vehicles for informing foreigners and less enlightened natives as to American traditions and values, and for helping to educate industrial designers in the proper use of line and proportion. Such an approach was a logical extension of the more passive arts-and-crafts view expressed earlier, that mere proximity to antiques could serve to improve both the taste and the morals of the masses.

The new approach was implemented by a generation of museum men that emerged at the turn of the century. Among them were Henry Watson Kent of New York, Edwin AtLee Barber of Philadelphia, and George Francis Dow of Salem, Massachusetts. Although some collected privately, they are important to the collecting movement for a different reason. Their contribution was to recognize antiques as evidence of an American cultural tradition, and to organize and present that evidence effectively. They set up museum exhibits that were orderly, understandable, and interesting. The jumble of nineteenth-century bazaar exhibition tables was replaced by careful chronological displays. And in Salem the unsorted clutter of sanitary fair and Centennial colonial kitchens grew into carefully conceived rooms whose American furniture, woodwork, and accessories were basically of the same period. The museum men concentrated on putting each object in a proper historical context. They emphasized its broad cultural significance, rather than its more limited associational value.

Temporary exhibitions, permanent acquisitions, and scholarly catalogues raised the public consciousness of American antiques. Furthermore, Dr. Irving W. Lyon's thorough and thoughtful book about colonial furniture, which had been published in 1891, was supplemented by several others on that and related subjects in the first decade of the new century. Though none rivaled Dr. Lyon's in scholarship, each new book introduced more people to American antiques. The public's familiarity was further increased by the inclusion of antiques in indoor scenes or portraits by contemporary painters and illustrators. As a result of these developments, early American decorative arts gained in both interest and respect, and the ranks of collectors swelled.

Collectors, too, became more committed to the idea that their antiques had educational value. Some, like Judge Alphonso T. Clearwater, collected what would best suit a museum's needs. Judge Clearwater often sought and followed the advice of the curators of the Metropolitan Museum of Art when he was considering adding to his collection, which he left to the museum upon his death.

When *The Evening Post* of New York reviewed *American Silver*, the catalogue to the loan exhibition held at the Boston Museum of Fine Arts from June to November 1906, it took a patronizing tone:

> To many, this handsome catalogue will appeal most strongly as a bit of painstaking antiquarianism. But the silver itself is of considerable artistic

merit. . . . We do well to remind ourselves of a time when American taste, if uninventive, was at least unvulgarized. This silver, with its obvious limitations, is better worth the while of an art museum than any subsequently produced among us.[1]

This was a landmark show, despite the condescending comment. It was the first time any of the decorative arts made in America had been given an exhibition by a major American museum and accompanied by a printed catalogue. The exhibition resulted from the effort and organization of Boston collector Francis Hill Bigelow. Some years later, Bigelow wrote:

> To my friend Mr. R. T. Haines Halsey must be accorded the credit of having inspired me to form the collection of American silver for the Museum of Fine Arts at Boston in 1906; and to his generosity is due the publication of the catalogue of that exhibition, which is one of the handsomest ever issued by any museum. His attribution to the silversmiths of the marks on these pieces has been invaluable in stimulating other investigations.[2]

The catalogue, beautifully printed by Walter Gilliss, was mentioned in the *Annual Report* of the Museum of Fine Arts for 1906: "The special exhibition of American Silver gave occasion for the publication of a catalogue which, next to the Catalogue of Japanese Pottery, is the best example of bookmaking yet issued by the museum."[3] This was the report's only reference to the American silver show or its significance.

Still, the fact that the Museum of Fine Arts was willing to lend its prestige —and its galleries—to such an enterprise was important. It helped to stimulate interest in the American arts, and to show that beautiful objects had been made by American craftsmen. In his introduction to the catalogue, Halsey argued against the existing prejudice that really fine silver must have been imported: "The Museum of Fine Arts, Boston, has demonstrated by this exhibition that the art of the silversmith was highly developed during our early colonial days, and that the craftsmanship of our early native born artisans deserves wider recognition by our Museum than hitherto accorded."[4]

A second important effect of this exhibition was that serious collectors gained initial access to information about American silversmiths. John H. Buck, who along with Halsey had been brought from New York to help with the exhibition, wrote six pages of "Technical description of objects," outlining the creative process and the development of style. Buck also provided basic information for each piece of silver shown: type of object, place of origin, maker, mark, inscription, and weight. He thus "set the form for such entries, which has been used ever since," as Henry Watson Kent commented in 1942.[5]

R. T. H. Halsey's introduction contained facts about the lives and work of the outstanding New England silversmiths. A major contribution to the field, it was chatty as well as informative. His comment on "whistling" tankards and cans provided a note that Halsey knew would add interest to the American past. These vessels were "a vivid reminder of early America's great social vice, tippling; the prevalence of which, while somewhat disastrous to health and morals, did much to promote the good fellowship and helping-hand policy so universal in the colonies."[6]

The next major showing of silver was a joint enterprise sponsored in 1911 by the Museum of Fine Arts in Boston and the Metropolitan Museum in New York. Again, Bigelow and Halsey did much of the groundwork. The theme was church silver, which Bigelow always considered the most important American type because it was so often well documented as to maker, date, and donor.

In Boston, the museum gathered over one thousand pieces of silver from churches throughout New England. Florence V. Paull of the staff wrote that besides the large number of churches in Boston and its vicinity which responded, those of Maine, New Hampshire, Rhode Island, and Connecticut had made possible a comprehensive exhibition of the silver of New England, rather than simply of Massachusetts. Miss Paull pointed out, however, that Boston was the regional silvermaking center in the seventeenth and eighteenth centuries,

Plate 1 in the catalogue to the exhibition of American silver at the Museum of Fine Arts, Boston, in 1906. (Courtesy of the New-York Historical Society)

and that as a result of the exhibition many new Boston names were added to the list of makers. George Munson Curtis, a Connecticut collector and member of the Walpole Society, wrote the introduction to the catalogue. Entitled "Early Silversmiths of Connecticut," it focused on the craft in that state, and provided collectors with much valuable information.[7]

In New York, the Metropolitan Museum, working in cooperation with the Colonial Dames, gathered silver from churches in New York, New Jersey, and the South. Henry Watson Kent of the museum's staff gave some of the background for that exhibition, which was the outgrowth of a small display of early American silver held at the museum in 1907. The exhibition itself, said Kent, was "brought together by the zeal and energy of the Colonial Dames of the State of New York." Halsey wrote a very useful introduction entitled "Early New York Silver Smiths."[8]

The New York exhibition was complemented by a concurrent showing of colonial portraits by Copley, Blackburn, and Smybert. Joining silver and portraits made very good sense, for often the people who commissioned the silver were also ones who could afford to have portraits painted by eminent artists.

As a result of the interest in early American silver aroused among the Colonial Dames, that organization employed the English expert E. Alfred Jones to write *Old Silver of American Churches*, published in 1913. Both Halsey and Bigelow aided Jones in this very valuable reference work, which furnished further proof of the artistic value of American antique silver. "From now on," wrote Kent, "exhibitions of silver began to multiply—in Providence, Philadelphia, Hartford and Washington."[9] The American public, through these and similar shows, was being introduced to the merits of its own colonial crafts.

New York's Hudson-Fulton Celebration was held in the early fall of 1909. It marked two important events in the history of the Hudson River: its discovery and exploration three hundred years earlier, and Robert Fulton's first successful steamboat trip in 1807. The commissioners voted for a cultural and historical, rather than traditionally commercial, emphasis. Education and brotherhood were the themes, and because "the Metropolis of the country was itself a vast exposition,"[10] no separate fair ground was built. One goal was to make New York history better known among all Americans, and another was to promote the assimilation of foreign-born or first-generation residents by inspiring a love of the city.

Interestingly, these motives also lay behind the activities of many local museum men and serious collectors of the period. There was a definite feeling that New York City's history, background, and traditions were not sufficiently honored in the world beyond. The artist Eliza Greatorex had remarked many years earlier that the claims of the old Dutch families of New York "to good birth and education are not readily granted by settlers of other nationalities in the United States."[11] Now, the New York collector Judge Clearwater took great pleasure in snatching rare pieces of early American silver from under the noses of his New England rivals. Part of this delight probably stemmed from a feeling that his distinguished Dutch and Huguenot forefathers were regarded by his New England contemporaries as inferior to their own Puritan ancestors.

Another facet of the Hudson-Fulton Celebration was the promotion of international friendship. Much was made of the variety of nationalities that had contributed to the discovery, exploration, and development of New York, both geographically and culturally. One especially dramatic and popular event was a journey upriver by replicas of Hudson's *Half Moon* and Fulton's *Clermont*. Ceremonies and celebrations accompanied the ships' progress. The journey ended at Cohoes, with parades and floats; there were also an Indian wigwam, an old Dutch homestead, evening illumination of the ships and buildings, and an impressive fireworks display.

Downriver in New York City, each night was marked by the lighting of ships, buildings, bridges, and public monuments. "The combined official and unofficial electric illuminations in New York City . . . ," reported the Commission, "were on a scale never before paralleled and were generally conceded to have marked an era in spectacular lighting."[12]

Many of New York's cultural institutions planned special events and exhibitions. In honor of Henry Hudson's Dutch birth and the original Dutch settlers, the Metropolitan Museum organized an unprecedented showing of Dutch old-master paintings borrowed from American collections. Over 140 such works were drawn from American business titans like Morgan, Widener, Havemeyer, Frick, and Altman.

Henry Kent of the Metropolitan suggested an exhibition of American decorative arts to balance the European paintings. Such a proposal took courage, since most members of the American cultural establishment regarded American art as negligible. The powers at the Metropolitan Museum were none too enthusiastic, but Kent's excellent relationship with Mr. and Mrs. Robert de Forest apparently led to the trustees' approval. Robert de Forest was not only the museum's secretary but also chairman of the celebration's Committee on Art Exhibits. His influence could hardly have been better placed for promoting this particular cause. Mrs. de Forest was the daughter of John Taylor Johnson, the museum's first president. With a collecting background and a particular interest in American antiques, she undoubtedly supported Kent in his efforts to display them at the museum.

In bringing together the objects that made up this first comprehensive and well-organized exhibit of American antiques, Kent relied on relationships developed during his years at the Slater Museum in Norwich, Connecticut. He also called upon R. T. H. Halsey, whom he knew from the Grolier Club, for advice and for loans of silver and furniture. Luke Vincent Lockwood, in those days the leading expert on American furniture, urged his Hartford friends to contribute; and he helped to select furniture from the outstanding collection of H. Eugene Bolles, which was an integral part of the exhibition. Francis Hill Bigelow suggested possible lenders in Boston, and provided introductions and arrangements there. Albert Hastings Pitkin was another intermediary for the Hartford collectors. And Edwin AtLee Barber, who had formed a wide circle of collecting friends and acquaintances during his travels to assess ceramics, suggested collectors in Pennsylvania, New England, and New York.

So, for the first time, a major exhibition of American decorative arts was held at a major American museum. Furthermore, it incorporated a new concept of display. Both Kent and Lockwood felt that an arrangement of objects chronologically, rather than by type—all the chairs together, for example—would be more interesting and instructive. The Essex Institute had set up a forward-looking exhibit of local furniture ordered chronologically in 1875, but that was limited in scope and impact, generating mainly local interest.

The Hudson-Fulton exhibition presented furniture, primarily of New England origin; silver from New York, New England, and other regions; ceramics; glass; pewter; and miscellaneous other objects, to a much wider audience. Its great influence resulted from its comprehensive scale, the care with which objects were selected and displayed, the thoughtfully written and informative catalogue, and the fact that the Metropolitan Museum had lent its prestige to the venture.

Nevertheless, the tone of many reviewers was condescending. Elisabeth Luther Cary, in *Art and Progress*, described the exhibition as lacking conspicuously in the "gayety, technical achievement, and loveliness of color that we find in the Eighteenth-Century French Rooms." But her review also indicates that she, like other art-conscious Americans, was beginning to recognize the merits of the native cultural tradition: "Seen in connection with the French section the most casual observer notes the difference between a sturdy people with their future yet to make, and that of a nation declining."[13]

American antiques displayed at the Metropolitan Museum as part of the Hudson-Fulton Celebration of 1909. (The Metropolitan Museum of Art)

Natalie Curtis reviewed both the Dutch masters and the American arts for *The Craftsman*. (Published by Gustav Stickley, this magazine had a strongly arts-and-crafts point of view toward all kinds of design; it described itself as "an Illustrated Monthly Magazine in the Interest of Better Art, Better Work, and a Better and More Reasonable Way of Living.")

We pass from the Dutch exhibit to the three rooms devoted to the art of the American Colonies. Here we are struck at once by the fact that any young community planted in the wilderness, whose whole effort must be to support life and establish industries among conditions of great hardship, can scarcely be expected to bring forth any other art than that devoted to making beautiful the necessities of life.

Having thus skeptically approached the American objects, Miss Curtis went on in a much more positive vein: ". . . one is struck throughout the exhibit by the element of refinement and good taste, the absence of display, and the dignity of line and curve that characterize Colonial workmanship." This was the view

that Clarence Cook had put forward in much the same words over thirty years earlier.[14]

Although reviewers made inevitable comparisons between sturdy American and sophisticated European art, both exhibitions were extremely popular. Winifred E. Howe, in her *History of the Metropolitan Museum of Art* (1913), described the two as the "most notable loan collections within their respective spheres ever brought together in America." Over three hundred thousand visitors appeared, and one result was fulfillment of Robert de Forest's hope that "a new emphasis may be given to the importance of our early workmen." Kent wrote that the exhibition of American art had inspired study of the work of individual American craftsmen and their methods, "as well as a veritable renaissance of the so-called Colonial styles. . . ."[15]

The arrangement of objects by period provided American antiques with a unified context for the first time. It showed, logically and clearly, how design had evolved in American decorative arts from the beginning of the colonial period until after the Revolutionary War. The catalogue, organized and partly written by Henry Kent, increased the value of the exhibition by providing detailed information about each object and picturing many of them.[16]

The Hudson-Fulton exhibition upgraded the importance of collecting American antiques, and accelerated the elevation of collectors to a position of respect and admiration. It also, Kent noted, brought collectors from New England, New York, and Pennsylvania together. A number of them subsequently formed the Walpole Society, where they began to exchange ideas and information, furthering the study of American antiques.

From pride in specific American heroes, events, and regions, America was moving toward pride in itself as a nation. As adulthood came into view, the artifacts of childhood and youth took on new significance and value. The Hudson-Fulton show summed up these trends. It succeeded admirably in pointing out to a wider public the importance of American antiques—from historical, cultural, and artistic standpoints.

As a consequence of the new enthusiasm and pride created by the show, the Metropolitan Museum soon acquired the Bolles collection of early American furniture and accessories, much of which had been part of the exhibition. This collection eventually became the cornerstone of the American Wing, which was to prove enormously popular and influential when it opened in 1924. But the immediate result of the Hudson-Fulton display was that American antiques were seen to be worthy of a major American museum. They had completed part of a transition from the private province of curiosities to the public domain of art.

Chapter 13

Judge A. T. Clearwater
Collecting for the Museum

JUDGE ALPHONSO TRUMPBOUR CLEARWATER (1848–1933) IS A TRANSITIONAL figure in the history of collecting American antiques. He stands as a bridge between two centuries and two orientations: his interest in early American silver stemmed not only from his respect for its associations and symbolism but also from an unusually keen appreciation of its beauty. Furthermore, he demonstrated a new commitment to displaying antiques for the public benefit, rather than maintaining them primarily for private enjoyment.

Like many of the collectors of Lyon's and Erving's earlier generation, Clearwater had a strong and pious regard for his ancestors and what they stood for. On the other hand, he shared a belief in the educational potential of antiques with the curators and many of the collectors of the first quarter of the twentieth century. The newer, emerging aspects of the attitudes that he represents are clearly set forth in his will:

> My reason for making this bequest [of his collection of American silver to the Metropolitan Museum] is that having been brought up from my boyhood with a great respect for the work of the human hand, and for that of American artists and artisans, I have made my collection in the hope of preserving

*Judge Alphonso T. Clear-
water. (The Metropolitan
Museum of Art)*

and transmitting to future generations specimens of the handiwork of our early American silversmiths so that it may be known that there existed in the American Colonies, and early in the States of the Republic, and among the members of early American families, not only a refined taste creating a demand for beautiful silver but an artistic instinct and skill upon the part of American silversmiths, enabling them to design and to make articles of Church and domestic silver which in beauty of line and workmanship well compares [sic] with the work of foreign silversmiths. And I bequeath this collection for the reason that not only is the Metropolitan a great Museum, but one of the greatest educational institutions in the world, freely opening its collections to artists and artisans, regardless of race, who there may study the artistic taste and craftsmanship of centuries.[1]

His obituary, on the other hand, implicitly points up his common bond with the collectors who had preceded him:

Throughout his long and useful life his faith in the old virtues and his love of early American handicraft never flagged. He was Kingston's benevolent patron, appealed to for advice in every emergency and called upon to speak at every public assembly. He would travel miles, even after he had passed his eightieth year, to speak at the anniversary celebration of a country church or the unveiling of a tablet commemorative of some event of Colonial times.

He edited a history of Ulster County and the addresses he delivered were remarkable for details of events long past. More than any other man of his time he kept alive in the old communities of the county a knowledge of their past and a pride in it.[2]

The Judge balanced his devotion to tradition with a whimsical touch and a nice sense of humor. In 1931, he sent a portrait of his great-granduncle, the Reverend James Melancthon Mathews, to New York for exhibition at the Metropolitan Museum. He had inherited the portrait, painted by Henry Inman, along with Dr. Mathews's own silver tankard, which was already on display. The painting, he felt, should be hung in the same room as the tankard. "If . . . Sir Oliver Ledge and Sir Conan Doyle and many others are right in their conjecture that the spirits of the departed return," the Judge wrote to Henry Kent, "I am very confident the old doctor will be glad to see his portrait in conjunction with the tankard. He will not come from that region where thirst is never allayed. If he does not arrive with a harp, he will with wings and a flowing gown."[3]

Judge Clearwater had acquired his faith in a hereafter with harps and flowing gowns as a boy in Kingston, New York, where he was born and raised, and spent his entire life. In his youth he frequently visited his grandfather, Thomas Theunis Clearwater, "who had a beautiful place at Twaalfskill, now within the limits of the city of Kingston." This grandfather was an elder of the First Dutch Church; he, Dr. Mathews, and their old friend Dr. Thomas DeWitt of the Dutch Reformed Collegiate Church of New York City—"one of the last clergymen who preached in both Dutch and English"—tested young Clearwater on his knowledge of the Dutch Church's catechism. Dr. Mathews and Dr. DeWitt decided that the boy should follow them into the ministry; but his grandfather Clearwater, who had been an officer in the War of 1812, wanted him to be a soldier. His mother and grandmother, however, believed that he should be a lawyer, and in the end these "dominant personalities" prevailed.[4]

Silver tankard by Jacob Boelen of New York, from the Clearwater collection. An English coin with the date 1696 is embedded in the lid. (The Metropolitan Museum of Art. Bequest of A. T. Clearwater)

Judge Clearwater read law in the Kingston offices of Senator Jacob Hardenburgh and Judge Augustus Schoonmaker, and was admitted to the bar in 1871. His career as a lawyer and judge was long and distinguished. Serving three successive terms as district attorney of Ulster County in the 1870s and 1880s, he was urged to run for the United States Congress; but he always declined because of commitments at home. Another similarity between Judge Clearwater and other collectors of his generation was his combining a busy professional life with many civic and charitable interests. He served on local and state boards of various kinds; beginning in 1918, he was president of the State Reservation Commission of Niagara Falls, to which he had a strong attachment. Here, his collecting urge and his dedication to civic duty proved complementary, and he gathered a series of aquatints of the Falls. After the legalization of beer in 1933, Judge Clearwater—no teetotaler—forbade its sale within the Niagara Falls reservation. Selling beer there, he said, would be "against the dignity of the fifth wonder of the world."[5]

Such was his influence among Kingston's citizens that they called upon him in almost any emergency. One day in 1931 a bear and her cub climbed a tree from which they could not be dislodged by police, firemen, or state troopers. In desperation, the authorities turned to Judge Clearwater. "If you will persuade the 2,000 people gathered in the vicinity of the treed bears to go home," he advised, "the bears will come down by themselves and be out of town in no time." The people proved as intractable, however, as the bears, who finally had to be lassoed and lowered out of the tree.[6]

Silver tankards, such as that of Dr. Mathews, seem to recur in the Judge's life with important associations. At the end of the War of 1812, his grandfather Clearwater had been presented according to custom with a silver tankard, which the Judge inherited. "My grandmother," he wrote,

> brewed a fine milk punch in this old tankard, of which Holland gin was an essential and much beloved component. Many a time have I seen my grandfather and the two dominies [Dr. DeWitt and Dr. Mathews, ministers of the Dutch Church] drinking my grandmother's punch and munching krullers which she had prepared by dropping the material into a pot of boiling butter. Always she insisted that lard was a poor shortening for oileykoeks, or krullers, or pie crust.[7]

Perhaps it was the tankards that developed in the Judge an affinity for silver. Although he began by collecting European pieces, he soon was concentrating on those of American origin. In this he was importantly influenced not only by his immersion in the American past but also by his friendship with John Buck, curator of metalwork at the Metropolitan Museum. After Clearwater had lent a number of pieces of American silver to the Hudson-Fulton show, he wrote of the reaction:

> Friends and acquaintances from Boston to Los Angeles have spoken to me of the collection of silver at the Metropolitan during the Hudson-Fulton with the utmost admiration. To many of them it was a revelation, and has done much to stimulate the collecting of the work of early American silversmiths. I owe much of my own interest in the subject to Mr. Buck for whom I have the highest and most affectionate regard.[8]

Clearwater relied on Buck's advice and judgment in the early years of his collecting. When Buck's health failed and he retired early in the second decade of the twentieth century, Clearwater turned to collector and Metropolitan trustee R. T. H. Halsey for advice.

Around 1910, Clearwater articulated his aims. One was to secure silver bearing the marks "of the earliest American silversmiths," even when the pieces themselves were of slight character. The other was to collect pieces "which may serve to demonstrate to this and the future generations that the artistic conceptions and workmanship of the American silversmiths of the

Silver teapot, made 1770–1810 by Paul Revere, Boston, from the Clearwater collection. (The Metropolitan Museum of Art. Bequest of A. T. Clearwater)

seventeenth, eighteenth, and early part of the nineteenth centuries compared not unfavorably with the similar work in other countries."[9]

Clearwater explored many different avenues for securing antique silver. He wrote to dealers up and down the Eastern seaboard; he exchanged information and duplicates with other collectors; he cultivated pickers and local dealers; and he went on buying trips. In 1913, in a speech at Vassar College, the Judge spoke about his methods:

> I am frequently asked—"do you think I can make a collection of American silver, would you advise me to undertake it?" It all depends. If one has ample means and a great deal of leisure there is no more delightful pursuit upon which to expend time and money, but without a fair share of both it is a hopeless undertaking. It was one of my early ambitions to buy a tin peddler's cart, stock it with tin and scour the country in search of old silver, old china, old furniture, old brass and pewter. The Fates have been so unkind to me that my nearest approach to a realization of this dream has been to take an occasional automobile journey in this fascinating pursuit, and in this way I have visited many towns from the Canadian border to the Delaware in search of additions to my collection. Doubtless I have derived more benefit from these journeys in other directions than I have as a collector for the appearance of a tourist on the scene leads to the most extravagant notions as to the value of any article no matter how trivial. Thus it is that I am compelled to entrust the gathering of silver to others with the result that its acquisition however pleasurable is immensely unprofitable.[10]

Reminiscing about life and collecting many years later, in 1931, Judge Clearwater commented:

> My grandmother was a famous cook, and seemed never happier than when
> the old gateleg table was surrounded by guests who always bowed defer-
> entially. . . . I never heard the subject of money talked of, and thus it was
> I was brought up without regarding the accumulation of money as the most
> important thing in life. In fact as I look back upon my career as a collector,
> I rather fancy the most important thing I learned was the expenditure of
> money.[11]

Many collectors of early American silver would have agreed with him. His
correspondence with members of the Metropolitan Museum staff indicates his
awareness of the fact that his willingness to pay high prices for pieces he
especially wanted inflated the whole market.

About 1911, Clearwater had written to the John Wells Company, dealers in
old silver on Fifth Avenue in New York: "There is but one salvation for me
that is never to take anything with me for the purpose of considering the
advisability of buying it. I always wind up by taking it no matter how strongly
I try to avoid doing so." H. E. Thorn of the Wells firm responded drily that
"bad as this habit may be, there are others who might be inclined to find more
fault with it than ourselves."[12]

Clearwater pursued the subject of money again, in a letter to the dealers
Potter and Stainforth of Boston:

> I am advised by Boston collectors that I am largely responsible for the gro-
> tesque notions of the value of silver held by Boston dealers in that I have
> paid extravagant prices for pieces for my collection. This sort of thing can-
> not go on indefinitely, and as I think I before have said, the time eventually
> will come when I will stop buying. Always there will be collectors and al-
> ways there will be fools. My brother collectors regard me as a specimen of
> both combined, and I have begun to think they are not far wrong.[13]

Clearwater continued his buying all through the second decade of the century.
In 1918, he wrote Henry Kent at the Metropolitan that he had had a pleasant
holiday, and had picked up "two or three interesting small pieces of silver."
They turned out to be extremely rare and valuable early American coins, and
Clearwater confessed that "I only secured them after a great deal of effort, and
took the entire collection at what I fear you would regard as a fabulous price.
. . . They seemed so admirably to supplement my collection of Colonial silver
that I followed that irresistible and ruinous impulse which like the road to
Sheol, leads a collector to perdition by imperceptible but steady gradation."[14]

Clearwater had relatives in Charleston, South Carolina. During the Civil
War, his immediate family and the Charleston branch had lost touch. In the

1920s, the Judge was invited to Charleston to give a speech at a Huguenot Church celebration. He was welcomed so warmly, and found the place and the company so congenial, that he made many return visits. In 1928, he wrote:

> You will be amused to learn that on my last visit to Charleston my relative Miss Ravenel casually handed me a very beautiful silver dish. . . . I asked her what she used it for. "Well," she said, "I usually use it to bake custard or make rice pudding." I asked her if I was to understand she put the dish in an oven. She said, "Certainly," her mother and her grandmother had done that. She asked if there was any reason why she should not do it.[15]

Judge Clearwater sent nearly all newly acquired pieces down to the Metropolitan Museum for exhibition, and his collection was thus on view from 1910 or 1911 onward. In 1916, the museum put the Judge's silver on exhibition in a new setting on the second floor. In connection with the opening, Halsey wrote an article for the museum *Bulletin*. The pieces were rare and many were unique, said Halsey, maintaining that the collection of over 140 pieces was so complete that "an exhaustive catalogue . . . would form a textbook of American silver and its makers." It was rich in examples from New England, said Halsey, going on to discuss some of the most outstanding and their history.[16] (After the American Wing was built, the corridor connecting it with the Morgan Wing was taken over for display of the Clearwater Collection of American Silver.)

Clearwater fought hard to procure some of the New England pieces, and he could not have been popular among the collectors of that region. He tells, in several letters, of battling for a piece of silver against a New England collector or institution. In 1911, he wrote of his triumph in securing a porringer by the Boston silversmith Zachariah Brigden: "I am the more pleased at getting this silver because of the fact that it was sold under sealed bids, and that the overseers of Harvard University were among the unsuccessful bidders. The silver was all appraised by Mr. Francis H. Bigelow of Cambridge who made the appraisement for the administrator of the estates."[17] Francis Bigelow was of great general assistance to him in obtaining fine pieces from old New England families; the question of whether Bigelow passed along information to Clearwater about what was in these particular estates and the amount of the appraisal remains unanswered.

Another time, Clearwater secured a tankard by the Newport maker Samuel Vernon at an auction where opposing bidders included the Boston Museum of Fine Arts, Dwight Blaney, Hollis French, Francis H. Bigelow, John Wells, and two gentlemen from Rhode Island. A man named Howe had won the bidding, but later, according to the Judge, repented of his extravagance and sold it to the Judge for the amount he had paid.[18]

Yet again, the Judge reported himself happy at securing "several fine pieces of silver which formerly belonged to Edward Holyoke, one of the early Presidents of Harvard College. . . . I am the happier at securing them for the reason that about all the New England collectors bid against me as did the overseers of Harvard. . . ."[19]

Whether it was the relish with which he snapped up fine New England pieces in competition with the Boston collectors, or just the fact of a New Yorker's making such an outstanding collection of *their* silver, the New Englanders apparently lost no love on Clearwater. He was never asked to join the Walpole Society, although he would seem to have been a perfect potential member—a dedicated collector who shared the backgrounds and interests of many members. Kent once remarked that it was a shame Clearwater had never joined, but since Clearwater had told Kent he would be glad to join if asked, it seems probable that he was blackballed by one or more of the Boston silver collectors.

In 1932, near the end of his life, Clearwater wrote to the director of the Metropolitan: "If you had had my experience with the Puritans and Pilgrims of Boston, you would have learned that they regard themselves as among the Lord's anointed, and they feel that it is an act of treason to send a piece of old

Judge Clearwater's silver, installed at the Metropolitan Museum in 1924.
(The Metropolitan Museum of Art)

New England silver to any place but the [Boston] Museum of Fine Arts."[20]

Clearwater had lent some of his silver to the Museum of Fine Arts, but his heart, as he told the Metropolitan staff many times over the years, remained with them. He usually let them know when some other institution—and there were many—asked him for loans or bequests. Clearwater left the Metropolitan 558 pieces of American silver and a number of objects made in other countries. He was strongly attracted to early American pieces because of their associations with historical figures and solid American values, but he was one of the first to concentrate on American antiques with the specific purpose of leaving his collection to a museum.

It gave Judge Clearwater great pleasure to see all his silver on display at one of the world's great museums. Whenever he could, he would slip away from his office and go down to New York to have a look at it. One final story from the Judge sums up his great pride in his collection and his feeling that, by lending and finally giving it to a great museum, he was making a real contribution, both patriotic and artistic:

> Shortly after the Ballard collection of Oriental rugs was placed on exhibition, I left the Museum with a gentleman. The day was disagreeable; we waited for a Fifth Avenue [omnibus]. He said, "I saw you looking over the rugs recently loaned to the Museum. What do you think of them?" I said I was not a judge of rugs, but they seemed to me valuable and interesting. . . . He said, "I think I heard someone address you as Mr. Clearwater. Are you related to the Judge who owns the wonderful collection of Colonial silver?" I told him who I was. He asked me what I was going to do with it. I told him that if no misadventure befell me I intend to present it to the Metropolitan, and so had bequeathed it by my Will. "Well," said he, "my name is Ballard. I own those rugs. I had thought of giving them to my hometown. Where do you live?" I told him. He said "Why don't you present your silver to Kingston?" I said I regarded the Metropolitan as one of the greatest educational institutions in the world, and that to present it to the Museum would prove more beneficial to a far greater number of persons than to place it anywhere else. "Well," said Mr. Ballard, "that is a new thought to me, and is worth considering." We parted at the St. Regis, where he was staying. Some day or other he may present us with some of those rugs.[21]

In May 1922, James F. Ballard left over 126 Oriental rugs to the Metropolitan Museum. Judge Clearwater must have been very proud.

Chapter 14

Francis Hill Bigelow

Renegade Among Loyalists

Scholar, collector, and dealer, francis bigelow (1859–1933) was long a member of the inner circle of Boston collectors. He organized the major 1906 and 1911 exhibitions of silver at the Museum of Fine Arts. For some years honorary curator of silver, he published his *Historic Silver of the Colonies and Its Makers* in 1917.[1] He was generous in lending antiques to important exhibitions. And he was a charter member of the Walpole Society.

Yet Bigelow remains an enigma. He collected avidly for himself, and apparently nourished the hope that his collection would be permanently installed in a museum; but he was willing to consider selling nearly all of it to Francis Garvan. And his working in secret to buy early New England silver from churches and old families, to resell to Garvan and Judge Clearwater, so offended his Massachusetts contemporaries that they are reported to have requested his resignation from the Walpole Society. (The Judge was not a New Englander; Garvan was, but his social credentials were far from impeccable.) There is a story about a group of collectors who, upon seeing a newspaper headline, "Francis Hill Bigelow Arrested," said, "Well, they finally caught up with him." They were disappointed when it turned out to be a different man with the same name.

In the end, whatever his priorities, Bigelow's outstanding contribution to the collecting movement was in helping to build the two greatest collections of early American silver. They were formed by men with a strong sense of their spiritual and educational significance, for eventual presentation to museums.

Bigelow was born in Cambridge, Massachusetts, where he spent the rest of his life. After graduation from public high school, he took a job in 1879 with Howe and Goodwin, Boston merchants who traded in India. According to the introduction to the catalogue of a 1924 auction of part of his collection, Bigelow became interested in American antiques in 1875, as a result of the exhibitions held in connection with the Lexington and Bunker Hill celebrations. He didn't begin collecting, however, until the end of the century, when "he was able gradually to discard the comfortable stuffed chairs and black walnut furniture that it had been his lot to live with, and to begin to substitute the more congenial Colonial antiques."[2]

American antiques from the collection of Francis Hill Bigelow, lent for an exhibition of colonial furniture at the Museum of Fine Arts in the Summer of 1912. According to the August 1912 Bulletin, *this was the first time the museum had exhibited early American furniture. (Courtesy Museum of Fine Arts, Boston)*

Having begun, Bigelow collected a variety of objects, among them furniture, clocks, mirrors, silver, glass, ceramics, and firearms. He especially liked furniture of the Federal period, but had some high-style block-front Chippendale pieces and simple earlier things as well. When the Walpole Society met in Boston in 1910, it was reported that some visited Bigelow's house in Cambridge and returned with tales of "ravishing furniture."[3]

Bigelow retired in 1906, at the age of forty-seven. That same year, word of the silver exhibition at the Museum of Fine Arts reached England, and the expert E. Alfred Jones journeyed to Boston to see it. He was so impressed that he urged Bigelow to "begin a systematic search among the churches of Massachusetts, while . . . the late Mr. George M. Curtis of Meriden, Connecticut, undertook a similar search in that state. A wealth of communion silver little dreamed of was revealed." Bigelow responded energetically, and his efforts contributed importantly to Jones's publication in 1913 of *Old Silver of American Churches*.[4]

In his pursuit of church silver, Bigelow also discovered "many notable" privately owned examples. It was these that he emphasized in his own book. And the valuable knowledge of their location enabled him to obtain fine pieces of New England silver—from both churches and individuals—for Clearwater and Garvan.

Although he told his clients that he wanted the Museum of Fine Arts to have first choice of his discoveries, he may not always have adhered to that

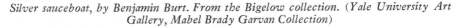

Silver sauceboat, by Benjamin Burt. From the Bigelow collection. (Yale University Art Gallery, Mabel Brady Garvan Collection)

intention. In 1911, Bigelow wrote Judge Clearwater that he was hoping to get him some church silver, "but this is confidential. I want the Churches to *give* their silver to the [Boston] museum but where there are *duplicates* by the same donor & maker I shall suggest their selling these."[5]

Later, when he sold Clearwater a church beaker, Bigelow asked him not to send it to the Metropolitan Museum for display with the rest of Clearwater's silver, because he needed to work surreptitiously if he was to get church pieces for the Judge from New England. Clearwater paid dearly for examples of ecclesiastical silver from Bigelow, who maintained that with names, dates, and donor history they were far more valuable than other objects of comparable quality but less certain origin.

In 1916, Bigelow began buying silver frequently, and at high prices, on Garvan's behalf. In that year he wrote Garvan, "There is a psychological moment in which to kill the owner and escape with the tankard which you do not appreciate. . . . I have to . . . approach stealthily—so you must be patient or we lose it altogether."[6] These hardly seem the words of a man dealing straight-forwardly.

"You must not get 'cold feet' on the prices," Bigelow wrote Garvan in 1916:

> When I talked domed tankards at $1000. to $1500 I meant the *ordinary* ones of which we will get plenty—but I have been working on the very impor-tant ones with inscriptions which are *historically* interesting and are not high at $2000.—I always recall Canfield's remark that "no price is too high for a good thing!" I feel that the more ordinary I can get *any* time and if price is not reasonable we will simply pass them.[7]

Again, when Garvan complained about high silver prices, Bigelow wrote him a stern reply: ". . . many of these things I can only get by taking them when the chance is offered and before the owners change their minds: this sometimes occurs on the telephone. Unless I know that you will take them and pay for them, I cannot afford myself to take the financial risk of such large purchases as I know you want." Garvan was not amenable to this arrangement and in-formed Bigelow in 1917 that "I am through collecting silver." He enclosed a check bringing his account up to date and revoked "any other commissions of any kind or description." He closed his letter, however, by saying that he *would* entertain offers of "the Sanderson, Dummer or Coney tankards, or any other pieces by them. . . ."[8]

Garvan, obviously addicted, was back in touch very soon; and as late as 1929, he was still securing choice New England silver from Bigelow: "You know the pieces my collection needs and I rely upon you to get the pieces for me at the lowest possible prices."[9]

Both Garvan and Clearwater heeded Bigelow's warnings, and kept quiet about their purchases so that he could continue supplying them relatively unhindered. Inevitably, however, these all-too-numerous sales to buyers in New York and other enemy outposts became known, and Bigelow was ostracized by the other Boston silver collectors. In general, they were loyal sons of New England who clearly regarded him as dealing in contraband. Among the most prominent of the group were Dwight Blaney and Charles Tyler—described earlier—and Philip Spalding and Hollis French. The latter two present intriguing contrasts, both to Bigelow and between themselves.

Philip Leffingwell Spalding (1871–1938), busy and successful businessman, used his spare time to become "a collector, an example to other collectors in the discriminatory character of his acquisitions. Spalding bought with quality and historical interest as his measures of merit, specializing in furniture and Willard clocks but particularly devoting his effort to American silver."[10] Upon his death in 1938, Spalding's wife and sons presented fifty of his choicest silver pieces to the Boston Museum of Fine Arts. Within the collection was "a remarkable group of thirty-two objects made by sixteen men of New England who were born in the seventeenth century."

Hollis French (1868–1940), neighbor and good friend of Dwight Blaney, also had a special love for silver among the variety of his antiques. "No Walpolean of the original 1910 group was more greatly loved and admired than Hollis French," wrote a memorialist. And Halsey described him as "a real collector . . . I remember how his eyes sparkled as he told of some acquisition in the line of American silver, the fascinations of which had caused him to transfer his interest from his previous hobby, our early furniture." Shortly before his death in 1940, French gave his collection of more than two hundred pieces of early silver to the Cleveland Museum of Art, "moved by the belief that the newer, inland cities of the country should share more largely in the products of the native culture which before their establishment had long been in being on the Atlantic fringe." In his concern for sharing the New England heritage with outsiders, French deviated from Spalding and the other loyalists, whose collections went either to their families or to the Boston Museum of Fine Arts. Thus, French may have been somewhat in sympathy with Bigelow's causing New England silver to be transferred elsewhere—if not with the manner of his accomplishing it.[11]

Unlike Spalding and French, Bigelow never provided in his own name the nucleus of an important museum collection. He seems to have been torn between the desire to do just that, and an almost overwhelming drive to maximize the monetary return from his antiques. Furthermore, although apparently comfortable financially when he retired, he may have found the effort to expand his own collection frustrated by rising prices.

In any case, Bigelow turned to selling antiques as well as buying them. He sold not only pieces for which he acted purely as middleman but others that he had long owned and presumably prized. Although a certain amount of dealing or trading went on among most collectors, Bigelow's primary activity eventually shifted from collecting to dealing.

As early as the Hudson-Fulton show of 1909, Bigelow let it be known that he would be happy to lend freely to the exhibition, and that a good many of his things were also for sale (Blaney, too, told Kent that he would sell the Metropolitan objects from his collection). Among Bigelow's offerings were a Paul Revere tankard bought for $800, and available for $1,000; and a sofa, "*the* finest of the period I have ever seen."[12] In 1910, Bigelow wrote a long letter to Kent offering for sale a number of pieces of furniture.

Bigelow's willingness to consider disposing of his antiques privately rather than selling or donating them to a museum is apparent in a letter of 1916 to an employee of Francis Garvan. The letter suggests an agony of conflicting hopes and desires:

> I am rather disappointed not to have Mr. Garvan see my house & the quality of the things. Photographs do not answer except for shapes . . . I rather am undecided as to what I want or am willing to let go. I *had* thought if [Gar-

Mahogany sofa, 1800–1810, Salem, Massachusetts. From the Bigelow collection.
(Yale University Art Gallery, Mabel Brady Garvan Collection)

van] was *really* interested in obtaining the best that I might consider letting nearly all of my claw & ball foot and pieces of that period go and making my own collection along the Sheraton lines entirely, for the Art Museum. But I thought it would be well to *see* what he would *care* for and consider the matter carefully. My pieces have not been spoiled by the finish that has been put upon them: and when I spoke to Miss [Florence V.] Paull, at the museum, about *thinking* of selling them she said she wished the museum might have a chance to purchase them. Then I have a lot of things in Worcester at the Salisbury house connected with the Art Museum there but they are considering their purchase. . . . I do not know *what* I would sell & what keep until I could find out *what* Mr. Garvan would consider and the price.

Several months later, Bigelow wrote directly to Garvan in a similarly uncertain vein:

The position on my furniture is this: I have been asked if I would consider selling it to a Museum to be installed under my supervision and to be known as the Bigelow collection. *Most* of it will be included but not all—as this is not necessary—If the matter is not closed by the time you come in January with Mrs. Garvan, I shall call the matter off and be willing to sell you much of my furniture. I have a fine collection of glasses for table use and various sets of plates that do not go with my *collection* anyway.[13]

In fact, the "Bigelow collection" never went to a museum. His antiques ended up being sold, in transactions with individual private collectors (like Garvan) and at two auctions, the one held in 1924 and another—three years after his death—in 1936. Bigelow, who never married, devoted much of his life to collecting, and the financial reward from his sales must have been sadly offset by a pervasive sense of loss. Yet he had the satisfaction of his considerable contributions to the field. As much as any of his Boston collecting contemporaries, Bigelow seems to have recognized the desirability of making early New England silver available for public appreciation. Through his scouting for two educationally oriented collecting giants, he worked indirectly to that end. More directly, he organized the first two comprehensive silver exhibitions in Boston—a city not noted in those days for its emphasis on the history of American decorative arts. And his repeated admonitions to Garvan and Clearwater, that they should concentrate on the finest and best-documented pieces, indicate a real concern for quality. In his own enigmatic way, Bigelow established for himself a unique place in collecting history.

Chapter 15

George Francis Dow

Bringing the Past to Life

*I grieved to see the connection between the last and
the present century so entirely lost. There is
something agreeable, if not great, in the primitive
manners. So much pleasure and peace at home, while the
great world is scarcely known. These things charm
upon the small scale, and when we see society
only in its first stages.*
The Rev. William Bentley, *Diaries*, 1796

ONE HUNDRED AND ELEVEN YEARS AFTER DR. BENTLEY LAMENTED THE DISAP-
pearance of any connection between the centuries in Salem, George Francis
Dow (1868–1936) did something about it. He felt as Dr. Bentley had, that it
was a shame to lose not only the old way of life but any sense of what it had
been like. Dow's three period rooms, opened on the second floor of the Essex
Institute in Salem in 1907, were an effort to catch hold of the past, to make it
tangible and understandable in the present. He used antiques and old (or old-
style) interior woodwork together to re-create the atmosphere of colonial and
early Federal days; then old houses, furnishings, tools, and other artifacts could
be understood in the proper context. This approach was innovative and exciting,
and Dr. Bentley would surely have been delighted with it.

Dow must have seen what Poore had done at Indian Hill, but his own work
was much more scientific and his purpose more serious. While Poore had been
interested in almost anything old, he did not share Dow's insistence on a historically accurate context. Dow differed from many collectors and scholars of his
own time, too. Bigelow, Halsey, and others who worked on the silver shows
and succeeding exhibitions were intent on demonstrating that America had an
artistic heritage—that the colonists had appreciated and lived with beautiful

George Francis Dow.
(Courtesy, Essex Institute,
Salem, Massachusetts)

objects made by American craftsmen. Halsey and Bigelow were historians *and* connoisseurs, while Dow was purely the historian and antiquary. He was interested in antiques almost entirely because they were old, not because they were also beautiful. He felt that rooms and houses furnished as they might have been in colonial times would automatically interest visitors, regardless of their artistic merits. The essence of such displays was what they showed about life in colonial and early Federal America.

Dow was heavily influenced by a European— Arthur Hazelius—who had created period rooms and an outdoor exhibit at the Nordiska Museum in Sweden. Their purpose was to save what was unique to Swedish, or Scandinavian, culture. Like Hazelius, Dow recognized the importance of preserving the old—and he very sensibly concentrated on the immediate vicinity of Salem, which contained an extraordinary wealth of material.

Dow wanted to know what antiques could reveal about daily life in the society that had created them. He wanted to know how American antiques— and to an even greater extent, old houses—had been made: with what tools, by whom, and under what conditions. His three period rooms were an attempt to reproduce the physical texture of past life, to provide an actual visualization of the past, as Halsey was to do in the American Wing of the Metropolitan Museum seventeen years later. But Dow's vision differed considerably from Halsey's. Dow used objects representative of everyday life among ordinary citizens. Halsey took only the best, and aimed at re-creating the environment of the élite. "Rooms furnished after the manner of the old time kitchen, the parlor, and the bedroom," said Dow, "should supply tangible illustration to the children of today. The relics of the Revolution and of the Civil War can then be intelligently arranged and studied."[1]

Dow's period rooms thus consisted of a kitchen furnished in the style of 1750, and a parlor and bedroom furnished in the style of about 1800. They were three-sided, and viewed through the glass of the fourth side. In building them, Dow used old woodwork if he could find it, but was perfectly willing to have the woodwork reproduced when necessary. He did not insist on genuineness; since he was trying to capture the *spirit* of the life of the past, he felt it was not crucial.

The illusion that one had wandered back into the past was strengthened by personal effects left casually on tables and benches—a pair of gloves, a newspaper of the correct date, eyeglasses resting on a book. It seemed that the eighteenth-century occupants had just stepped out of the room for a moment.

The sensation of being transported to another time was not an entirely new experience to visitors in 1907; there had been the New England kitchens, historical tableaux, and panoramas in increasing profusion throughout the second half of the nineteenth century. What was new was the museum location of the tableau, and the accuracy and consistency of its components—New England woodwork, furnishings, tools, and household utensils, all of about the same date.

Dow's explanatory label mounted on the wall near the rooms stated that the institute's collections in this arrangement illustrated "in an almost unique manner, the every-day life of our forefathers . . . which *cannot fail to serve as object lessons* and convey an historical illustration far more effective and impressive than could be secured by any text book." Dow believed that if the collections were properly interpreted and explained, their intrinsic worth would become obvious to the public.

Dow's contribution was thus to go beyond simple antiquarianism—what's old is interesting—to a more scientific and scholarly use of antiques and old rooms than had been previously attempted. By trying to understand and recreate the total context of the period in which things owned by the Essex Institute had been made, Dow made history come alive. He used antiques and architecture together so that people looking at his exhibits would say: "*Now* I see. *Now* I understand why these things are interesting and important."

The period rooms met with great success. Dow then wrote, "It seems not only fitting but necessary that every effort should be made, now, while it may be possible, to collect every object that illustrates the life and environment of our New England ancestors." Urging the membership of the institute to secure the future of their heirlooms by giving them to a museum, Dow warned that otherwise those heirlooms might eventually be scattered and even "unknown to you, adorning the homes of people who never knew of [your grandmother's] existence."[2]

From 1910 to 1913, Dow was occupied in setting up his own small outdoor museum behind the Essex Institute. This, he felt, was a logical step after the period rooms: "The fine collection of objects illustrating the daily life and environment of our New England people should be increased and made to show not only the house and its interior but the occupations of the people,—agricultural implements, and the tools and finished work of the carpenter, the cooper, the shoemaker, and the smith."[3] It was just what Hazelius had done on a larger scale in Sweden.

Dow obtained the seventeenth-century Ward House; an old shoe-repair shop; and two porches and a cupola from local houses. He completely restored the Ward House and furnished it to give, as he said, "a truthful picture of an interior of the year 1700."[4] Once again the overall picture had to be truthful, as Dow saw it, but each part did not have to be original. If the actual article was not available, Dow commissioned a reproduction—a point of view that stemmed from his vision of the larger truth as not exclusively dependent upon the use of authentically old components.

To explain the Ward House and its contents to visitors, Dow engaged live-in guides. "Miss Sarah W. Symonds and her assistants occupy the second floor and act as custodians," he wrote, "showing the house to visitors when the cow bell signals its call from the front entry. They will be dressed in homespun costumes of the time when the house was built." Dow's approach to displaying the Essex Institute's collections is employed to this day, and, according to one museum man, Dow was the first to understand and implement the principles that underlie modern historic-house and period-room displays.[5]

In his work on the Ward House, Dow hit the peak of his powers and enthusiasm. His respect for the past led him to approach this and other restorations with care and patience. A fellow Walpolean, writing about him in the Walpole Society's fiftieth anniversary publication, said:

> As a restorer of old houses he was distinguished for knowing when to leave things alone. It could not be said of him what an old carpenter remarked . . . in disparagement of architects. Old buildings, he said, with freely flowing profanity, should be left as they are, "strengthened, but not all shored up and be-Judased." . . . Those of us who knew Dow well when he was among our number can see him in imagination now, minutely inspecting every nail-hole, every mortise or cut in the old frame-work, or prying beneath later applications of lath and plaster in order to seek out patiently each shred of evidence. . . . Under the guidance of Dow's knowledge of old construction and finish, the added work of subsequent years was removed and bit by bit the original features which had been long concealed again made their appearance; ultimately it was as though a mask fell from the old house, and it stood revealed in all its pristine beauty.[6]

Dow's commitment to preservation took another very important form: the collecting of over five thousand engraved prints and photographs of Essex County scenes, buildings, and historical places. Speaking of these views in 1900, he said: "The value of such a collection is inestimable when preserved for reference and the inspection of future generations. To walk the pictured streets of Salem a hundred years ago, how delightful to the historian and the antiquary. We are the builders and the preservers for those who are to come after us."[7]

Dow served as secretary of the Essex Institute from 1898 to 1918, and from 1919 to his death in 1936 he filled several important posts at the Society for the Preservation of New England Antiquities. He restored many fine old New England homes, including the Parson Capen house at Topsfield, Massachusetts; transformed Salem's Pioneer Village into a permanent exhibit; helped with the

Parlor furnished in the style of c. 1800 by Dow in 1907.
(Courtesy, Essex Institute, Salem, Massachusetts)

Bedroom furnished in the style of c. 1800 by Dow in 1907.
(Courtesy, Essex Institute, Salem, Massachusetts)

early New England rooms in the American Wing; and edited and published materials both on his own and for the organizations that employed him. He wrote several books on historical and marine topics. Among the best remembered—and still vital—are *Domestic Life in New England in the Seventeenth Century* (1925), *The Arts and Crafts in New England, 1704–1775* (1927), and *Every Day Life in the Massachusetts Bay Colony* (1935). "He was a *Pioneer* in the study of Early Colonial history,"[8] said a friend.

By showing how interiors of a given period could be used to complement antiques interestingly and informatively, Dow had a crucial influence on the trend of collecting. On a broader scale, his ability to bring alive things of the past encouraged others to see and take seriously the American—or at least New England—cultural tradition. He was one of the first to interest Americans in their own past, at a time when most were hardly aware of its existence.

Parlor of the seventeenth-century John Ward House. The house was moved to the grounds of the Essex Institute, furnished, and staffed with costumed guides under the direction of George Francis Dow; photograph c. 1912. (Courtesy, Essex Institute, Salem, Massachusetts)

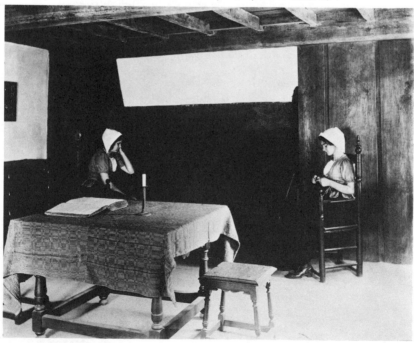

Chapter 16

Henry Watson Kent

Museum Man with Vision

Henry Kent (1866–1948) was an educator, not a collector. He spent most of his working life at the Metropolitan Museum of Art, where for thirty-five years he was one of the most innovative and far-sighted administrators in the museum's history. He also remains one of the best friends American decorative arts have ever had.

Kent was a visionary, crucial in shifting the balance from private toward public collecting of American antiques, and—though a New Englander in origin—in making New York the collecting center. These changes resulted from his organizing the Hudson-Fulton display, arranging the Bolles purchase of early American furniture, and envisioning the American Wing. He made many other contributions in the museum world, but it is his imagination and determination with respect to American decorative arts that must be underscored here. A major installation of such arts would have been undertaken eventually by a major museum; but without Kent's resolution and energy, it would probably have happened much later. His friend George Palmer wrote him in 1918, after the Metropolitan had acquired the cream of Palmer's Chippendale furniture: "I rejoice with you that now the Museum has at hand all of the possibili-

*Henry Watson Kent in his
office at the museum. (The
Metropolitan Museum
of Art)*

ties of making a wonderful showing of American craftsmanship, and I fully
realize that it never would have been possible without your active and per-
sistent—if I may say so—efforts."[1]

Kent's involvement with early America came from his New England up-
bringing. His memoirs begin:

> I am of Yankee stock, all of my forebears having come to Massachusetts in
> its beginning, and I was brought up on stories of these ancestors, their ways
> and manners—Watsons and Winslows of Plymouth, Hobarts of Hingham,
> and Kents of Kent's Island, Newburyport. Puritans, Pilgrims, Indians, and
> royal governors were all subjects of the talk I heard in my early days. My
> father was a good storyteller and singer of early Yankee songs, like "Captain
> Jinks of the Horse Marines," who had inherited his gift for this sort of thing
> from his father. My maternal great-grandfather had thirty ships plying be-
> tween Boston and China, my grandfather was a captain in the War of 1812,
> and some of my Kents were at Bunker Hill. So, you see, I was started out
> in life in true New England fashion, with a love of the past and enough of
> the characteristics of Puritanism in me to make life miserable or interesting,
> according to circumstances.[2]

Born in Boston, Kent was sent to school in 1881 at the Norwich Free Academy
in Connecticut. He maintained in later life that the town had solidified his love
of the American past:

> Norwich had been one of the most influential towns of the state in Colonial
> and Revolutionary times, and after the Civil War it became an important
> manufacturing city, but the old part of the town, Norwichtown as it is now

called, kept its Colonial character, in houses, people, manners, and customs. The houses around the old green (green is the Connecticut name for what in Massachusetts is called a common), originally of the seventeenth century, had gradually been renovated to suit the later fashions in dwellings, but many of them had kept their original woodwork, paneling and shutters, and chimneys. Everything about the place recalled the old times, and to a boy from the city who was naturally impressed by such things, it was a delight.[3]

After the Academy, Kent returned to Boston to work in the public library. His superior there, "an exacting taskmaster," supervised him in what he described as boy's work. "All employees of the Library in those days," wrote Kent over sixty years later, "from the top to the bottom, were required to change their shoes for slippers on entering the building in the morning, and their coats for 'dusters,' as they were called. All of this routine was good discipline, teaching quietness and consideration for others—excellent training for public servants."[4] To the end of his life, Kent considered himself a public servant, an educator who was under an obligation to use the collections in his charge to provide the greatest possible public enlightenment.

Kent's training in sorting and cataloguing was carried to a much higher level when he left Boston for Columbia College in New York. In the fall of 1884, he enrolled in Melvil Dewey's first course in Library Economy, along with "some ten or twelve men and women, of all sorts and kinds, eager to become librarians, some of them later to be distinguished in that profession."[5] Under Dewey, who devised the renowned Dewey decimal system, Kent learned to classify and catalogue, skills that he later took with him to the Metropolitan Museum. There he modified them for museum use, creating a system that is still the standard not only at the Metropolitan but throughout the museum world. This precise, reserved, and distinguished gentleman remains a legend among the Metropolitan's staff, who marvel at the continuing efficiency of the cataloguing and filing method he set up nearly seventy-five years ago.

In 1888, Kent was invited to return to Norwich as librarian of the Norwich Free Academy and curator of the just-completed Slater Memorial Museum. In this dual post he was able to use much of his library experience and to extend it into the museum field. As the museum's curator, he soon discovered that special exhibitions were necessary to sustain interest after the initial flurry upon its opening. Among the thirty-seven exhibitions Kent arranged were several related to Norwich's colonial heritage: portraits of men and women connected with the town's early history, the work of Norwich silversmiths, historical Norwich publications, and early printed children's books. "Norwich," wrote Kent, "lived up to its reputation in producing old objects out of its collections."[6]

During these years Kent was also traveling to Europe to observe museum procedures. Unlike many American museum men, he never got carried away by the arts of Europe and the Orient, however. He was preoccupied with a lively and respectful interest in the arts of colonial America, and attuned to their importance in the past life of Norwich. There, "One couldn't turn around without running up against interesting historical facts and names."[7]

Despite his devotion to his field, Kent seems not to have collected for himself. He mentions one incident, however, that shows he was not immune to the excitement of discovery:

> I went one day with Mr. Wells behind his Arab stallion to Yantic, to a real old-fashioned vendu, or auction, in the Backus House, after the death of the last one of a family that settled Norwich and, later, Ohio. It was known how full the house was of old things, and great crowds of dealers came to the barbecue, and then to bid. I swept up a mass of papers, thrown out by the executors, and having put them in a barrel and two soapboxes, asked the auctioneer to put them up for sale. This he did, and I got the lot for a dollar. Among the treasure trove were many rare books, pamphlets, and maps, the Battles of Concord and Lexington engravings by Doolittle in color, and other engravings of real value and rarity. Best of all was a diary written by a Backus boy, Elijah, Jr., when a Senior at Yale in 1777, a priceless piece of Yale memorabilia. . . .[8]

Whether Kent was acting for the museum or for himself, he took obvious pleasure in his find.

With great reluctance Kent left Norwich in 1900 to accept a post as the first paid librarian of the Grolier Club in New York—"A great honor for the boy from Boston's public library."[9] He stayed until 1905, happily engaged in "things bibliographical." Then he made the decision that would profoundly affect the history of American antiques. He accepted a post at the Metropolitan Museum as secretary to Robert de Forest. In 1913, when De Forest became president of the board of trustees, Kent moved up to replace him as secretary of the board, a position that he occupied with unsurpassed distinction for twenty-seven years.

His first memories of the museum were of three curators who had served under its first director, the colorful and authoritarian General Cesnola, and who were constantly warring among themselves. One day, to his amazement, Kent heard one of the curators ask another to step outside. This proved to be to argue, not to fight, but soon the two were chasing each other through the galleries. "I called the policeman at the door," wrote Kent, "and he stopped the exciting performance. I have never known professional feelings to run so high." In his own office, which he described as "about as big as a closet," he and his secretary, H. F. Davidson, proceeded more decorously, if no less energetically.[10]

Kent took his profession very seriously. He came on the scene when there was no specific training for museum workers—when each had to decide how best to prepare himself for what he wished to do. It was, correspondingly, a time of exciting change in conceptions of the American museum's place in society. "The old idea of the museum as a storehouse of art laid it open to the criticism that it would become a mausoleum in fact unless it was made to be actively serviceable," Kent observed.

> In other words, the European idea of a museum of art which housed the treasures the country had accumulated by hook or by crook, museums like the Vatican and the Louvre, did not fit the needs of this country, which had its own arts to develop. The American museum should show collections of what other civilizations had done, under religious or civil influences, of course, as a lesson to those whose business it was to produce similar kinds of things for us, to show what . . . might be done, by our own artists and craftsmen. Thus the museum would become a teacher in the truest sense, which was a new idea in this country—the active teacher instead of the inactive opportunity.[11]

Kent's greatest contributions to the American antiques collecting movement came early in his career at the Metropolitan. Although his devotion to the museum's public caused him to move away from this area in later years, the groundwork he laid affected the collecting movement enormously. He believed strongly in the necessity for wider public recognition of the intrinsic merits, both historical and aesthetic, of American antiques. He noted how little the great educators of the nineteenth century knew of the arts of their own country:

> It is interesting to reflect that at the opening of the Slater Museum [in 1888] even a person like President Gilman [of Yale], familiar with Norwich and quick to see the possible influence of a museum on the arts and crafts of an industrial city, did not mention the examples of American arts and crafts of an earlier period of which the town was so full. Still less did Mr. Norton [Charles Eliot Norton, professor of fine arts and cultural history at Harvard] have anything good to say about American art. Bewailing the lack of beauty and taste in American houses (*sic!*), furniture, and articles of daily use, he seemed unaware that a native tradition existed, with surviving examples all around him. The collectors . . . had begun to be aware of these things, but it was to be many years yet before early American decorative arts would come into general acceptance and public acclaim.[12]

Kent brought early American decorative arts to public notice dramatically with the exhibition at the Metropolitan Museum during the Hudson-Fulton Celebration in 1909. He wrote of his original idea, and its realization:

> Norwichtown gave me an interest in American history, architecture, arts and crafts, all of which, as I said before, were exemplified there, and this interest stood me in good stead; for instance, it led me to recommendations made to Mr. de Forest at the time of the Hudson-Fulton celebration in 1909, when the Curator of Paintings had advised a showing of Dutch paintings. I said to Mr. de Forest, who was then Secretary of the Metropolitan Museum, that it seemed to me a museum which showed Greek, Roman, Egyptian, Chinese, and other Eastern things surely ought to show to its public the things America had accomplished. He saw the point, and appreciated the soundness of the argument, and so to the exhibition of Dutch paintings representing Hudson's period was added an exhibition of American furniture, silver, pottery, etc., representing Fulton's period, which I brought together, with the help of Miss Florence Levy, borrowed from my collector friends, Palmer, Bolles, Blaney, Halsey, Flagler, and others. This was the first time American "antiques" were ever shown in New York, and they made a great hit with public and dealer alike. The Hudson-Fulton effort resulted eventually in the American Wing. . . .[13]

Kent's contacts with old and new friends involved in the Hudson-Fulton exhibition put him at the center of the antiques-collecting movement in 1909. Although he never made collecting a main focus of his own personal life, he had strong professional associations with American antiques, and felt that the collectors drawn together by the Hudson-Fulton show should remain in touch. As a result, he suggested to Lockwood and Bolles that the three of them organize the Walpole Society, then and now a select group of collecting gentlemen. Kent was one of the most active and respected members of the society from its first meeting in Hartford in 1910 to his death in 1948.

Another landmark in the history of collecting that resulted from the great success of the Hudson-

American furniture, silver, ceramics, and paintings exhibited at the Metropolitan Museum during the Hudson-Fulton Celebration of 1909. (The Metropolitan Museum of Art)

Fulton show was the Metropolitan's purchase of the Bolles collection in 1909, just after the close of the exhibition. As early as 1907, Kent had had American decorative arts in mind as a potential field of acquisition. He wrote his old friend George S. Palmer, whom he knew from Norwich, to ask whether Eugene Bolles (Palmer's cousin) had made a catalogue of his furniture collection, and whether there was "any possibility of it, or any part of it coming on the market for sale. I am writing entirely on my own initiative without any authorization or right, but I have my own reason for asking the question." Palmer replied very encouragingly:

> I am glad to write you a few points concerning Mr. H. Eugene Bolles' collection of furniture.
>
> Mr. Bolles has no children, his wife is a confirmed invalid, and he himself far from strong. He has spent a large amount of time, and considerable money, in the last twenty-five years building up a collection of representative pieces of American Colonial furniture, supplemented by some pieces of English furniture of corresponding types. He has collected such a mass of material that he now begins to find it a burden, and in spite of his great

affection for it and absorbing interest in it, he is inclined to look for a suitable place for its permanent keeping. As he cannot afford to furnish such a place himself and cannot afford to present his collection to a public institution, he is approaching the point where he will be willing to sell it to be kept together in some public place.

So far as my knowledge goes his collection is far and away superior to any other collection of American Colonial furniture, and it would be practically impossible to match it in a long course of years with unlimited expenditure. Mr. Bolles has been fanatically conscientious in keeping only such pieces as are absolutely typical and genuine, so that no element of suspicion can arise in connection with his things. This I regard a most important point, especially as the art of faking has reached such a development as to produce pieces which deceive the very elect.[14]

The day after receiving this letter, Kent wrote Palmer again, repeating his request that their correspondence be kept secret, even from Bolles, as "I shall not mention it to anyone here until I am in a position to give them the full facts and exact data."[15] That fall Kent did go to Boston to see Bolles's house and collection, but he took no further action for a year and a half.

In March of 1909 Kent wrote Palmer once more, saying he had learned from Bolles that he was about to lend a large part of his collection to the Boston Museum of Fine Arts, just when Kent was hoping to get loans for the Hudson-Fulton exhibition. Kent decided that the time had come for action: "I shall now recommend the purchase of the collection, if the price seems to be one which would come within the possibilities of consideration. Can you give me tentatively the price which Mr. Bolles would be apt to ask?"[16]

Exactly what happened from this point is not clear, but many of Bolles's antiques were included in the Hudson-Fulton exhibition, and Kent later wrote of a trip that probably convinced Robert de Forest to recommend buying the Bolles collection:

To emphasize the importance of the collection to the Museum, I invited Mr. and Mrs. de Forest and R. T. H. Halsey to go with me as my guests to Boston, where we would see what Boston and its vicinity had to show of American arts and crafts. We went, and had dinner at the Copley-Plaza Hotel, to which I had invited Hollis French, Joseph Chandler, Sumner Appleton, prominent collectors of American things, to meet my friends. The next day we motored to Salem, and then to Danvers, Topsfield, and Beverly; we devoted our attention to seventeenth-century buildings and other things, saw the Essex Institute, the Rebecca Nurse house, the Parson Capen house, and lunched with Charles Tyler and had a real fish chowder, which these New Yorkers had never eaten before. Back in Boston I showed them Christ Church, the Paul Revere house, and the old State House. Then we came

Antique American interior woodwork and furnishings exhibited at the Metropolitan during the Hudson-Fulton Celebration of 1909. (The Metropolitan Museum of Art)

home, I think with my purpose already accomplished, namely, to emphasize the importance of showing the history of American objects in an American museum.[17]

The Metropolitan Museum acquired the Bolles collection as a gift from Mrs. Russell Sage, who bought it for $125,000 in the fall of 1909. Robert de Forest was her lawyer and "proposed to Mrs. Russell Sage that she should pay the bill. She did so." Although Mrs. Sage was not noticeably interested in American decorative arts until the time of the Bolles purchase, she was heir to a $70 million fortune from her husband, a Wall Street speculator, and was happy to contribute to worthy causes. A few months after her gift, Kent wrote Bolles: "You must have been interested in the very widespread notice that has been given the collection. Clippings come to us from all over the country. Mrs. Sage, as I understand from Mr. de Forest, is much pleased with the interest shown."[18]

The Bolles purchase, remarkable for its size and comprehensiveness, gave another boost to the status of American antiques among the public at large. In an article on the collection, published in the January 1910 number of the Metropolitan Museum *Bulletin*, Kent offered his own sharply focused view of why such a collection belonged in a major museum:

With [a few] exceptions, no activity has as yet been displayed by our public museums in the conservation and exhibition in a dignified and discriminating manner—such as would be displayed in the treatment of the art of any other country—of the art of our own land. It is to Mrs. Sage's wise liberality that we, in New York, are enabled to save the evidence of our forefathers' appreciation of art before they shall have been scattered beyond recall and to show with becoming respect the work of their hands.[19]

Kent immediately began thinking of period rooms in planning a permanent display of the Bolles collection. As early as 1908, he had written De Forest asking whether it might not be "thought desirable to furnish in the manner of the German museums three or four rooms with objects in use in this country during the period of the colonies. . . ." In 1909 Kent wrote Lockwood, who had helped with the Hudson-Fulton exhibition and with the initial organization of the objects purchased from Bolles: "I have talked with Mr. de Forest with regard to the installation of the Bolles collection, and I have suggested that you and I might be able to pose a scheme for the arrangement of the pieces according to the German method, or 'room' arrangement." Finally, Kent himself did the first sketches for the American Wing, which was not to come to fruition until 1924.[20]

Henry Kent rarely wrote of his private life; and little is known of it aside from his love of all kinds of music, mentioned by several friends and acquaintances, and his fondness for the Cotswolds in England and his house in New Hampshire. A friend described him as "remarkable for elegance of mind as well as for a perfection of dress which, indeed, was almost dandiacal."[21] He was a popular diner-out as well, and since he never married, he was often in demand as an unattached man at parties. When he first came to New York, the well-meaning wife of a friend asked him to dinner with an attractive young woman; he was polite but perfunctory, and the experiment in matchmaking was not repeated.

As Kent was so active in many different professional associations and clubs such as the Grolier—where his propensity for elegance and accuracy was shared by printers, designers, and book collectors—and the Walpole Society, he probably had little free time left. It seems reasonable to conclude that his energies and affections were fully involved in his work.

Some years after his death, Kent was paid a compliment difficult to match:

At a meeting where tribute was being paid to Kent, Carl Rollins said "Many years ago, a very dear friend of Mr. Kent's and mine said to me, "You know, Kent is the finest man in New York!" Years later, repeating the remark to another mutual friend, with the observation that perhaps it was a bit extravagant, he said, "Well, he *is*, you know!"[22]

Chapter 17

The Walpole Society
"A Guild of Workers in the Collector's Noble Craft"

THE FORMATION OF THE WALPOLE SOCIETY, LIKE THE HUDSON-FULTON CELEBRATION from which it had evolved, represents a milestone in American collecting history. This was the first club for collectors and students of American decorative arts. The name itself is highly significant; it was taken from the eighteenth-century collector Horace Walpole, because, as a member later explained, "he was the discoverer of English arts and crafts at a time when polite society could appreciate only the foreign. Similarly, early Walpoleans directed public attention to the merit of American work in an era when the foreign was the thing."[1]

The idea originated one day in the fall of 1909, as Henry Kent and Luke Vincent Lockwood were lunching with Eugene Bolles after completing arrangements for the Metropolitan's acquisition of the latter's collection. Kent described the occasion:

> Bolles asked Lockwood and me to luncheon with him at the Union Club. Here, in a front room overlooking the Common, with a magnum of champagne between us, the suggestion was made that steps be taken to bring the collectors of Americana together in closer association. The idea met with approval. Then and there it was decided to form such a group for the purpose of sharing enthusiasms, exchanging views, and so increasing the knowl-

edge of the arts of our early days. A list of the names of men known to the three of us, to the number of nineteen, was drawn up, and since it was found that those nominated lived in several states, it was determined to make the proposed society a peripatetic one, with meetings in different places, from time to time, wherever there might be things of interest to see—houses, collections, collectors—anything under the definition.[2]

The society—which is still active today—flourished from the first. Leading collectors and museum men were invited to join, and most were delighted to accept. The following is a list of the original members, nearly half of whom had been lenders to the Hudson-Fulton exhibition:

Samuel Putnam Avery
Edwin AtLee Barber
Francis Hill Bigelow
Dwight Blaney
H. Eugene Bolles
Richard Canfield
Thomas Benedict Clarke
George M. Curtis
John Cotton Dana
Henry Wood Erving
Harry Harkness Flagler
Hollis French
Henry Watson Kent
Luke Vincent Lockwood
George Shepard Palmer
Arthur Jeffrey Parsons
Albert Hastings Pitkin
Charles Adams Platt
Frederick Bayley Pratt
Charles Hitchcock Tyler
Frederick S. Wait
Theodore S. Woolsey

The majority were from New York, Massachusetts, and Connecticut; almost all meetings in the early years were held in one of those three states.

Each member had previously had at most a few friends who were engaged in the same eccentric pastime, but now each gained the fellowship of numerous

others who shared his collecting interest. Casual associations, created by participation in the Hudson-Fulton show, grew into valued friendships. Henry
Wood Erving wrote of the society's impact:

> The founding of the Walpole Society in 1910 was to all of us the beginning
> of congenial and new friendships and the cementing of the old. There
> usually comes the desire to perpetuate and distribute the good in one's hob-
> bies, and information and knowledge can certainly be classed among the
> things which are good. The benefits, and certainly happiness, we have
> each—I think—derived from the association, have made the inauguration
> and maintenance of the Society one of the most worth while things of life.

Most of the others were comparably enthusiastic. Dwight Blaney went so far as
to say that "life began to carry on" once he became a member. Sharing similar
backgrounds and outlooks, the early Walpoleans delighted in one another's
company; the society was very important to them.[3]

The Walpole Society *Note Books* record not only this reaction but also a
common belief that preservation of the group's unique character required careful attention to the compatibility of new members. From the beginning, the
society was very exclusive, reflecting the consciousness of status that had become pronounced in the collecting movement during the 1890s. Membership
was clearly limited, not merely to collectors of American antiques but to men
with the "right" backgrounds. In a letter to the society on the occasion of a
meeting he could not attend, Hollis French articulated this attitude: "Our future
depends on the proper selection of our members, who not only must have the
requisite knowledge in our various lines, but must have in the future, as in the
past, a broad general culture which stamps a gentleman and a scholar."[4]

As primarily professional men, of respectable but not aristocratic origins,
the Walpoleans were susceptible to the snobbishness that often accompanies
social aspiration. Although several of the charter members worked to spread
awareness of American antiques among the general public, the society itself
was not democratic. This was less evident in the early days, when potential
membership candidates tended to be from acceptable families of old native
stock. But it became obvious in the 1920s, when men like the Irish Catholic
Francis P. Garvan and the perhaps too brashly successful Henry Ford were
among those dominating the collecting scene. Both were passionately interested
in the American cultural tradition, and ranked among the most prolific and
dedicated collectors of the time. Neither, however, was asked to join the
Walpole Society.

On the other hand, one of the charter members was Richard Canfield, the
society's "gorgeous gambler." Although his "profession" was considerably less
conventional than those of the others, his avowed aim in collecting was to
surround himself with the trappings of a gentleman. The Walpoleans tended to

share Canfield's perception of collecting as a method for the elevation of status, although some might not have recognized or admitted it. In any case, they admired his success in achieving the goal. Besides, he was a white Anglo-Saxon Protestant from New England, who had made some desirable social connections. So Canfield was included among the original members, and doubtless placed an extremely high value on the association.

The élitist, exclusionary attitude of the Walpoleans toward membership was accompanied by a failure to undertake any organized program for the widespread dissemination of their accumulated knowledge. Most were satisfied with the society as a haven from the world outside, and as a vehicle for the pleasure and edification of the members alone. And, in the old English club tradition, there have been no female members. Walpoleans were delighted to visit the ladies, to see their collections, and to take refreshment in their gardens, but serious female collectors who might otherwise have qualified were not considered for membership.

Yet some Walpoleans—of whom Henry Kent was an outstanding example —have stressed the greater responsibility of the group, which has included leading authorities on most aspects of American art. And its very formation

had a significant influence on the world of American antiques. That influence stemmed most immediately from the opportunity for association among the members, from the exchange of ideas, and from the encouragement of the collecting urge. Each member, in turn, was bound to have some impact on the world beyond the society—an impact greatly reinforced by his contacts within. And a few members, like Kent and Halsey (who joined after the founding), were pivotal figures in developing a broader enthusiasm for the American decorative arts.

In an "imperfect way," as Kent described it, the society also contributed from the outset to the published scholarship on American antiques. It sponsored several glossaries, including one for furniture (1913) by Lockwood and one for ceramics (1914) by Edwin AtLee Barber. Hollis French's *Silver Glossary*, which appeared in 1917, was actually a history of early American silversmiths and their works. All were printed by Walter Gilliss, the eminent New York printer.

The glossaries are an example of what, in a larger sense, the formation of the Walpole Society represents: the cataloguing, categorizing impulse of the first decade of the twentieth century. Thus, men with a shared interest in the

American past and its artifacts were brought together into an organized group. But Kent's hope that the society would initiate a program of serious publication was never fulfilled. Other institutions—some of them, like the Winterthur Museum, created by Walpole members—have filled the gap. And the society is no longer the sole formal meeting place for collectors and students of early American decorative arts. It is only one élite group in a vastly expanded field. However, Walpoleans can still gain access to almost any collection they might wish to see—quite an advantage, in view of collectors' and curators' now-chronic fear of theft.

The Walpole Society has brought out books in addition to the early glossaries. In 1926, it began issuing annual reports of each year's meetings and trips. These *Note Books*, often delightful to read, are a valuable reference for historians of the collecting movement.

The Walpole Society on an outing sometime around 1913. Among those shown are Henry Erving, Luke Lockwood, Albert Pitkin, Richard Canfield, and Dwight Blaney.

There is information about members, about the content and importance of their collections, and about historic houses. And in 1921, five years before the start of the *Note Books*, the society published a single report of a trip to northwestern Massachusetts. It conveys the air of conviviality and companionship, and the joyous sense of making new discoveries, that pervaded the early meetings. After a pleasant drive through an autumn landscape, the members arrived for dinner at the home of Judge John Woolsey:

> What a great reunion! and such a good time! and what a fine collection of clocks and old furniture all in good condition and guiltless of the restorer's hand. In a rear room was a display of ironwork and household implements including a pie-fork of unusual form that at first set the party guessing. The dinner will be long remembered; the table set with old pewter, flat-topped tankards and silver and ornamented with bright colored fruits and gourds; and all the sweet cider we could drink and such a chatter of voices. . . . We had learned discussions about paneling, etc., and then bidding goodbye to Mrs. Woolsey and the boys, we packed into our cars and started for Greenfield by way of Athol. The discussions on the way would fill many volumes. Learned conversations on genealogy by Seymour and Isham; profound lectures on furniture by Erving and Lockwood, made every moment of value. Approaching Greenfield we went through many covered wooden bridges with their "bowstring" trusses and as it grew darker we enjoyed the sunset across the lovely valley of the Connecticut river. . . . One car was entertained by ancient songs by Isham, Blaney and Seymour, and long to be remembered will be Seymour's singing "The Sword of Bunker's Hill."[5]

Chapter 18

Edwin AtLee Barber

Missionary Museum Man

Edwin Atlee Barber (1851–1916), like his colleague Henry Kent, was an educator—though unlike Kent he was a collector as well. Barber was interested in displaying and interpreting the arts of early America in a way that would encourage their study by contemporary manufacturers. In particular, he felt strongly that early ceramics produced in America should be properly appreciated by his countrymen. In his generation, collectors focused on the European—mainly English—wares that had been used by Americans. But, according to Diana and J. G. Stradling, "in attempting to stimulate interest in Americana," Barber encountered "an overwhelming disinterest, even an 'unreasonable prejudice . . . against all American productions.' "[1]

To combat the prejudice, his primary weapon was the publication of *The Pottery and Porcelain of the United States*. In a preface to the first edition in 1893, Barber set forth his immediate goal:

The main purpose of the work is to furnish an account of such of the earlier potteries as for any reason, possess some historical interest, and of those manufactories which, in later days, have produced works of originality or artistic merit. Confining myself necessarily to these limits, I have endeavored

Edwin AtLee Barber.
(Philadelphia Museum of
Art)

here to present a condensed but practically complete record of the development of the fictile art in America during the three centuries which have elapsed since the first settlement of the country.[2]

Barber's ultimate hope was to encourage American potteries of his own time to produce useful and attractive wares. In *Pottery and Porcelain*, he set forth his ideas on the state of the industry. American manufacturers, in his opinion, were turning out sets of china inappropriate to the refinement of post-Centennial America. "It is no longer necessary," said Barber,

to make butter dishes and gravy boats large enough to serve the purpose of vegetable dishes, nor the latter of a capacity sufficient for an ordinary soup tureen. The increasing refinement of our modern civilization rebels against the continued use of the capacious and clumsy utensils of pre-Centennial times. While the quality of our domestic table wares is not inferior to that of the foreign, the commercial element in design and workmanship must be made secondary to the artistic before our manufacturers can expect the more cultured classes to abandon, to any great extent, the imported for domestic manufactures.[3]

Not satisfied with completion of the monumental *Pottery and Porcelain*, Barber moved on to the publication of *Anglo-American China* in 1899 (an enlarged edition was issued in 1901), *Tulip Ware of the Pennsylvania German Potters* in 1903, and *Marks of American Potters* in 1904. This last work is described by the Stradlings as continuing to be "the best handbook for the collector of American ceramics."[4] In addition to his research and writing, this remarkably energetic man carried on his professional duties and traveled widely, cataloguing American ceramic collections.

Barber began his career in 1874 as Assistant Naturalist with the United States Geological and Geographical Survey. In 1875 he accompanied part of the Survey team to ancient ruins in Colorado, Utah, and Arizona, as special correspondent for *The New York Herald*. Returning to Philadelphia, he was appointed in 1879 to the honorary position of chief of the department of archeology of the Permanent Exhibition in Fairmount Park. After serving in this and a number of civil-service capacities in Philadelphia, he made the intriguing disclosure that he had gone into the investment business. By 1892, Barber had become honorary curator of the Pennsylvania Museum's new division of American Pottery and Porcelain. His interest in early American ceramics had surely been stimulated by the archeological expeditions, for ceramics play an important part in piecing together information about earlier civilizations.

To further his goal of attracting Americans to their own ceramics, Barber advocated pottery courses, published many articles besides his books, and formed an outstanding collection of Pennsylvania pottery for the museum. He also had his own noteworthy collection, which he lent generously for exhibition. Once, an acquaintance devised a series of "American Luncheons" as a way of promoting American ceramic tablewares for Americans. This enthusiast fed her friends royally—on American china. Printed below each of the many courses on the menu were the name and origin of the china on which it was served. Blue points on halfshell, for example, were served on "Oyster Plates of Mazarine Blue, made by the New England Pottery Co., East Boston, Mass." Sweetbread pâtés arrived on "Fluted China Shells, made by International Pottery Co., Trenton." Barber endorsed the china, and therefore the idea. "No foreign productions could be more dainty and artistic than this combination of domestic wares," he said.[5]

When Henry Kent was organizing the Hudson-Fulton exhibition in 1909, Barber responded energetically and helpfully. Having been appointed director of the Pennsylvania Museum in 1907, he offered objects both from its collection and his own. He also sent the names of potential lenders from Pennsylvania, New York, and New England. He wrote the text to the catalogue, not only for ceramics but also for glass and pewter. "Among the prominent Philadelphia [pewter] makers whose marked work I have gathered together," he wrote Kent, "may be included the names of Parkes Boyd, B. Barns, T. Danforth, and others." Regarding Barber's knowledge of early glass, the New York collector A. W. Drake told Kent: "He knows dates of Colonial and American glassware better, probably, than any other person in the country."[6]

Barber was a charter member of the Walpole Society. He wrote *The Ceramic Collectors' Glossary*, whose publication the society sponsored in a small edition in 1914, and which has recently been reprinted in combination with the furniture and silver glossaries. The Walpole Society took on the ceramics project in response to "the need of a uniform ceramic nomenclature as an aid to the correct labeling and cataloguing of collections of pottery and porcelain. . . ."[7] Since Barber had been advising museums on the display and labeling of their ceramics for many years, he was the logical author.

Barber was the rediscoverer of the charming slip-decorated and *sgraffito* wares produced by the Pennsylvania Germans. He tells, in *Pottery and Porcelain*, of the help he received from one Thomas B. Deets,

whose explorations through the old farm-houses in my behalf have resulted in the discovery of many a rare old piece, whose existence would never have been suspected had not my attention been drawn to this untrodden field by an old pie plate which I procured from him, the first example of the kind that I had seen. . . . His knowledge of Pennsylvania German, which is generally spoken in this section of the State, enabled him to penetrate the mysteries of ancient closets, and place at my command the hoarded treasures concealed therein.[8]

Although he worked hard to encourage the use and appreciation of American-made ceramics, Barber was considered the leading American authority on those of *all* countries. A contemporary newspaper article described him:

Dr. Barber, with his shock of white hair, his piercing black eyes and his straight, alert figure is a wizard in his discernment of "what's what" in china, for with a glance of the eye and a touch of the fingers he is able to tell almost immediately the pottery from which the pitcher, cup and saucer, vase or other articles came.[9]

Among the many collections Barber was called upon to assess and catalogue were those of the Boston Museum of Fine Arts; the Essex Institute in Salem, Massachusetts; the Chicago Art Institute; the Albany Institute of History and Art; and the Wadsworth Atheneum in Hartford. At the Atheneum, he was particularly impressed by the "wealth of ceramic treasures" that had been gathered by Dr. Lyon's friends Stephen Terry and Horace Fuller.[10]

Another impressive Hartford collection was formed by Barber's friend Albert Hastings Pitkin, who shared in his pioneer effort to interest Americans in their own ceramics. Pitkin's collection is now also at the Wadsworth Atheneum, where he was curator for some years. The first to study early New Eng-

Sgraffito dish from Barber's collection. (Philadelphia Museum of Art; gift of John L. Morris)

Slip-decorated red earthenware platter from Pitkin's collection. (Courtesy of Wadsworth Atheneum, Hartford; gift of Mrs. Albert Hastings Pitkin in memory of her husband)

Glazed red earthenware lion by John Sanders. From Albert H. Pitkin's collection of American folk pottery. (Courtesy of Wadsworth Atheneum, Hartford; gift of Mrs. Albert Hastings Pitkin in memory of her husband)

land redware pottery, Pitkin described the beginning of this interest in his posthumously published *Early American Folk Pottery . . .* (1918):

> In the Spring of 1884, while "China hunting" near Hartford, Conn., I picked up, at a farm house, two pieces of "Red Clay Pottery," lead glazed and slip decorated. Little information could be obtained regarding them, except, that they were, probably, more than fifty years old, and at one time, quite common. At that time, I knew of no such pieces in the hands of either dealer or collector. Convinced from the first that they were of home manufacture, I began to study into the matter, and to quietly collect all similar pieces available.[11]

Pitkin's study showed that such pottery had been made in New England from about 1771 to 1850. He went on collecting it, and "by the time I had obtained some sixty or seventy examples, I observed other collectors, as well as dealers, giving their attention to these wares. As a result it became scarce and rapidly increased in value. Today, it is being sought for, for Museum Collections." Kent wrote Pitkin at the time of the Hudson-Fulton exhibition, to which the latter lent furniture as well as ceramics, that his redware was "an astonishment to me in its completeness and interest. I did not know that any one had so many American pieces."[12]

In 1911, Barber caused an uproar in Albany. He was invited to inspect and catalogue the collection of over five thousand pieces given by James Ten Eyck

*Ten Eyck collection on
display at the Albany
Institute early in this
century. Barber catalogued
it in 1911. (Collection,
Albany Institute of History
and Art)*

to the Albany Institute of History and Art in 1909. After careful study, Barber suggested that some two hundred objects be eliminated, as either not genuine or else inferior specimens. *The Knickerbocker Press* seized upon and published the story, headlined: "Counterfeits in Ten Eyck China/ Collection Presented to Albany Historical Society Has Spurious Specimens/ Dr. Barber's Discovery/ Over Two Hundred Pieces, for Which High Price Was Paid, Not Genuine." The pieces, said the *Press* reporter, "were very clever reproductions of the original designs and were so carefully executed that even a connoisseur might easily have been deceived, and it was not until the arrival of Dr. Barber, one of the most celebrated authorities in the country, that this fact became known."[13]

The commotion caused by the sensational headline and the revelation of a few fakes prompted Barber immediately to draft a reassuring letter, published five days later in the Albany *Times Union*. "In the first place," wrote Barber, "this collection, as freed from reproductions, counterfeits and undesirable specimens, is a representative collection of English wares, and in some features stronger than any other collection of its kind in this country, particularly in its group of English lusters and Staffordshire blue printed wares." Barber mentioned a number of rarities, including a group of blue-and-white Staffordshire pieces decorated with scenes from the opening of the Erie Canal. Emphasis on such pieces was particularly appropriate for an Albany resident like Ten Eyck; and many china enthusiasts had pursued a similar kind of specialized collecting in local wares. Even by 1911, however, this group within the Ten Eyck collection was unusual enough for Barber to note that it must have been assembled at an early date, "before such designs became so rare and expensive."[14]

He also set the record straight with regard to "counterfeits" and "reproductions." Most of the pieces removed at his suggestion, Barber said, were genuine but of poor quality. The actual fakes were few, and "the [Ten Eyck] collection is freer of forgeries than almost any other collection, public or private, which I have examined."[15] Thus subsided, presumably, the tempest over the teapots.

Barber's death in 1916, as noted by the Stradlings, "almost coincided with the outbreak of World War I, which effectively put an end to ceramic activity in the United States for many years to come."[16] This reference to the activity of contemporary American art potters applies, more or less, to the collection of old pottery and porcelain as well. Its popularity seems to have diminished as the twentieth century progressed. The single-minded devotion to old china so prevalent in the nineteenth century faded, like the horse and buggy and the sentimental rural scenes of E. L. Henry, with the coming of a new, gasoline-powered collecting generation.

Chapter 19

George Shepard Palmer
High Style in Connecticut

Ⓘ N 1909, MORE THAN TWENTY YEARS AFTER HE HAD BEGUN TO COLLECT, GEORGE Shepard Palmer (1855–1934) set forth his motives: "I have been moved by two purposes, one to furnish a home in a distinctive way, the other more serious and important, namely, to demonstrate the but imperfectly and recently realized artistic tastes of our forefathers."[1]

By including American (as well as English) antiques among the furnishings for his home, Palmer exhibited a serious interest in his own heritage. But in acquiring only the finest examples of eighteenth-century work, he took another significant step. Even other collectors and students did not yet recognize the skill of eighteenth-century American craftsmen. Palmer sought to demonstrate it, living elegantly with his high-style colonial furnishings. Like Canfield, Pendleton, and Perry, Palmer aspired to live with the best—and he had the necessary judgment and money to do it.

"When the Walpole Society was founded," wrote Luke Vincent Lockwood, "it was inevitable that his [Palmer's] name was among the small group that headed the first roster. He was older than most of us, and the dean of the world of grandeur in our field."[2]

From his work at the Slater Museum in Norwich, Henry Kent knew Palmer

George Shepard Palmer.
(National Cyclopedia of
American Biography)

well. Palmer's first collecting venture, according to Kent, was to assemble a series of chairs that showed the range of styles from Byzantine times down through Chippendale. An exhibition of the chairs at the museum in the late nineteenth century attracted much attention. As Palmer's interests widened to include other forms of furniture and a variety of antique silver, pewter, glass, and pottery, his house filled up. He displayed the overflow in his attic, which he remodeled for the purpose.

"George Shepard Palmer with his wife and son, then a schoolboy, came to Norwich from Montville in order, as I understand, to be near his mill in Fitchville, a neighboring village," wrote Kent. "He and his three brothers were in partnership in the manufacture of bedquilts, with mills in Palmertown and Fitchville, and eventually they came to have a monopoly of this business. He took a house on one of the principal streets, Broadway." It was during the Norwich years that Palmer acquired many of his best antiques: "Some of his most important pieces came from the home-

steads of the Huntington, Carpenter and Backus families, famous people in Colonial days. He specialized in the elegancies of the house furnishings of 'first families'—block fronts and 'Philadelphia' pieces were his standards."[3]

Although he lived with only the best antiques, Palmer was never too grand to search them out himself. He wrote of the day he and his cousin Eugene Bolles went calling on the Hartford collector and cabinetmaker Walter Hosmer:

Admittance to the house was seldom granted and then most grudgingly. [Hosmer] had never been known to sell a piece except one to me sometime before; but that misstep was fatal to him. The thought suddenly struck me one day, buy his whole collection, and the next morning accompanied by

Left: *Philadelphia Chippendale lowboy, mahogany, 1760–1775, from the Palmer collection. (The Metropolitan Museum of Art, Kennedy Fund, 1918)*

Below: *Connecticut blockfront cherry desk signed "Benjamin Burnham 1769." This was part of Hartford cabinetmaker Walter Hosmer's collection, all of which was purchased by Palmer and Bolles in 1894. (The Metropolitan Museum of Art, Kennedy Fund, 1918)*

The famous Philadelphia Chippendale "Pompadour" highboy,
c. 1765, from the Palmer collection. (The Metropolitan
Museum of Art, Kennedy Fund, 1918)

my friend [Bolles] I was banging to and fro his disconnected door-pull. At length we were admitted and straightway began our attack by boldly stating that we wanted prices put upon everything in the house. We had come to purchase the whole. A fleeting smile, somewhat sad and almost ghastly (for his face was always very pale), spread over his countenance, but he made no direct refusal, which to us was a great encouragement.[4]

Hosmer capitulated. Palmer took the mahogany and cherry, and Bolles "the early coarse Colonial stuff."[5] This was in 1894, and Bolles and Palmer were among the first to buy entire collections. (Ben: Perley Poore is reported to have operated in a similar fashion.) During the 1920s men like Francis Garvan and Henry Ford snapped up whole collections without a second thought, but in the nineties it was something unusual.

"No one," wrote Norman Isham, "worked more intelligently, more systematically than he, and he was the first to play the game in a large way—not merely here a little and there a little, but in whole collections already formed—and to set a goal before him which involved an exact knowledge of a definite period to which the pieces he sought should belong."[6]

Palmer pursued a particularly fine matching highboy and lowboy through three generations of the family in which they had descended. On one occasion, when he had traveled all the way to St. Louis to examine the highboy, Palmer "admired the center finial so much that the dear old lady took it off and insisted that he should keep it. She wanted to give it to him, but he was fine enough to utterly refuse it and tell her never to let the piece be dismantled."[7] By the time Palmer was finally able to buy the pair, after stalking it for twenty years, the highboy had lost its finials and central cartouche to some less scrupulous admirer. In spite of the serious loss, these two lavishly leaf-and-shell-carved pieces are among the most beautiful in the group of superlative Philadelphia furniture that Palmer gathered.

Both Erving and Lockwood wrote of Palmer's visits to William Meggat's shop in Wethersfield, Connecticut, near Hartford. Lockwood marveled: "My first memory of Mr. Palmer takes me to Mr. Meggat's where a very beautiful kettle-shaped high desk was priced at the peak of my experience in extravagance in 1893, at $300.00, and that desk was purchased by Mr. George S. Palmer of Norwich. It sounded to me just like the Kohinoor diamond for riches and daring." Palmer's Norwich house "remains in my memory as a very charming place," continued Lockwood. "The furniture kept in perfect condition and artistically arranged. There were also delightful arrangements of flowers in the house, which Mr. Palmer did with his own hands."[8]

After his first wife died, Palmer left the Norwich house for one in New London. It was "a beautiful example of the work of Charles A. Platt, [and] was furnished chiefly with these eighteenth-century objects . . . it is doubtful if a more perfect expression of the richness of the period could be made." In New

London, Palmer turned his collecting energies to paintings by American artists ("many of them the work of friends, members of the colony at Lyme"), and to books related to American history.[9]

Palmer later moved to Goshen Point, beyond New London; there, except for furnishing his new house, he apparently stopped collecting. In 1918, he allowed the Metropolitan Museum to buy its choice of his finest American and English furniture. He was favoring the preservation of his name over his purse, for the collection would surely have brought more if sold complete. In an article published on the Palmer furniture in 1918, R. T. H. Halsey wrote:

> As a fellow-collector of Mr. Palmer, it has been a joy to see this collection grow slowly piece by piece. To many of us there had been no idea that such beautiful furniture as that in the Palmer Collection had ever been made in America. Year by year Mr. Palmer kept on surprising us. His weapons of chase consisted of a love and appeciation for the beautiful, untiring quest, infinite patience, persistence, and a long pocketbook—a formidable battery.[10]

By securing a permanent home for his best pieces at the Metropolitan Museum, Palmer was realizing a dream. He had written Henry Kent years earlier that he and Bolles were making complementary collections in the hope that they would eventually be displayed together at a museum. And as early as 1893, Palmer had written to Henry Waters of Salem:

> I, myself, am trying to get together fine specimens of eighteenth century furniture with the expectation that they may remain together in some public institution for the profit and pleasure of future generations. It seems to me that the old things which have come down to us from the first settlers in our country should be carefully gathered together and preserved in places where they may be studied advantageously by large numbers of people. . . .[11]

Thus, Palmer was in the vanguard of those who collected with a definite educational purpose.

In 1913, Palmer's European—mainly English—silver had also enriched the Metropolitan Museum's collections. He had been gathering this silver, which was of the same quality as his furniture, for about twenty years. Palmer pointed out that he was selling it to the museum for what it had cost him, not its increased worth at the time of sale.

Palmer amassed a notable collection of American silver as well. One of the earliest and most important purchases, the Madame Sarah Knight communion cup, occurred in Norwich, where he had been so successful in buying furniture. Kent tells the story:

I had found one day in a cupboard in the Pastor's study of the old church, a communion cup of silver, with wire handles, but as black as your hat. Cleaned, it allowed one to read the name of its maker, John Dixwell of Boston, and an engraved inscription which said, "The gift of Sarah Knight to the/ Chh of Christ in Norwich/ Ap^r 20, 1722." This I placed in a case in the [Slater] Museum. Later, when the church needed money, George S. Palmer bought it and took it away. In time he sold it to Philip L. Spalding of Boston, another early collector of American silver, and at his death it was given to the Boston Museum and is now one of its treasures.[12]

Of all his antiques, Palmer may have preferred his American silver. It was eventually sold by Tiffany's to Mr. and Mrs. Edsel Ford, and became the nucleus of their collection.

Lockwood once said that Palmer "always regarded his collection in the light of a capital asset and not as his soul's necessity."[13] But Palmer was unquestionably motivated by a real belief in early American artistic achievement. He set out to show that there were artists in colonial America whose work in wood and silver equaled that of Europe's finest craftsmen. From his limited early interest in gathering a series of chairs, Palmer moved on to become one of the grandest collectors of his generation. He established beyond question the excellence and elegance of the best early American craftsmanship.

The Madame Sarah Knight communion cup, silver, by John Dixwell. It was discovered in Norwich by Kent, and bought by Palmer for his collection. (Courtesy, Museum of Fine Arts, Boston)

IV

All-American Antiques for All Americans

The prices of antique furniture, glass, china, metal, samplers, fabrics,
and so on, have increased astonishingly in the last ten
years. It used to be that the term "collector" was synonymous with
lunatic, or at least one slightly touched. Nowadays he is
legion and she is legioner. . . .
Ten or twenty years ago people sold century and more old furniture
as they now sell worn-out golden-oak or mission, for what
it would bring, or wring, from the secondhand dealer—anything. "My,
my," our middle-aged visitors tell us, "you paid sixty
dollars for that piece? I remember when we refurnished our home
in 1905 or was it 1906?—we gave at least twenty pieces
like that to our ashman's wife." And they did.
M. L. Blumenthal, "Antiqueering," The Saturday Evening Post, *1924*

THE TRENDS AND ATTITUDES REFLECTED IN THE HUDSON-FULTON CELEBRATION OF 1909 were consolidated and intensified in the twenty-year period that followed. In particular, the feeling that American antiques were important because of their artistic qualities, as well as their associations, became firmly rooted. Henceforward, it would be some combination of the two that motivated private collectors and museums alike. But the relative importance of artistic and associational motives differed from collector to collector, and from one curator to another.

The rising national awareness that had nourished the Hudson-Fulton exhibition grew stronger as a result of World War I. Feelings had run high during the war: German-Americans were herded into concentration camps in huge numbers, and often cruelly treated no matter how staunchly they supported the American cause. The war left a legacy of bitterness, a sense that many Americans had died to protect European countries thousands of miles away in both fact and spirit. Xenophobia was widespread by 1920, as Americans in all walks of life turned inward to shut out the rest of the world and its problems.

But this reaction also had a positive counterpart. Many Americans were able to shake off their feelings of national inferiority because it was clear to the whole world that without their intervention Germany would be ruling Europe. With new pride, they became more interested in their own, as opposed to the European, cultural heritage. More than ever before, Americans were prompted to look backward—to try to understand their beginnings, and how they had grown. The critic Van Wyck Brooks, writing of his retreat to Westport, Connecticut, after the war, described the contemporary climate:

> This note of the native Connecticut air meant much to the newcomers who were settling in abandoned farmhouses and remodelling barns, aside from the tranquility one found there in a war-torn world and the charm of old hand-hewn beams and drooping elms. For in many cases the artists and writers had grown up in a still raw West or had returned from Paris in search of "roots," that shy and impalpable quiddity the lack of which, they felt, had made them frequently shallow and generally restless. No word was more constantly on their lips unless it was the native "soil" or "earth," and this obsession lay deep in the minds of urban cosmopolitans whom one saw toiling now with spade and pick. . . .
>
> No European could understand this constant American talk of roots, or why it was that expatriates discussed expatriation—a word that scarcely existed in any other country,—wondering about their "responsibilities" when they were abroad and how long they could safely stay in Europe.[1]

The need for roots, and the desire to turn away from Europe, enhanced the appeal of American antiques. There was a readiness, even an eagerness, to find beauty in the arts of early America, and enough national pride to make them especially desirable because of the American associations alone. By now, these associations were usually very broad, although they still occasionally involved a specific person or event. What was important, in the nationalistic decade of the twenties, was that the antiques were *American*.

This commitment to the national heritage brought increased status to ownership of American antiques. It was heightened by the growing belief that, although less ornate than European antiques, American pieces had their own artistic validity. Rising national confidence strengthened the impulse toward using American antiques for educational purposes, and confirmed the conviction that they were worthy of museums.

Early American home life, craftsmanship, and artistic achievement were the themes of museum displays and exhibitions, building toward the opening of the Metropolitan's American Wing in 1924. Paramount among the new developments in displaying and interpreting antiques was the period room, the most popular and striking method of presentation in the 1920s. George Francis Dow's innovation of 1907 was splendidly expanded in the American Wing. By exhibiting objects with a unity of time and space, this approach conveyed a concentrated impression of the past and its spirit.

Wallace Nutting.

While plans for the American Wing were being discussed and put in motion behind the scenes at the Metropolitan Museum from 1910 to 1924, exhibitions of American furniture and silver testified publicly to the museum's commitment to the arts of early America. In December 1916, Judge Alphonso T. Clearwater's collection was rearranged to form the first permanent public display of early American silver.

According to R. T. H. Halsey, this collection was important for three more broadly applicable reasons, which he and others continued to stress during the years to follow. American antiques were links to a rich cultural past; they were artistically successful; and they could serve as models for contemporary designers and craftsmen.

Many advocated the simple reproduction of American antiques. None was more fervent in this view than Wallace Nutting, one of the most famous figures in the history of American collecting. Preacher, photographer, publisher, promoter of old houses and new "antiques," Nutting summed up his philosophy as follows: "Copy and avoid bad taste. Not all the old is good but all the new is bad."[2]

Nutting's workshop produced the copies that would save his countrymen from the sin of bad taste. From 1917 until the late 1930s, he specialized in reproducing American furniture of the seventeenth and eighteenth centuries. In his catalogue, Nutting wrote of the "Romance of Furniture":

> There is enshrined in the forms of furniture used by our ancestors a spirit absent from the exotic shapes that come from Italy and France. We love the earliest American forms because they embody the strength and beauty in the character of the leaders of American settlement. These forms are the only tangible relics of our ancestors. . . . But those pioneers were a small band. We carry on their spirit by imitating their work. The major influence of a museum should be the stimulus it affords to the taste of this generation. Not to copy these approved types is a crime, because the only alternative is the making of mongrel shapes.[3]

Nutting's attitude toward American antiques combined the nostalgia and hero worship of the nineteenth century with the nationalism of the twentieth. For him, associations weighed more heavily than pure artistry. His loyalty to early America and his desire to recapture its taste led him to compile the most ambitious illustrated book ever attempted on American antique furniture. Con-

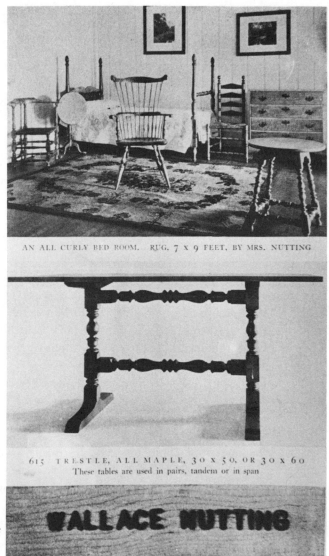

AN ALL CURLY BED ROOM. RUG, 7 X 9 FEET, BY MRS. NUTTING

615 TRESTLE, ALL MAPLE, 30 X 50, OR 30 X 60
These tables are used in pairs, tandem or in span

WALLACE NUTTING

A page from Nutting's catalogue of reproduction furniture, 7th ed., 1928. "Not all the old is good but all the new is bad," said Nutting.

taining five thousand photographs, nearly all taken by him, Nutting's *Furniture Treasury* has remained *the* pictorial archive of early American furniture since publication of the original two volumes in 1928.

In looking ardently to the American past for both spiritual and artistic models, Nutting was representative of his generation. But in choosing the earliest oak and pine furniture as best embodying the American spirit, and in longing nostalgically for the quaint cottages and picturesque lanes he loved to photograph, he was a throwback to the nineteenth-century collectors.

• • •

Before the Metropolitan bought the finest of George S. Palmer's high-style American eighteenth-century antiques in 1918, there was considerable discussion among the various museum people involved. The price seemed stiff to many, and not everyone was convinced that early American objects had real artistic value. But, as Palmer wrote to Halsey in 1918,

> I worked in unison with my cousin Mr. Bolles, whose collection the Museum now owns, for twenty years or more, more or less with the hope that our things might be placed in permanent relation with each other in some museum. Since his death, many of the finest things I offer have come to me, so that his things and mine together form such a complete representation of American artist craftsmanship in wood as can never be matched.[4]

In a memorandum to Robert de Forest, then the museum's president, Henry Kent pointed out that besides containing superlative pieces, the collection was important for its "undoubted examples of the work of cabinetmakers of particular localities, especially of Newport and Philadelphia." One group of three highboys, three lowboys, and one console table, said Kent, established beyond doubt the comparability of American and English workmanship, and the entire offering was worthy of purchase for this reason alone.[5]

The outstanding quality of the Palmer pieces decided the question. Both Henry Wood Erving and Luke Vincent Lockwood were asked to value them, and each appraised them at more than Palmer asked. Although some of the museum's officials were shocked at the price—$107,250 for sixty-six pieces—they paid because of a consensus that the quality was truly extraordinary. Palmer's furniture thus joined Bolles's, as the two men had hoped when they hunted antiques in a horse-drawn buggy nearly forty years earlier.

The museum made much of its new purchase. The furniture was put on display in a special temporary exhibition, and several articles were devoted to it in the *Bulletin*. The museum's commitment to displaying, studying, and explaining the arts of early America was becoming increasingly clear. This key Palmer acquisition, which came just as the United States was emerging from World War I, was doubtless influenced by the intense nationalistic pride that was to dominate the 1920s.

In 1922 the Metropolitan Museum mounted another exhibition of early American furniture, presenting the work of the New York cabinetmaker Duncan Phyfe. Over one hundred examples of furniture were included. All of it was attributed to the hand of the master, although today's students are much more careful, assigning undocumented pieces to his workshop or simply using the phrase "in the manner of" Duncan Phyfe. This show was important not only because it featured the work of one man but also because that man was from New York. Most early American furniture was attributed to other parts of the country; as late as 1929, in the catalogue to the Girl Scouts Loan

Exhibition, Louis Guerineau Myers stated that there was no identifiable New York furniture style except for Phyfe's. The entire seventeenth century and most of the eighteenth were thus a void, insofar as what was known about New York cabinetmaking. That is undoubtedly the reason New York collectors were so interested in Phyfe; luckily for them, there was a sizable reservoir of Phyfe-style furniture. It was elegant enough to furnish a townhouse or a luxurious apartment, and well-to-do New Yorkers who collected it were able to display local antiques with pride.

The show was organized by Halsey, one of the earliest and most avid collectors of Phyfe furniture, and Charles Over Cornelius, a young man who had been hired to help Halsey with the installation of the American Wing. Containing furniture on loan from many prominent collectors, the exhibition occupied a gallery whose vast space was broken by partitions into manageable segments. This gave the impression of rooms, which were furnished in the period manner. Halsey and Cornelius described them:

> On the walls are hung paintings and prints by artists contemporary with Phyfe, looking-glasses, girandoles, and sconces. Silver and porcelains are set on the tables. The true effect of the fine mahogany upon which Phyfe lavished such careful attention can thus be seen in association with the colors and gilding characteristic of the period.[6]

The Duncan Phyfe exhibition at the Metropolitan Museum, 1922. (The Metropolitan Museum of Art)

Halsey and Cornelius were obviously trying out the display technique that was to be seen on a much grander scale when the American Wing opened two years later.

The theme of inspiration for manufacturers and designers recurred in the *Bulletin*'s introduction to the show: ". . . while rendering homage to one of our few distinguished master-craftsmen, the collection should prove of value to our present-day designers, as well as to the collectors of the American arts and crafts." One collector, at least, dissented from a view prevailing among Nutting, Halsey, and others that pure reproductions were an answer to the problem of creating well-designed modern furniture. The New York lawyer and collector Allan B. A. Bradley wrote an opinion much more in accord with today's thinking than that of the twenties: "I realize that the purpose of the exhibition was largely to encourage the production of modern furniture of a high standard of quality and workmanship, but the repeated reproduction of . . . antique furniture may greatly tend to lessen the interest of the original."[7]

In 1916, Halsey had written that American antiques were coming into their own largely as a result "of the development of collections of American decorative art by the Metropolitan, Boston, and Providence museums." Their examples, he said, were being followed "by the managements of other museums, notably the Brooklyn Institute and some of our large western museums."[8] The Boston Museum of Fine Arts, unlike the Metropolitan, never pursued a policy of active acquisition. Most of their now-notable holdings were donated by collectors, or by families in which American antiques had descended.

Providence, of course, had the collection gathered by Charles Pendleton in the last quarter of the nineteenth century. But Brooklyn, without the resources or munificent donors of the other museums, acquired through active purchase furniture and interior woodwork that eventually furnished a series of permanently installed period rooms. As early as 1917, the Brooklyn Museum held a small exhibition of early American furniture, acquired over the preceding three years. The magazine *Good Furniture* took note, stressing that it was educational, that it presented good design and could be a force for quality and beauty in daily life.[9]

The idea of a series of period rooms representing the architecture and decorative arts of one's own country had arisen in Europe in the nineteenth century. George Francis Dow (who had created the series of three New England rooms in Salem in 1907), Kent, and other museum people were well aware of this development; their putting it to use in America indicated the same interest in national culture and artistic achievement that Germans, Swiss, and Swedes had shown. Feelings of patriotism and nationalism, which ran high in the Western world in the second half of the nineteenth century and again—

certainly in America—in the 1920s, contributed to public appreciation of period-room displays.

Henry Kent was proposing the period-room concept to his colleagues at the Metropolitan Museum as early as 1908. In 1910, he tried to buy colonial American woodwork; after seeing a passage about the Schuyler House in a circular advertising a new book, he wrote, "Would it not be possible to get one of these fine *historic* rooms?"[10] Apparently it was not. Although Kent wrote the author of the book and one or two other people he thought might be connected with the Schuyler House, he was unsuccessful. That difficulty was remedied in 1914, when the museum began under Halsey's direction to acquire the antique woodwork that eventually furnished the American Wing's three floors.

Period rooms also appealed to Luke Vincent Lockwood. Under his direction, Brooklyn by 1914 had joined the Metropolitan in searching out old interior architecture. Lockwood was assisted in this endeavor by the dealer André Rueff, who traveled the East looking for suitable interior woodwork. These were the days when old houses languished, neglected and decaying, their beautifully carved mantelpieces, stairways, and paneling being destroyed by insects and the elements. Although there was occasional public resentment upon the removal of the interior architecture from a particularly fine house, approval or indifference were more usual. Under the circumstances, museum people felt they were preserving the woodwork from eventual destruction.

In a report of about 1917 to the Brooklyn Museum describing his search for old woodwork and antiques in Maryland, André Rueff wrote:

> The dealer, generally, is not welcome: I do not say that the owner has suffered at his hands, but the feeling that he is taking the lion's share has made the people cautious. On the other hand I found almost immediate responsiveness from those to whom the Museum idea had been presented. . . . Panelled interiors are fairly common, especially eighteenth-century specimens covering the lower part of the walls. . . .[11]

The fruits of collecting interior architectural elements were apparent when the museums revealed their American period rooms in the 1920s. The first, and most influential, opening was that of the Metropolitan Museum's American Wing. By giving American antiques prominent place in a major museum, it confirmed once and for all their status as art and as cultural documents. By permanently applying to American decorative arts the technique of the Hudson-Fulton display—organization according to period and style—it set the **trend of the future.** And by showing furniture, silver, ceramics, and pewter in a room with architecture of the same style, it made both the objects and their surroundings come alive. In fact, the opening of the American Wing in 1924 caused a sensation.

The new Wing revolutionized the collecting movement. Americans were

The Almodington Room, as it was installed and furnished in the American Wing, 1924.
(The Metropolitan Museum of Art)

ready to appreciate the art and architecture displayed. The restraint and simplicity of indigenous furnishings, often considered drawbacks before, were now seen as reflecting prized components of the American character. According to Halsey, no visitor to the Wing could fail to perceive that "the old American arts and crafts, in their simple elegance, are in thorough harmony with the mental attitude of our people; they lack the pomp and splendour of the Old World, which reflected conditions which the builders of this country came over here to escape."[12]

Furthermore, the American Wing showed people how to relate antiques to their daily lives. Instead of collecting randomly, they could collect with a purpose and a focus, using antiques to create mini-American Wings in their own homes. The fashion for buying colonial houses was one result of this new awareness. Such houses could be furnished with antiques to both delight the eye and complement the architecture. Their owners could then aspire to the earlier, simpler, more peaceful way of life presented in the American Wing as characteristic of colonial America.

Among the converts were wealthy collectors like Henry Francis du Pont and Katharine Prentis Murphy. They were so impressed by the American Wing that they evolved their own personal and very influential variations of the period room (now preserved in what they left to the public). The prospect of gathering antiques for such rooms gave collecting a whole new dimension. Both rich and middle-class Americans were intrigued by the possibility of creating charming, beautifully appointed period settings; and they flocked in unprecedented numbers to museums, auctions, exhibitions, shops, and shows in the 1920s. During this period, propelled by the renown of the American Wing, New York City supplanted New England as the country's antiques center. It was already the financial and fashion capital, and the prices and fashionableness of American antiques rose with their status. Nearly all the important auctions of the twenties were held in New York, where most of the influential dealers had shops. By 1930, both *The Magazine Antiques* and the celebrated dealer Israel Sack had moved their operations down from Boston.

Today, many observers feel that the period rooms of the 1920s conveyed an exaggerated, romantic vision of life in colonial America. Those responsible, while trying to be accurate within the limits of their knowledge, were influenced by a desire to authenticate and enhance the American artistic tradition. In their charming rooms, colors always harmonized and bad taste was banned. If the validity of the resulting picture suffered, it was not intentional.

Boston, Brooklyn, and Philadelphia, when their period rooms opened later in the 1920s, could not approach the comprehensive coverage of America achieved in the American Wing. Only the Metropolitan encompassed the arts of colonial and early Federal New England, the Middle Colonies, and the South. All ten American period rooms at the Boston Museum of Fine Arts were from New England. The omission of other regions reflected an attitude widely held in Boston. "The Proper Bostonian," as Cleveland Amory puts it, "is not by nature a traveler. . . . The Beacon Hill lady who, chided for her lack of travel, asked simply, 'Why should I travel when I'm already here?' would seem to have put the matter in a nutshell. . . ."[13]

Brooklyn made more of an effort to span the colonies and the centuries, but owing to restricted funds its coverage was considerably more limited than the Metropolitan's. Philadelphia had four rooms in the art museum itself—all but one from Pennsylvania—and three historic Philadelphia houses in Fairmount Park furnished in the period-room manner.

The serious interest evident in these museum activities led to the birth of *The Magazine Antiques* in 1922. Beyond the museums as well, American antiques were attracting more attention than ever before; the new publication confirmed the existence of an audience for scholarly information. Its three founders, Homer Eaton Keyes, Frederick E. Atwood, and Sidney M. Mills, saw the need for a reliable magazine in which collectors and scholars of American antiques could share their knowledge. Keyes, who edited the magazine until his death in 1938, was committed to substituting facts for traditional or romantic stories. As a former professor of English and, later, business manager of Dartmouth College, he was well suited to a position that required financial and organizational abilities as well as editorial skill.

Keyes's interest in American antiques developed as a result of his acquaintance with a group of collectors in Hanover, New Hampshire. Among them was Alice Van Leer Carrick, author of popular books on the subject. Together they toured the surrounding countryside and took summer trips to Europe, looking for antiques. When the editorship of the new magazine was proposed to him, he knew it was right. Moving into his "Editor's attic" in Boston, he furnished it with treasures picked up on trips with his Hanover friends. He had "a Hepplewhite secretary, some Sheraton fancy chairs, tin sconces and bits of pewter and glass, and the Caswell carpet (now in the Metropolitan's American Wing), which he used as a wall hanging."[14]

Alice Winchester, editor. of *Antiques* from 1938 to 1972, wrote of the magazine's beginnings: "The other founders were Frederick E. Atwood, a Boston printer and publisher, and a stamp collector, who became publisher of the new monthly; and Sidney M. Mills of Beverly, Massachusetts, a collector of early American furniture, and later a dealer, who acted as New England representative. . . . Together they worked out policies that have guided *Antiques* ever since."[15]

Homer Eaton Keyes, editor of The Magazine Antiques, *surrounded by antiques in his Boston office. Hanging above the desk is the renowned Caswell carpet, which is now in the Metropolitan Museum's American Wing. (Photograph courtesy of Alice Winchester)*

One difficulty, at this early date, was the lack of serious, reliable writers in the field. Keyes solved that problem by developing them. For example, he encouraged Lura Woodside Watkins of Winchester, Massachusetts, to turn her interest in collecting early New England pottery and glass into serious study. Mrs. Watkins went on to complete authoritative books, based on ground-breaking material she had researched and written for the magazine. Among the many others whom Keyes influenced were Faith and Edward Deming Andrews, pioneer collectors of American Shaker furniture. They wrote: ". . . we knew that the founding editor, Homer Eaton Keyes, was publishing original studies on various phases of American folk art and craftsmanship, that he was encouraging scholarship wherever it emerged, and opening the magazine freely to new discoveries in a hitherto neglected field."[16]

According to Alice Winchester, *Antiques* became a unifying factor, as the founders had hoped. It served as a permanent repository of information, brought dealers and collectors together, and created much interest among others less involved. From the beginning, one of the magazine's biggest assets was Keyes's own very acute and distinctive analysis. Throughout his editorial career he sorted, catalogued, and criticized the rapid flow of developments relating to American antiques.

Miss Winchester noted that Keyes "wrote a great deal himself on a great variety of subjects; his chief personal interests were American furniture and China Trade porcelain. He had a broad knowledge of the whole field, a sound background in art history, a lively curiosity and a keen eye, and a great sense of humor."[17]

Occasionally, Keyes's love of lush language triumphed over the subject at hand:

> When July bestrews with pallid dust the verdant domes of wayside shrubs and overarching trees; when the erstwhile roistering stream, shrunken to timorous diminishment, picks its way among rocks and stones, like an ancient gaffer hobbling through thick urban traffic; when the collie dog seeks panting respite on the shadowed doorstone beside the farmhouse kitchen— then it is that city folk amuse themselves with rural pilgrimages. Then, too, occurs the hot blooming of red geraniums and salvia fringing the petticoats of white cottages with vulgar glory, and, vying with them in torrid conspicuousness, the scarlet banner of the auctioneer.[18]

In general, however, he concentrated on weeding out beguiling but misleading myths about American antiques. Because of his dedication, the magazine was essential reading from the start for anyone interested in the field, setting standards for accuracy and comprehensiveness. Its only real rival, *The Antiquarian*, folded in the Depression, and *Antiques* remains the one long-standing and comprehensive reference for information about American decorative arts.

Increasingly, too, temporary exhibitions of early American arts were accompanied by articles in the museum bulletins, both adding new material and drawing on what had previously been published. Besides scholarly articles on American antiques, there was a great deal of lighter reading available during the 1920s in popular magazines and newspapers; and books on the subject, most of them addressed to the novice collector, proliferated. *The Saturday Evening Post*, whose editor, George Horace Lorimer, was an avid collector, began to run such articles. Some were written in a humorous vein by the novelist Kenneth Roberts, one of Lorimer's collecting friends. They were aimed at a wide audience that was interested and enthusiastic, but often not serious about antiques. In one entitled "Antiquamania," published in 1922, Roberts warned what was in store for the gullible buyer:

> Many antique dealers . . . persist in attempting to sell the associations that cluster around their antiques as well as the antiques themselves; and some of them are unusually talented at making up associations for antiques that have none of their own. If one furnished a three-room apartment with antiques purchased in these antique shops, he would be more than likely to have about three hundred dollars' worth of furniture and objects of art and about thirty thousand dollars' worth of associations—which may be all very well for the sentimental owner, but which holds less interest for his visitors, who like to sit in chairs because they are comfortable, and not because they are the ones in which the boy, Millard Fillmore, was accustomed to sit when roasting apples in the kitchen stove.[19]

By the 1920s, Henry Ford's Model T and other inexpensive cars had put millions of Americans on the roads. "Antiquamania" was fostered by the resulting easy access of city dwellers and dealers to country byways, where they envisioned old farmhouses with attics and storerooms full of undiscovered treasures. Ease of movement contributed also to the public's attendance in large numbers at museums, auctions, and loan exhibitions.

American antiques were given added cachet by the super-collectors, who charged the scene with excitement during the 1920s. Among them were Henry Francis du Pont, Henry Ford, and Francis Patrick Garvan; some had great fortunes, imparting glamour to collecting. They battled at auctions, even though they might vow cooperation and a solid front against the dealers beforehand. They paid unheard-of prices that made newspaper headlines. They created lovely home settings with their early American objects, and gave splendid parties for distinguished guests.

Two spectacular auctions, involving many collectors as well as dealers, resulted in enormous publicity: the Reifsnyder and Flayderman sales of 1929 and 1930. Although the antiques offered were from Pennsylvania and New England, it is significant that the auctions were held in New York. According

Henry Francis du Pont paid $44,000 for the Van Pelt highboy, made of mahogany, 1765–1780, at the Reifsnyder sale in 1929. It was, said Keyes in Antiques, *"among a very small group of the most perfectly conceived and executed highboys made in pre-Revolutionary Philadelphia." (Courtesy, The Henry Francis du Pont Winterthur Museum)*

to Keyes, the Philadelphia Queen Anne and Chippendale furniture offered at the Reifsnyder sale represented "the most brilliantly ornate achievements of American cabinetmakers in the richest and most luxurious colonial city of the Revolutionary period." When the Walpole Society visited Mr. Reifsnyder in 1926, John Hill Morgan wrote: "one was almost oppressed by the beauty of the furniture. Practically everything he has is of museum standard."[20]

Prices at the two auctions stunned everyone. The most sensational was $44,000, paid by Du Pont for the Van Pelt Philadelphia Chippendale highboy at the Reifsnyder sale. It was the most ever brought by an American antique up to then; the whole Reifsnyder collection went for $600,000, the Flayderman collection for $429,840 with fewer objects. As Keyes noted, this averaged out to about $815 per lot for Reifsnyder and $836 for Flayderman. The atmosphere at both sales was electric. Besides Du Pont, Garvan was bidding, Ford was bidding—everyone seriously collecting high-style American antiques attended, and most were in the heat of the battle.

What stands out clearly is that certain American antiques were regarded as artistic masterpieces, and not just as fragments of history or embodiments of tradition. On the basis of style, materials, and execution, some pieces—of furniture and silver especially—were regarded as examples of American artistry outstanding enough to command extraordinary prices. Keyes, commenting on the significance of the two auctions, made the point that the buyers were connoisseurs, who had made artistic merit the dominant factor:

> To the man in the street, perhaps, the newspaper accounts of the [Flayderman] sale might suggest that the collecting public had gone mad. But anyone who followed the event through its three successive sessions must, eventually, have realized that, in the main, the bidding showed very careful discrimination. With a few exceptions, the articles which brought high prices were literally priceless rarities, some of them beyond hope of duplication. The sums which they commanded pulled up an average which, during the first two sessions, had shown a tendency to sag in spots. At no point, furthermore, was the eloquence of the director of the sale sufficient to arouse any enthusiasm for the less desirable offerings. Thus, an elaborate mahogany card table of the late Empire period stuck at $120; a really choice maple butterfly table whose turnings lacked the elegance demanded by particular connoisseurs brought $460, as against $1,500 for another more closely conforming to special tastes. An unusual mahogany claw-and-ball foot chair from Rhode Island would almost certainly have surpassed its $150 figure, had the top rail of its back more perfectly composed with the rest of the piece. . . . So I urge my more inexperienced readers to bear in mind that, among the hundreds of carefully selected items in such a group as the Flayderman collection, only a relatively small number—the cream of the cream— bring the prices chronicled by the press; and that these prices are seldom paid except upon the advice of experts.[21]

The Girl Scouts Loan Exhibition, held in 1929, indicated the state of the collecting movement at the end of the decade. No longer were the collectors of New England pre-eminent, as they had been at the Hudson-Fulton show. And no longer was the emphasis on furniture from the Pilgrim and Puritan era, of New England manufacture. Queen Anne and Chippendale pieces—many of them made in Philadelphia—and New York furniture by Duncan Phyfe (or in his manner) were featured in the Girl Scouts show. These antiques were lent mostly by New Yorkers, or by others who kept apartments in the city.

The loan exhibition, sponsored by the Girl Scouts and held in New York's American Art Galleries from September 25 to October 9, 1929, provided, according to *The New York Times*, "aid for those interested in the fine points of American antiques. Presenting only genuine examples of the work of master craftsmen in their various lines, the displays will furnish much material, it is hoped, to enable students to differentiate between the merely old and the true collector's piece."[22]

Here was a connoisseur's show. Its focus, like that of many leading collectors, was the artistic aspect of American antiques. It attempted to show a wide range of objects, all selected as the best of their kind. By the time of the Girl Scouts exhibition, there was no question of the value—either artistic or historical—ascribed to American antiques. That had been established and demonstrated time and again during the twenties by the spectacular buying activities of some of the richest men and women in America.

The point was to show only top-quality and authentic pieces, so that the interested student or collector could begin to distinguish the bad from the good, the better, and the best. As a show for collectors, this differed markedly from the Hudson-Fulton exhibition. The latter drew its objects from dedicated donors, but without the degree of selectivity that had been developed twenty years later; and it aimed at the general public. The Hudson-Fulton had been an attempt to establish the worth of American art, while the purpose of the Girl Scouts show was to further refine the education of people already convinced. The exhibition of 1929 brought together an array of pieces distinguished for their artistry and craftsmanship that could serve as touchstones of quality for aspiring connoisseurs. It was, as Charles Messer Stow wrote in *The New York Sun*, "the finest display of early American furniture ever got together in one place at one time."[23]

In summary, the twenty years between the Hudson-Fulton and Girl Scouts exhibitions were the era of the museum, of wealthy individuals amassing enormous collections, and of many devoted collectors with more modest means. By the end of the 1920s, American antiques had at last fully achieved honor in their own country.

Chapter 20

R. T. H. Halsey

and the American Wing

RICHARD TOWNLEY HAINES HALSEY (1865–1942) IS UNIQUELY QUALIFIED TO represent the status of the collecting movement in the early twentieth century. His participation reflected the trends of the time, and the influences that lay behind them. He also had a pervasive and permanent impact on the field of American decorative arts.

Halsey's life spanned the period during which collecting American antiques went from an amateur occupation to a primary concern of major museums. The transition, in fact, was speeded by his efforts—capped by his making the American Wing a reality. He vigorously promoted the idea that American antiques are important. Their history and associations were of great interest to him, but he emphasized even more their artistic worth. He did not go so far as to rank them with masterpieces of the European decorative arts; but he believed strongly that American antiques embody a true tradition of artistry.

As Halsey turned from his own collecting to museum work, he concentrated on communicating this belief in the existence of an American artistic tradition. To further the goal he stressed, always, the *best* furniture, silver, and other colonial or early Federal objects. This orientation governed his advice to Judge Clearwater on the purchase of early American silver and his insistence on quality in the rooms he installed for the American Wing.

The arts-and-crafts notion that the spirit of an age resides in its artifacts was central to Halsey's convictions. He also believed that immigration was a threat, and that the example of past American craftsmen could help in mustering resistance to imported alien tendencies. Thus, the products of those craftsmen were valuable potential tools for education. Used together in settings to form a three-dimensional picture of early home life, they would inspire the traditional American spirit in the viewer, whether native-born or immigrant. This approach could be implemented through the tasteful simplicity of exhibits like the American Wing. To Halsey, and others of his generation, it was a key to preserving what was unique in the American character.

Richard Townley Haines Halsey (Walpole Society Note Book, 1941)

This was a constant theme in Halsey's speeches during the 1920s. It is inherent in his talk to a group of Republican women, given after the opening of the American Wing in 1924:

> . . . unquestionably some of the appeal made by our American furniture is first because it was made by some of our forefathers by whose united efforts this Republic was made possible, and second because it represents the home furnishings of our people in the days when our country was struggling to get on its feet, of the homelife of those who protected this country from enemies within just as you women in this country in this last campaign did such convincing work to preserve us from the dominating influence of foreign ideas.
>
> For a real appreciation of colonial furniture it must be considered as one of the sub-divisions of colonial art, and should be considered and studied with the general atmosphere of the colonial home.[1]

"Always," according to William Ivins, a colleague at the Metropolitan Museum, "behind and above everything else, was his major enthusiasm for the lives and writings of the Fathers of the Republic."[2] In this, Halsey resembled Henry Erving of Hartford, who liked to sit among his antiques and imagine the original owners still moving about the room. It was nostalgic, this yearning to draw the spirit of early Americans from objects they had once used, but in both Halsey and Erving it inspired serious research as well as sentimentality.

Halsey was one of the first New Yorkers to gather collections of American antiques that later went to museums. He began to collect in the 1890s; although his major interests were to be centered in New York, he described how he started in Maryland:

> It was just twenty nine years ago that I first came here [to Annapolis, Md.]. You must believe me when I tell you that I was very young. . . . It was on a visit to a sister, who had just made her home here. . . . Knowing that I was just starting out to furnish a tiny apartment [in New York] with old furniture she planned a trip to Annapolis for me . . . I can never forget the impressions of that day. I did not then know the glories of colonial architecture. It was in the spring of the year, the trees were just budding, New York was still cold and gloomy. The play of sun and shadow on the fine old brick houses with their white doorways, cornices, and window frames gave me what I really believe was my first aesthetic thrill.[3]

Halsey's friend and colleague Henry Kent suggested that William Henry Huntington's gift to the Metropolitan Museum of over two thousand American portraits—most of Franklin, Washington, and Lafayette, "of every conceivable kind on every conceivable material"—stimulated Halsey's interest in early American portraiture and craftsmanship. Bequeathed to the museum in 1883 and kept on display until 1906, the Huntington Collection was the result of thirty years of collecting, most of it done in Paris during "a thousand golden afternoons." The 1889 Centennial of Washington's Inauguration very likely increased Halsey's appetite for history and for American antiques.[4]

Another important influence on Halsey, wrote Ivins, was "the delightful personality of William Loring Andrews, for forty-three years a Trustee [of the Metropolitan Museum] and long its Honorary Librarian."

> A careful and discriminating collector of the older school, Mr. Andrews amused himself by writing and printing for private distribution a series of beautifully produced little books or essays, in which were reflected not only his tastes but his very genuine curiosity about origins and histories. Gradually there formed about him a group of younger men, a number of whom, imbued with his enthusiasm, had the fortitude to undertake work of longer breadth than he was capable of.[5]

Halsey was among those younger men; he was also a member of the Grolier Club and the Society of Iconophiles. Mr. Andrews was the founder and "guiding spirit" of the latter, which was devoted to preserving a disappearing New York City through engravings and lithographs of its scenes. Halsey's friends at the Grolier and in the Society, which he joined in 1900 and 1904 respectively, provided both collecting companionship and a sense of rivalry.

The two organizations were among the most active centers in New York for collectors—of objects as well as books and graphic arts. Halsey's collections reflect the influence of his fellow members, and his dedication to American

Blue-and-white Staffordshire plate showing the burning of the Merchants' Exchange, New York. From Halsey's collection. (Pictures of Early New York on Dark Blue Staffordshire, *by Halsey*)

history. At their peak, the collections included an outstanding group of English political cartoons relating to the American Revolution; blue-and-white jasperware portrait medallions of Revolutionary heroes by the great English potter Josiah Wedgwood; miniatures and engravings by colonial artists; blue-and-white Staffordshire pottery printed with New York scenes; and furniture made by Duncan Phyfe, or in his style, which Halsey was one of the first to collect. Like many of the other Iconophiles, Halsey dealt with Ernest Hagen, the New York cabinetmaker whose own interest in Phyfe was very likely the original source of Halsey's.

Halsey reserved his greatest loyalty, however, for early American silver. Kent wrote that a teapot by Paul Revere "which always stood on a shelf in Mr. Andrews' library . . . I am sure, did more than anything else to fix Halsey's enthusiasm for our colonial artisans in silver."[6] As a result, Halsey accumulated one of the most notable collections of early American silver of his day, with special emphasis on New York.

In 1896, Professor Theodore S. Woolsey of Yale had published an eloquent plea for the study and display of American colonial silver, pointing out that no one had uncovered and set forth the information necessary to collectors. In the first decade of this century, Halsey took up the gauntlet. All early students of the subject give him credit for substantial contributions to our knowledge of American silver marks and makers. He cooperated with Francis Hill Bigelow in organizing the first major exhibition of such silver, at the Boston Museum of Fine Arts in 1906, wrote the introduction to the catalogue, and paid for its publication. Bigelow later said that the catalogue was "one of the handsomest ever issued by any museum."[7] Halsey also helped organize the church silver show held at the Metropolitan in 1911. Once again he wrote the introduction to the catalogue, adding further to the store of published knowledge.

In 1909, Halsey contributed both antiques and expertise to the Hudson-Fulton exhibition. It may have been the influence of William Loring Andrews, or Halsey's enthusiasm for American silver and for its public display, that caused him to take an interest in the Metropolitan. As early as 1906, he gave the museum money for "the development of the Americana side." In 1914, he was appointed to the Metropolitan's board of trustees and, according to Kent, was immediately

> appointed chairman of its Committee on American Art. Later he was ap-pointed Chairman of the Committee on the American Wing, after the plans for that building, the conception of which came with the exhibition of 1909, had been completed. He took over, first with Durr Friedley, of the Museum staff, and, afterwards, with Charles Over Cornelius, the difficult task, in-volving study and research in many fields, of installing the rooms and collec-tions in the building, devoting all of his time to this work.[8]

The ultimate success of the Wing, when it opened in 1924, made Halsey much sought after as a consultant on the restoration and furnishing of old houses. He briefly considered moving to Williamsburg to work on its restoration, but decided instead to undertake what Kent described as an experiment at St. John's College in Annapolis. From 1928 to 1932, Halsey was a professor in the

Silver bowl, 1745–1760, by Richard Van Dyck of New York. From Halsey's collection.
(Yale University Art Gallery, Mabel Brady Garvan Collection)

Department of American Culture there, conducting a course which combined the study of American arts and crafts with that of American history.

Halsey's lead was followed by John Marshall Phillips, curator of the Garvan Collection at Yale from the 1930s to the 1950s. Their approach to American decorative arts as an aspect of American history and culture was later used to teach students in the nation's first program for graduate study in the decorative arts, instituted at the H. F. du Pont Winterthur Museum in 1953. It became the standard way of introducing students to American antiques —another example of Halsey's significant impact on the field.

Halsey grew up in Elizabeth, New Jersey. He went to Princeton, graduating in 1886. William Ivins wrote that during his student days, Halsey acquired two abiding interests: tennis, which he was among the first to play in America, and "the history and heroes of the American Revolution."[9]

From college, Halsey proceeded straight to Wall Street, and by 1899 he had become a member of the board of governors of the New York Stock Exchange. Until 1923 he was an active partner in the firm of Tefft, Halsey & Co., but after 1914 and the start of his trusteeship at the Metropolitan, he devoted more and more of his time to museum affairs.

His personal life had as much color and variety as his career among antiques. He was devoted to his first wife, who died in childbirth in 1903. Her loss so distressed him that he swore he would wear only clothes of the kind he had worn during their life together, and would eat only what they had eaten. The wound healed, however, and he married again in 1909.

The second marriage ended in 1927, when he divorced Effie Underhill Halsey on the ground of insanity, and on condition that he furnish a $100,000 bond to provide for her. An article in *The New York Herald Tribune* for September 9, 1927 from Reno, Nevada, stated: "From the courtroom Mr. Halsey went to the County Clerk's Office and obtained a license to marry Elizabeth A. Tower, who gave her address as Reno but who is understood to be from New York." Elizabeth Tower was Halsey's assistant at the Metropolitan Museum.

Possibly because of the financial strain from his divorce and then starting a family, Halsey sold much of his collection toward the end of the 1920s. Many of his things had been on long-term loan to the Metropolitan, but surprisingly few came to rest at the museum to which he had devoted so much time and effort. Halsey wrote to H. F. Davidson of the Metropolitan in 1932 that he had sold "a lot of my collection" to Francis Garvan "some three years ago."[10] Halsey's furniture and silver are now at Yale, as part of the Garvan Collection; his prints are at Brown University. Other than a few scattered objects, the only part of the Halsey collection now at the Metropolitan is a group of forty-two Wedgwood medallions that the museum bought from his estate.

There is modest but persuasive evidence that Halsey occasionally dealt in antiques. As adviser to restorations and museums, he was in a position to act as middleman in providing furnishings to a number of buyers. His awareness of possible sellers, especially in New York and probably in Maryland, had been developed over many years of buying for himself and for the Metropolitan. Combining the practices of dealing, collecting, and advising institutions would be considered unprofessional today; there was a different atmosphere in the 1920s, however, and fewer ethical restrictions on possible conflicts of interest. Here, too, Halsey is representative of his era in the collecting movement. Like several of his contemporaries, he seems to have turned his consuming interest into a part-time business.

Halsey accepted the teaching post at St. John's College in June of 1928. Although he continued to visit New York frequently, he went on, after four years in Maryland, to New Haven, where he worked as a research assistant in the Frankliniana Collection at the Yale Library. In 1942, he was hit by a car while crossing a street near his home, and died soon afterward. His friends and colleagues in the Walpole Society paid him a final tribute:

> Though sometimes not presenting a picture of sartorial, or tonsorial, perfection, Halsey's most impressive characteristic was his elegance. . . . From his clothing, which has been described as "incidental," to the old Ford car which he drove dangerously there was nothing of exterior elegance about Halsey, but the presence of that quality within him was affirmed by his collections, his writings, and his judgments.[11]

The American Wing is properly regarded as Halsey's crowning achievement. Much of the framework was already in place, however, when Halsey came on the scene. Kent had conceived the idea of putting American decorative arts on permanent exhibition, had made the finest private collection of American furniture then in existence the property of the museum, and had decided on its display by the most effective method of his day. And it was Kent who influenced the De Forests to make the museum a gift of the Wing.

Halsey's task was to fill out the framework and breathe life into the exhibit. "It is doubtful," wrote Marshall B. Davidson of Halsey, "that the Museum has ever had a more active and dedicated trustee." In 1914, when he was appointed to the board, Halsey took charge of the museum's search for early American interiors and furnishings "that would be most widely representative of early American achievement."[12]

Colors for walls, woodwork, floors, and fabrics; window and floor treatments; paintings, prints, and looking glasses—these were a few of the matters Halsey had to decide before rooms and furnishings could be combined. He

*Mahogany side chair by
Duncan Phyfe, 1810–1815.
From Halsey's collection.
(Yale University Art
Gallery, Mabel Brady
Garvan Collection)*

turned to wills and inventories, old newspapers, and other early documents to create for himself a picture of life in these old rooms. Although scholars have since discovered much to change Halsey's picture, it was a remarkable effort.

To make the rooms more appealing, Halsey added more than three hundred small decorative objects from his own collection. The administration was unwilling to use the museum's own possessions; one of the American Wing's notable features was that most of the time its rooms were completely open. Since visitors could wander through at will, it seemed very risky to leave small, pocketable objects lying about. But Halsey took the chance; and, at least for the first six months, nothing was taken.

Halsey got so caught up in his research that he sold his seat on the New York Stock Exchange in order to devote himself entirely to the American Wing during the final year of its preparation. The opening, which occurred on November 11, 1924, evoked such enthusiasm that it must have surpassed Halsey's wildest dreams. Royal Cortissoz, a leading art critic, began thus his glowing review for *Scribner's Magazine*: "To explore the American Wing is to apprehend in singular vividness the spirit in which those men who made the Colonies and those who founded the Republic lived their lives at home and superimposed urbanity upon the site of primeval wilderness."[13]

Halsey might have written that sentence himself. As he had hoped, the American Wing was generally seen as a patriotic lesson in history. Furthermore, it was widely perceived as representing artistry, characterized by the sterling simplicity that distinguished the New World from the Old. Halsey's own subsequent assessment appeared in *The Homes of Our Ancestors* (1925), a book that he and Elizabeth Tower expanded from the handbook written for the opening by Halsey and Cornelius:

> The American Wing has convincingly demonstrated that the love of the beautiful has long existed in America; also that American art has a strong background of tradition behind it. There was an appreciation of beauty here which was not confined to our craftsmen. It thrived in the houses of many of the men by whose efforts our country

Right: *Federal-period room from Baltimore, Maryland. Installed in the American Wing; 1924 photograph. (The Metropolitan Museum of Art)*

Below: *Bedroom from Hampton, New Hampshire, 1725–1750. Installed in the American Wing; 1924 photograph. (The Metropolitan Museum of Art)*

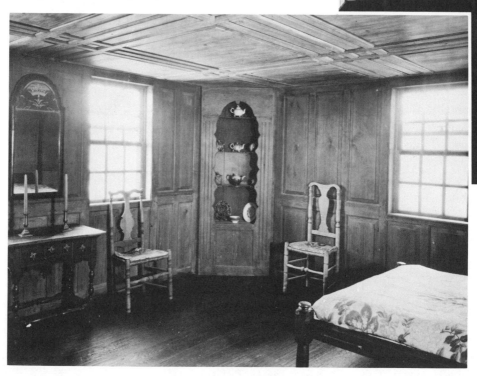

was developed and our Republic founded. Without patrons our craftsmen could not have successfully carried on their trades.[14]

Although Halsey's goal had been to give the American Wing rooms a feeling of warmth and immediacy, one important critic complained of their coldness. Homer Keyes initially withheld editorial comment from *Antiques* for months after the Wing had opened. When he finally pronounced on the new display, he was severe. He had no argument, he said, with regard to quality or quantity, for both were present. His concern was that the installation lacked warmth, and failed to inspire in a visitor the ability which Halsey had striven to impart:

"not merely to *see* but likewise to *feel* the character of the homes of his ancestors." One arrives at the museum, said Keyes, filled with great expectations; but he soon realizes that something is missing:

> In the cold gray dawn of subsequent analysis he begins to realize the nature of his difficulty. He has approached the exhibits of the New Wing as one with keen appetite approaches an anticipated feast; he has retired from the encounter filled, yet with a disturbing sense of having received inadequate nourishment. And this phenomenon—to pursue the dietetic figure—he perceives is attributable to an insufficiency of mental and spiritual vitamines in the pablum provided.[15]

Today, Keyes's point seems well taken; for photographs made in 1924 show that the rooms were formally arranged and devoid of the lived-in sense that had characterized Dow's exhibit in Salem. At the time, however, this deficiency was generally lost in the sensation caused by the Wing's sheer size and scope. To most visitors, it came as a revelation.

The American Wing was innovative: nowhere else in America was there a series of period rooms covering the entire range of the decorative arts in *any* country. Its sixteen rooms, plus three large exhibition halls and several alcoves, documented the natural evolution of style during two hundred years. The building contained three floors, devoted respectively to the seventeenth and early eighteenth centuries, the mid-eighteenth century, and the early Federal period. Architecture and furnishings of the same era were combined to present a three-dimensional picture of American home life in New England, the Middle Colonies, and the South.

The influence of the Wing was enormous. It affected other museums, art critics, and the art-conscious public in general. It changed the appearance of home-furnishing displays in department stores and the arrangement of antiques shops. And, most important of all, it influenced both existing and potential collectors. Besides presenting Americans with overwhelming evidence of their own artistic tradition, the Wing excited them about the prospect of collecting. It also provided a wonderfully ingenious method of display: the period room was ideal for adaptation to home use. Collectors could be as authentic or eclectic as they wished, but most began to aim at capturing something of the atmosphere in the American Wing.

It was, in short, a landmark in the history of American antiques, not only recognized today but acclaimed at the time. That alone, because of Halsey's major contribution, would have established his significance to the collecting movement. He must have been elated to see his long crusade dramatically supported in a newspaper headline after the opening: "American Art Really Exists."[16]

Chapter 21

Luke Vincent Lockwood

Quiet Effectiveness

Luke Vincent Lockwood (1872–1951), author, collector, and museum man, was one of the leaders of his generation of scholars in the decorative arts. He was part of the classifying, cataloguing, and educational impulse that prevailed in the first quarter of the twentieth century. Neither innovator nor true connoisseur, he was nevertheless a talented adapter and organizer.

Lockwood played key roles in the Hudson-Fulton exhibition, in the subsequent Bolles purchase by the Metropolitan, and in the later installation of period rooms at the Brooklyn Museum. At a time when there was a distinct need for a comprehensive reference book on American furniture, Lockwood provided one. *Colonial Furniture in America*, published in 1901 when he was only twenty-nine, testifies to his serious interest in the field, and he was for many years *the* expert on American antique furniture.

Born in Brooklyn, New York, he attended Trinity College in Hartford. While there he became acquainted not only with the influential Hartford collecting fraternity but also with his future wife. Her mother had a house full of antiques, both inherited and collected, and Lockwood was so smitten (with the antiques, as well as the daughter) that he began searching them out for himself. One of his prime hunting grounds in Hartford was the local funeral parlors.

Luke Vincent Lockwood.
Black crayon on paper, by
John Singer Sargent, dated
1913. (Photograph courtesy
of Donald Peirce)

Undertakers, with occasional access to many houses, sometimes knew the location of antiques available for purchase. Then, too, an undertaker unable to collect cash for services rendered had to accept other forms of payment, which could include antiques. After his student days, Lockwood visited country shops, patronized the New York dealers, and "went antiquing wherever he was," according to his daughter.[1]

Upon graduating from Trinity in 1893, Lockwood went on to the New York Law School, where he received a degree in 1895. Eventually, he became a partner in the New York firm of Lockwood & Redfield. In the 1890s the Lockwoods took a townhouse in Brooklyn Heights, a rewarding area in which to collect:

The old mansions there had many fine antiques that constantly found their way into the shops of three dealers, Jacob Ring, Caspar Sommerlad, and Charles Morson. The Lockwoods found these places excellent informal laboratories for learning about antiques. When anything of importance was acquired by any of the three dealers, the Lockwoods saw it promptly.[2]

The Lockwoods moved their New York City residence in the 1920s to East 70th Street in Manhattan. Their twelve-room apartment was filled with antiques, like the house in Riverside, Connecticut, to which they migrated during the summer. Each winter they journeyed to Charleston, South Carolina, where Lockwood loved to continue the hunt.

His collection was not confined to one period, nor to American objects. A photograph of the drawing room in the Lockwoods' Greenwich, Connecticut, house (bought when Lockwood retired from practicing law) shows an assortment of high-style eighteenth-century American and English furnishings. The introduction to the catalogue of an auction held upon Mrs. Lockwood's death in 1954 stressed the American portion, however, calling it "undoubtedly one of the finest small collections of American furniture and paintings." There was, said the introduction, an unusually fine group of New England furniture made between the years 1675 and 1710. "A single, but notable" Queen Anne chair provided a bridge between these and furniture of the Chippendale period, "in which lie many of [Lockwood's] greatest rarities. . . ."[3]

In its seventeenth- and early eighteenth-century furniture, the collection reflected the influence of the collectors Lockwood had known in Hartford. The bias of Canfield and Pendleton, both of whom he represented as attorney, was evident in the sophisticated Chippendale pieces. The fine group of paintings and drawings was very likely gathered in consultation with Lockwood's close friend John Hill Morgan, the expert on American painting. (Morgan, who lived for many years in Brooklyn Heights, was also a collector and lawyer. In addition, he was a fellow trustee of the Brooklyn Museum and a fellow member of the Walpole Society.) The Lockwoods had put together a notable collection of English pottery and porcelain as well, and they presented an important group of Dr. Wall Worcester pieces to the Metropolitan Museum in 1942.

Lockwood became the foremost authority on American antique furniture as a result of examining so many pieces in preparing for his book. *Colonial Furniture in America* went beyond Dr. Lyon's work in scope, if not in scholarship, to include the major forms produced from the seventeenth century through the early part of the nineteenth. Lockwood had classified them according to period and style, with the objective, he said, of furnishing the collector, "and

The Lockwoods' living room in Greenwich, Connecticut. It is filled with English and American antiques. (Photograph courtesy of the Photographic Archives of the National Gallery of Art)

other persons interested in the subject of American colonial furniture, with a trustworthy handbook on the subject, having especially in mind the natural development of the various styles, and arranging them in such a way as to enable any one at a glance to determine under what general style and date a piece of furniture falls."[4] The volume was richly illustrated with photographs of pieces from most of the important collections of the day; thus, Lockwood's research had brought him into contact with people seriously interested in American antiques in the 1890s and early 1900s. The book was revised and enlarged for reissue in two volumes in 1913; it has since been reprinted several times.

Lockwood was of great assistance to Henry Kent in organizing the furniture section of the Hudson-Fulton exhibition in 1909, getting in touch with several of the Hartford collectors and writing to Bolles. Before the exhibition, he went to Boston to advise on the selection of furniture from the Bolles collection, and after the Bolles sale to the Metropolitan Museum, Lockwood was consulted as to which pieces were to be kept and which "counted out." When the Hudson-Fulton Celebration was over, Lockwood received a medal for his participation.

Although the Metropolitan turned to Halsey rather than Lockwood to organize a department of American art, Lockwood remained on good terms with those in power there; from then on, however, he devoted his attention to the Museum of the City of New York and to the Brooklyn Museum, where he and John Hill Morgan became trustees in 1914. They were put on the advisory committee for American art, and the museum began to purchase American antiques and interior architectural elements. Although day-to-day supervision was in the hands of André Rueff, Lockwood was in overall charge of the installation.

Above: *For the Brooklyn Museum period rooms, Lockwood bought interior woodwork and furnishings which had come down in the Porter and Bidwell families of Wethersfield, Connecticut. Here, Miss Esther Bidwell is sitting on a Queen Anne chair from the same set to which the chair in the museum's Porter-Bidwell Room belongs. (Courtesy, Brooklyn Museum)*

Right: *South parlor from the Porter-Bidwell house, Wethersfield, Connecticut. Installed at the Brooklyn Museum under Lockwood's direction in 1929. The Queen Anne chair and the Hadley chest are said to have descended in the family of Dr. Ezekiel Porter. (Courtesy, Brooklyn Museum)*

Perhaps in part because of tips from friends in the Walpole Society, Lockwood learned of opportunities to buy woodwork, paneling, and furnishings for the Brooklyn Museum; Rueff was also sent on scouting trips. Without the benefit of a major gift like that of the Bolles collection to the Metropolitan, or major benefactors like Mr. and Mrs. de Forest, Lockwood assembled, with Rueff's help, a remarkable series of American period rooms. In this effort he was probably influenced by the Metropolitan's plans for the American Wing. Supplementing the Brooklyn Museum's purchases with gifts and loans from friends involved with American antiques, Lockwood supervised the installation of nineteen rooms, which opened in 1929.

The museum had occasionally set up period rooms before 1929, but none had been permanent. The press was extremely complimentary about this new display in Brooklyn, and there was a certain amount of criticism of the American Wing implicit in the praise. The Albany *Times Union* wrote that Lockwood had "endeavored to give these rooms the feeling of actual homes instead of museum exhibitions. . . . For there is a warmly human air about these interiors that is completely lacking in the metropolitan museum."[5] The striking repetition of this point in newspaper articles must reflect the emphasis Lockwood himself gave it in preparing material for the museum's press release. Perhaps he derived considerable satisfaction from favorable comparisons with the Manhattan rival that had once seemed to underestimate his value.

What distinguished the Brooklyn rooms from the American Wing was partly Lockwood's stress on documented work over masterpieces—or history over connoisseurship. He did not insist on the finest examples, but on pieces of good quality whose history was firmly established. The Brooklyn Museum, as a result, has an excellent collection of documented American furniture.[6]

A second difference between Brooklyn's rooms and those at the Metropolitan resulted from Lockwood's decision to give something of the feeling of the whole house in his installations. He accomplished this by using part of the clapboard exterior in the display, by including two or more adjoining rooms from the same house, and by giving the illusion of daylight pouring through the windows. One reporter noted that "A feeling of harmonious relationship between the old houses which framed these delightful settings and fittings themselves is realized throughout the group."[7] The entrance to the exhibition was through a colonial doorway flanked by white clapboards. Once inside, the visitor moved from one house to another, sampling the architecture and decorative arts of New England, New York, New Jersey, and the South from 1730 to 1830.

Another innovation at Brooklyn was period rooms that contained furnishings both of the date of the house and earlier. Just as most of us live with some new furnishings and a variety of older ones, so, Lockwood proposed, our ancestors combined new and old. Charles Messer Stow, writing in *The New York Sun*, was delighted with this aspect of the Brooklyn rooms:

Somebody a long time ago ought to have done that which has just been done at the Brooklyn Museum, namely, to arrange a display of early. American interiors from the standpoint of the period of living rather than from that of the period of the furniture. . . . This is done by showing, as far as possible, the type of furniture and sometimes the pieces themselves that were in the houses at a time when it was remodeled, so that, as in the case of a house that is actually lived in, there is a variation of styles with many pieces retained from earlier times.

It has always seemed to me that in the pursuit of "period," we have been a little too eager to discard. I doubt if even the wealthiest households, when it came to refurnishing with more modish furniture, always threw out the comfortable old pieces altogether. This was a thrifty country. . . . Then, too, the intimacy with old furniture tends to preclude its abandonment.[8]

Stow seems to have been criticizing the American Wing's practice of adhering very closely to one period and style in its rooms. The same inference can be drawn from the comments of Homer Keyes, who wrote that Lockwood had been guided by "something quite as precious as archaeological information . . . good common sense."[9] Keyes seems to have felt that the Brooklyn rooms embodied the warmth and vitality that were missing from the American Wing.

Lockwood was also involved in organizing period rooms at the Museum of the City of New York, acting as president of the Municipal Art Commission, and working for numerous other antiquarian and charitable organizations. He was a founder, devoted member, and long-time chairman of the Walpole Society, as well as the author of its *Furniture Collectors' Glossary*, published in 1913. Affectionate references to him in the society's *Note Books* through the years bear witness to his popularity.

In a sense, Lockwood is an unsung hero of the collecting movement during the early twentieth century. No single one of his achievements has come to be regarded as monumental, but he made many significant contributions to the study of the decorative arts. Personally shy, he impressed not by the force of his personality but by his ability to get things done.

Upon his death, his friend William Mitchell Van Winkle wrote a warm, admiring memorial tribute:

. . . with the members of his beloved Walpole Society he was among the most entertaining and interesting. To his friends and associates his interest in their pursuits was always keenly appreciated and one knew that he was willing to give to them from his vast knowledge anything that might be of aid to them. His kindliness, his quiet humor and his courage under adversity were never better shown than during his long and trying illness.[10]

Chapter 22

Henry Francis du Pont
Creative Collector

THE CONSENSUS IS THAT HENRY DU PONT (1880–1969) WAS THE GREATEST COL-
lector of his generation. For him, aesthetic considerations were paramount; and
his talent for selecting, combining, and arranging antiques was prodigious. In
1951 he wrote of the origins of his interest:

> The house at Winterthur, Delaware, my family's home where I was brought
> up, was furnished with miscellaneous foreign and American Empire pieces,
> predominantly of veneered mahogany, and these to me had seemed heavy
> and often lacking in grace. A visit to Mrs. Watson Webb's house in Shel-
> burne, Vermont, in 1923, was therefore a revelation. This was the first early
> all American interior I had ever seen and it captivated me. I still remember
> in detail the contrasting colours there of pink Staffordshire against a lovely
> pine dresser. Seeing Harry Sleeper's house at Gloucester, Massachusetts, a
> few days later crystallized my desire to start collecting Americana on my
> own. In retrospect, I realize how important was this particular week in shap-
> ing the course of my life.[1]

The Webb and Sleeper houses impelled Du Pont to say to his wife, "Why
don't we build an American house? Everybody has English houses and half the

furniture I know . . . is new. Since we're Americans, it's much more interesting to have American furniture."[2] So one Sunday, instead of attending church, the Du Ponts visited a dealer named Lindsey in Media, Pennsylvania. They bought their first piece, a Pennsylvania walnut chest with the date 1737 inlaid in the top drawer.

Lindsey later offered interior paneling and woodwork from old houses on the eastern shore of Maryland, which Du Pont bought and incorporated into his house in Southampton, New York. It was called Chestertown House, after the Maryland town from which many of the rooms came. To furnish it, Du Pont bought more American antiques. He told of his first auction, the George F. Ives sale, in Danbury, Connecticut, in June 1924: "[I bought] my first iron floor lights, and a slant top desk with various manifold later embellishments which by now have turned a completely different color. I luckily was not the successful bidder on a straight leg wing chair with curly maple wings, which at the time I thought was the ultimate."[3]

Henry Francis du Pont. Oil on canvas, by Ellen Emmet Rand, 1914. (Courtesy, The Henry Francis du Pont Winterthur Museum)

Du Pont confined the furniture for Chestertown House to pieces made of pine, walnut, and various fruitwoods because of his distaste for the veneered mahogany furniture of his childhood home. He wrote that, during this period,

> I came in contact with widely divergent early American materials of all kinds. The problem of giving them appropriate recognition inevitably came to my mind. After the opening of the American Wing at the Metropolitan Museum in New York in 1924, and another such wing in the Brooklyn Museum . . . it occurred to me to undertake a similar venture, and I decided to add an "American Wing" to Winterthur, which I had inherited at about this time.[4]

Thus began what was to be one of the nation's great museums of the decorative arts. For Winterthur, Du Pont secured paneling from old houses in Virginia, Pennsylvania, and Maryland, to "provide authentic settings for display purposes."[5] As this woodwork was from the Chippendale period, it promoted purchase of Chippendale furniture, which appealed to Du Pont because it was sturdy. "Also, I was interested in its many different variations, not only let us say, those of the Philadelphia chairs, but also in the great difference between the influences of Boston, Newport, New York, and Philadelphia. As Queen Anne furniture crossed my path, naturally I could not resist it."[6]

It was this pine dresser filled with pink-and-white Staffordshire pottery that inspired Du Pont to begin collecting American antiques when he saw it in Electra Webb's Vermont house in 1923. The dresser and pottery are now at Winterthur, the gift of Mrs. Webb's children. (Courtesy, The Henry Francis du Pont Winterthur Museum)

While the first rooms were gradually furnished, Du Pont decided to "Americanize" the rest of the house. Structures from the original thirteen colonies provided interiors that served as backgrounds for Du Pont's furnishings. Geographically, they ranged from New England to South Carolina; chronologically, from 1640 to 1840.

As he became engrossed in collecting and in creating period rooms, Du Pont concentrated increasingly on historical accuracy. Although later scholarship has sometimes contradicted him, he was trying to do things in the true eighteenth-century fashion with the documentation available. He wrote in November of 1930: "I am doing the house archaeologically and correctly, and I am paying the greatest attention even to the epoch of the fringes."[7]

It is clear from the rooms at Winterthur, and from many of Du Pont's letters, that he was astonishingly patient and exacting in working toward blending all the elements of a room into one harmonious, uplifting whole. His stress on that goal is evident from his statement to an interviewer that no one object should stand out: "It's one of my first principles that if you go into a room, and right away see something, then you must realize that that shouldn't be in the room."[8]

Du Pont's approach to arrangement and decoration had been strongly influenced by the Boston decorator Harry Sleeper, whose Gloucester house he so admired in 1923. He had asked Sleeper to help him furnish Chestertown House, and the two men remained in touch until a parting of ways in 1931.

Henry Davis Sleeper (*c.* 1873–1934) was born in Boston and trained in Paris as an architect in the Beaux Arts tradition. He began his house, Beauport, about 1907. Inspired by Ben: Perley Poore's nearby Indian Hill, Sleeper combined early American rooms and furnishings to create a charming and unusual environment. Like Poore, Sleeper was especially drawn to antiques associated with famous people, and several of the rooms at Beauport were created around the theme of a romantic or heroic figure: Shelley and Byron, for example, and Lord Nelson.

Sleeper did not have a scholarly interest in American antiques and architecture. Preoccupied with achieving the right atmosphere, "he saw each room as a composition complete to the last detail," write one enchanted visitor. "As a painter works with oil or a sculptor with stone, Sleeper worked with colors, textures, architectural fragments, furnishings, and hundreds of decorative objects to create his works of art."[9]

Part of Beauport's fantastic, magical quality derived from Sleeper's uninhibited enjoyment of color and light: he could create an especially stunning effect with old colored-glass objects set on glass shelves in a clear window. He loved surprises—a dark, plum-colored room leading into one that fairly dazzles with light and luminosity. He combined objects of different materials but a similar ambience; an old-time kitchen with pine, pewter, and pottery stayed in the minds of thousands who saw it as the "colonial" archetype.

Besides being master of the delightful surprise, Sleeper was the consummate decorator, with a sure eye for the right juxtaposition of pattern, color, and line. A Beauport room was usually based on a major theme, sometimes reinforced by minor ones. Besides a famous person, the motif could be a certain color, or something like strawberries or the sea.

From Sleeper, Du Pont absorbed a love of dramatic decorating techniques and themes. He also came to share Sleeper's understanding of the importance of mixing just the right elements, and his willingness to spend whatever time,

At Beauport, Henry Davis Sleeper combined objects old and new to create a "colonial kitchen" that, for many who saw it, summed up early America. (Society for the Preservation of New England Antiquities)

effort, and expense were needed to find them. But Sleeper's intention was to create an amusing and original statement, whereas Du Pont's purpose was much more serious. He wanted not only beauty but historical authenticity.

Du Pont was such an apt learner that Sleeper ultimately paid him the compliment of ranking Du Pont's gifts with his own: "I always think of you as one of my clients who has just as much energy and imagination in these matters as I have. I am pleased and flattered when you want my help, but between ourselves, I think you are about as capable as I am." The rooms Du Pont created at Winterthur, like Sleeper's at Beauport, were works of art in themselves—tributes to the taste, thought, and patient arranging of their creator. Du Pont had an instinctive flair for the right line, mass, and mixture of colors, the same flair evident in the gardens that he designed for Winterthur and worked on throughout his life. He recognized this gift, for he wrote that just a few years after he had begun to transform Winterthur,

I realized that the collection was too good to be dispersed after my death and hence the idea of the museum gradually came to me. I have had countless expert advice, and still do, but when it comes to arranging furniture, some how or other, I seem to feel where each piece should go, and have changed countless of my friends' rooms to their satisfaction, but this is not for publication as after a short time they seem to feel it was their idea.[10]

Some of his friends may have forgotten who perfected their interiors, but others did not. Wilmarth S. Lewis, a fellow collector, wrote:

> After a visit from Harry du Pont, the house was never quite the same again. Perhaps the furniture had been moved; perhaps an object was on its way to Winterthur; perhaps Harry had merely tapped a familiar piece and repeated what he had said on former visits. "Very nice," an encomium that the owner would treasure the rest of his days.
>
> The changes that he effected in my house are a daily joy to me. . . . Two accessions were found for Winterthur, some ferns were growing on the shady side of a tool house, and until Harry spotted them with a cry of astonishment and delight I am afraid they had not figured in my life. The spinning wheel was languishing in the twilight of a barn and I had never noticed it. Harry spotted it at once, gave it the accolade, and in no time a Winterthur truck arrived and bore it away flanked by the ferns.[11]

In making artistic decisions, Du Pont often consulted Mrs. Harry Horton Benkard. Mrs. Benkard was an old friend of Du Pont's sister, Louise du Pont Crowninshield, and the three sometimes went antiquing together. Bertha Benkard (1877–1945) had begun collecting for her own home in New York City after her marriage in 1903. When she moved to a house on East 9th Street in 1915, she started to buy furniture in the style of Duncan Phyfe, becoming one of the most renowned Phyfe collectors and a respected authority on early American things in general. In her sensitivity to line, proportion, and color, she was a perfect collecting companion for Du Pont. When the Walpole Society visited Mrs. Benkard on Long Island in 1940, one of the members described her house as

> A delightful little place, close by the road, where she has done what so many have tried to do, but she has done it superbly,—made charming interiors of the days when our Constitution was just being introduced. They are lovely to complete illusion. We look about and feel that the worthies, Aaron Burr, Jefferson and John Marshall, may be trailing right at our elbow. What all would want but had failed to achieve.[12]

It was just such an atmosphere that Du Pont sought at Winterthur. He valued Mrs. Benkard's opinion so much that he is said to have lost interest in collecting after her death in 1945.

• • •

By the late twenties, Henry du Pont had come a long way from the enthusiastic novice who nearly bought an easy chair with tiger-maple wings. At both the great auctions of the period, Reifsnyder and Flayderman, he was one of the most active and discriminating buyers.

According to *International Studio*, the Reifsnyder sale in April 1929 generated "an air of drama . . . far more thrilling from the theatrical—nay, the dramatic—point of view, than the show shops of Broadway, grinding out their monotonous and conventional little shocks. . . . This battle of collectors will probably never be duplicated in any American salesroom." Du Pont was one of the chief actors in the drama. Bidding under the pseudonym H. F. Winthrop, he battled William Randolph Hearst for the Van Pelt highboy, described by Homer Keyes as one of "the most perfectly conceived and executed highboys

This pine kitchen, formerly installed at Winterthur, shows that Du Pont shared Sleeper's gift for creating atmosphere through artistic arrangements of a variety of forms, textures, and materials. But it also shows his concern for using only genuine antiques—a concern not shared by Sleeper. (Courtesy, The Henry Francis du Pont Winterthur Museum)

made in pre-Revolutionary Philadelphia." Hearst finally dropped out, and the highboy went to Du Pont for the staggering sum of $44,000. Although this was the highest price paid for an American antique until then, Keyes suggested that since all comparable highboys were "either held by museums, or in private collections where they are likely to remain indefinitely, the record sum paid for this distinguished specimen . . . is not particularly surprising."[13]

At the Flayderman sale in January 1930, Du Pont added two other master-pieces of American furniture to his collection: a Rhode Island tea table for $29,000, and a labeled secretary by Boston cabinetmakers John Seymour & Son for $30,000. Keyes wrote: "Everybody knew that the tea table made by John Goddard would create a sensation: but few, if any, expected that the desire for its possession would create so intense a rivalry as to fetch a closing bid of $29,000." Keyes explained that the table was one of the chief prizes because of its "intrinsic quality, its rarity, its condition, and its well attested ownership by a distinguished Rhode Islander [Jabez Bowen]." The Seymour secretary, ac-cording to Keyes, "perhaps marks the high point of achievement by New England cabinetmakers of the early Federal period."[14]

Du Pont's seriousness as a collector and connoisseur of American antiques—and particularly of the Queen Anne and Chippendale furniture that were his favorites—is graphically demonstrated by these purchases. He was committing huge amounts of money, even for a man of his wealth, to the arts of early America, because of his belief in their artistic merit.

When the Girl Scouts Loan Exhibition was being organized in 1929, Louis Myers asked Du Pont to lend many pieces. He consented, even though a New York dealer advised him that the exhibition had allegedly been concocted by Myers and others to boost the prices of Duncan Phyfe furniture. Du Pont further agreed to arrange his furniture in the vast rooms at the Anderson Galleries where the exhibition was held; when the time came, he took off his jacket, rolled up his sleeves, and pitched in to get the job done.[15]

This same energy is evident in Du Pont's collecting. Just ten years after beginning, he had gathered such a vast quantity of American antiques that he wrote:

> I thought at one time of having an elaborate catalogue made of [the con-tents of Chestertown House in Southampton] and had even begun it, but when I discovered that there were about three times as many articles there as in the Metropolitan Museum and that it took all sorts of different people to write a catalogue, I decided to bring the best things back from there to [Winterthur] and eventually include them in the write-up of this house which sooner or later will have to be done.[16]

Du Pont was elected to the Walpole Society in 1932, and the group's fall meeting that year was held at Winterthur. The richness of the collection, its extraordinary quality *and* quantity, dazzled even this group of distinguished experts and collectors. Luke Vincent Lockwood was awed:

> Imagine a house which records the decorative history of our Country, and that in supreme terms! Are you interested in architecture? Here you will see choicely chosen examples of interior woodwork covering two centuries. Is it silver? The finest examples of distinguished Colonial makers. Pottery? Everything the Country affords. Pewter and brass? A fine collection. Porcelain, especially that brought from the Orient by the East India Company? A bewildering array. Looking glasses? Fine specimens of every kind. Textiles and needlework that show once more what beauty and color picked out the households of the Colonists.[17]

In a second description of the meeting, three other society members responded to Winterthur. Their appreciation of the rooms' warm, welcoming air contains an implicit comparison with the colder, more formal American Wing—and perhaps with other museum installations:

> We have seen restored houses, beautifully done, like that of Mr. Perry, or new houses like Mr. Palmer's, both unforgettably delightful as homes. Yet never have we seen so many old American rooms under one roof—the number seemed endless and we have serious doubts if any of us saw them all—possibly Mr. du Pont himself may sometimes forget a few of them. Nor could we imagine that there could be put into one house so many rooms so different in size, period and character, in such way as to make it livable— to make a home of it. But Mr. du Pont has done it. Here are rooms that welcome the guest, furniture which seems glad to receive him. There is nothing of the museum in the air. We are not among the dead.[18]

Henry Francis du Pont made a great contribution to the collecting movement not only because of his rare talent but because he was in the right place at the right time. Like Ford and Garvan, he had the money and the desire to go after the highest-priced American antiques. But he had a much more specific idea than his contemporaries of how he would use each piece—and he always did his own buying. His eye for line, proportion, and color has become legendary; he rarely bought an ugly piece, and he bought more than his share of great ones.

The result was a collection of the finest and rarest, shaped and arranged in enchanting period rooms by his taste alone. Without the arrangement, his collection would never have achieved so much fame and influence; but to him the antiques and their settings were inseparable, after he had been inspired by the combination of pine dresser and pink Staffordshire pottery in Mrs. Webb's

Du Pont's taste and connoisseurship are nowhere more apparent than in the Chinese parlor at Winterthur. (Courtesy, The Henry Francis du Pont Winterthur Museum)

house. At Winterthur he far transcended his original inspiration, creating visual symphonies. "Since the world began," wrote a friend, "there has been no more ardent, informed, and creative collector than Harry du Pont."[19]

Du Pont believed that Winterthur's settings were realistic re-creations of early American rooms. Today, however, many experts feel that the Winterthur he conceived represents a romantic twentieth-century vision, with far too much perfection to be historically accurate. Its original rooms have therefore come to be valued primarily for reflecting Du Pont's sensitive and passionate appreciation of the beauty of American antiques. His legacy to the nation was to communicate that appreciation, proving on a major scale that the best American pieces *are* beautiful, and—through his own artistry—that they can be combined in rooms as charming and elegant as any in the world.

Joseph Downs, Winterthur's first curator, wrote upon its opening as a museum in 1951: "Winterthur represents the largest and richest assemblage of American decorative arts, especially of furniture, ever brought together." As the visitor enters one room after another, said Downs, he "feels the richness of life at its best in successive periods of our early history." Downs, like Du Pont, considered Winterthur a tribute not only to the taste and ability of early craftsmen but also to the merchants, shipbuilders, and others who had commissioned their work—to "those who had the means and perception to command the best and, in so doing, encourage artisans to realize their talents to the fullest."[20]

The rarity of the objects at Winterthur is underlined by the following story:

Some years ago, when the director of a famous London museum was visiting Winterthur as a private guest, Mr. du Pont started to lead him across a rug which was woven in Portuguese India in the early 1600's. The museum man took one step and jumped backward as though his foot had touched hot coals. "I can't walk on that," he pleaded. "If we had that rug it would be hanging in a gallery of its own!"[21]

Chapter 23

Francis P. Garvan

Sharing the Wealth of Antiques

Francis Patrick Garvan (1875–1937) was a pioneer in his approach to the educational potential of American antiques. In 1930, on the occasion of his twentieth wedding anniversary, he donated the cream of his collection to Yale University as the Mabel Brady Garvan Collection. By the terms of his gift, selected examples were to be lent to any institution or organization that asked for them. This was an extraordinary concept: a collection of five thousand objects as a kind of circulating library, containing rare and valuable "textbooks" of American art and design. "Every man, woman, and child in America," he said, "is entitled to the extent of their capacity, to all the inspiration that can be derived from the works of art it is our good fortune to possess in this country."[1]

Along with many other collectors of his generation, Garvan felt that machine-made furnishings were tasteless, graceless, and dehumanized. An old silver bowl that had been raised, embossed, and engraved by hand seemed to him vivid proof of the beauty of the old over the new. He thought that making such examples of hand craftsmanship available to the American public would result in a vast improvement in taste. Therefore, Yale was to be the custodian of the Garvan antiques, but it was to share them freely with responsible exhibitors

Francis Patrick Garvan. (Yale University Art Gallery, Mabel Brady Garvan Collection)

throughout the nation. The university's role was "to keep them moving through the country so that as great a number of people . . . may study them as it is possible to interest."[2]

In this purpose, Garvan was a direct descendant of the early arts-and-crafts advocates, who believed that simply being exposed to well-made objects would improve one's taste. Like Halsey, Clearwater, and others, he felt a responsibility to educate Americans through antiques. But Garvan went a step beyond. It was not enough to give the antiques to an institution, where they could be seen only by a relative few. It was unrealistic, he thought, to expect the people to come to his antiques, and much fairer and more effective to send them out to people. "Let us start the art of the country in circulation where it can be rendered accessible to every owner of a Ford car."[3]

The reference to Ford is appropriate. Both Ford and Garvan, who was the son of an Irish immigrant, had relatively humble beginnings. Because he had done well, Garvan saw America as the land of opportunity. In giving his antiques to Yale to be used as a lending collection, he was trying to share part of his good fortune with the masses. His was a democratic attitude, compared with the relatively frightened or élitist view of men like Halsey. The latter perceived the waves of immigration as a menace to the native spirit, an alien influence to be resisted. They offered American antiques and period rooms as an aloof form of propaganda, while Garvan regarded antiques as a positive and direct channel of communication.

Garvan's public-spiritedness was evident in other areas of his life. After attending the Hartford, Connecticut, public schools and graduating from Yale University (1897) and New York University Law School (1899), he joined the New York County District Attorney's staff, where he stayed for several years. During World War I, he served the national government as Alien Properties Custodian. His most important act in that post was confiscating German dye patents, with the approval of Congress and President Wilson. To distribute these valuable formulas to American manufacturers, Garvan established the American Chemical Foundation, Inc. As its president, he worked extremely hard to encourage and facilitate the growth of the American chemical industry. His zeal eventually led to difficulties, when he was sued by the federal government, as the foundation's head, for the return of the dye patents; he did, however, finally win the case. The American chemical industry naturally saw the issue differently, and Garvan was the first layman to receive the Priestley Medal, the highest award of the American Chemical Society.[4]

Besides his public posts, private law practice, and active collecting, Garvan had many other interests. He was a philanthropist. He was an enthusiastic horseback rider and owner of prize-winning thoroughbreds. He had been an athlete at Yale; and years later, his competitive spirit complemented by his sense of humor, Garvan entered a race with three Olympic track champions. Having incurred a two-yard penalty by jumping the starting gun, he overcame the handicap in the rerun by cutting across the field to arrive first at the finish line.

Over the years, Garvan participated in a number of sensational lawsuits. The first and most notorious, in which he was a member of the prosecution team, was the Stanford White–Harry Thaw trial of 1907. As one historian has said, "Probably the most famous of murder cases involving America's super rich was Harry K. Thaw's murder of the architectural genius, Stanford White."[5] Both the motive and the method were sensational. Thaw's wife, a former Floradora girl, had been White's mistress before her marriage. Thaw brooded and planned revenge for years. His chance came in June of 1906,

This maple banister-back arm chair, 1750–1800, from coastal Connecticut, shows Garvan's interest in forming a collection representative of simple, as well as sophisticated, tastes. (Yale University Art Gallery, Mabel Brady Garvan Collection)

when the Thaws encountered the architect at a Madison Square Garden musical. Making his way to White's table, Thaw shot and killed him. It seems appropriate that Garvan's rise to prominence began in this case, for White had been one of the major forces behind the revival of interest in American colonial architecture.

Garvan began collecting as a means of furnishing his apartment, after he was married in 1910. His bride was Mabel Brady, daughter of Albany financier Anthony N. Brady, whose fortune at the time of his death in 1913 was said to approach that of J. P. Morgan. The Garvans started buying old English pieces on their wedding trip. Before long, they had $40,000 worth of English antiques, which Garvan promptly sold when he discovered that some fakes had crept in.

He began again about the time of World War I. From then on, he was careful to have each piece of furniture checked by a cabinetmaker before he bought it. And now the Garvans' specialty was American antiques, to which Garvan said he was drawn by the example of R. T. H. Halsey. For some reason, he felt that fakes were less likely to turn up among American pieces. There is a story that Garvan arrived home one day proudly bearing his first American antique—a cowbell.[6] From this unpromising beginning, he went on to amass one of the outstanding collections of American decorative arts.

Garvan maintained that his courtroom experience served him well in collecting. "I had eight years . . . in the District Attorney's office," he said, "and I try every piece as I would a murderer." Following this unorthodox method, he developed the ability to make educated judgments. "There is no necromancy in collecting," he said. "It is merely a question of the education of the eye, or rather of the eye and hand, because the feeling of a piece is as essential as the appearance. . . . Just as a prosecutor sometimes achieves remarkable results merely by his intuition, so the collector reaches conclusions by his instinct." Garvan studied auction catalogues, books, magazines, and photographs of pieces in his own collection. The study, he believed, rested him as nothing else could.[7]

Garvan's transition from private collector to public benefactor seems to have occurred gradually, as he was periodically asked to lend to museums. At some point he decided to collect, like Ford and Clearwater, for eventual public display. From then on, he concentrated—except in silver—on representative examples rather than masterpieces. Many collectors and museums restricted themselves to only the most elegant antiques; but Garvan aimed to be encyclopedic, spanning the range from modest to exceptional. Thus, he wanted ultimately to circulate American antiques as comprehensive in their coverage as library books.

The result was a collection of great variety. It included furniture, silver, pewter, glass, ceramics, ironware, paintings, and Currier and Ives prints. Most of these categories individually showed the diversity characteristic of the whole. For instance, the furniture was described by Meyrick Rogers, one-time curator of the Garvan Collection at Yale, as "richly representative of the more fashionably sophisticated achievements of the early American cabinet-maker." Overall, however, Rogers felt that the collection embodied the individuality—and often the whimsy—of craftsmen "less restricted by formal fashion."[8]

An outstanding exception to the variety of quality among Garvan's antiques was silver, which was his passion. "For two decades after his initial purchases," wrote Graham Hood in the catalogue to the Garvan silver collection, "he collected with almost insatiable appetite." He sought the help of the best scholars and dealers, including, besides Bigelow, the English authority E. Alfred Jones, George Gebelein of Boston, Robert Ensko of New York, and Maurice Brix of Philadelphia."[9]

In 1930, Garvan wrote to Henry du Pont to suggest trading for some of Du Pont's silver:

> If I have anything in the furniture line which you are particularly desirous of, I wish you would let me know. My one real ambition is to make my silver collection at Yale a comprehensive, permanent educational one for all times and I am quite willing to sacrifice any of my other Americana in exchange for anything which will strengthen my collection. . . . whenever I want a piece I am threatened with it being sold to Mr. du Pont if I do not pay an extravagant price for it, and undoubtedly the same thing is being said to you.[10]

Garvan had many ways of acquiring antiques. He bought whole distinguished collections, including furniture and silver from Halsey; furniture from the heirs of Irving W. Lyon; silver from Lockwood; pewter from Louis Myers; and glass from Rhea Mansfield Knittle, an authority in the field. When his antiques had overflowed his home, Garvan rented a loft downtown in New York City, and reportedly he would leave his office on Madison Avenue every afternoon, step into his car, and be driven down to the loft to meet with dealers. He would look over the antiques being offered to him, and is said to have bought up to a limit set by his stock-market gains of the day.

Garvan regularly appeared at his loft to inspect what the dealers had brought, but he also purchased extensively at auctions—including the famous Reifsnyder and Flayderman events of 1929 and 1930. In the Flayderman sale, Garvan bought Paul Revere's anvil for $9,700, and paid $5,500 for a charmingly pierced and scrolled silver strainer made for the eminent Jabez Bowen of Providence.

Above: *Silver punch strainer, 1765, made by Jonathan Clarke of Rhode Island for Jabez Bowen. Garvan bought it for $5,500 at the Flayderman auction in 1930. In* Antiques, *Keyes called the strainer "a collector's treasure* par excellence." *(Yale University Art Gallery, Mabel Brady Garvan Collection)*

Left: *Garvan had his portrait painted standing beside this impressive and important two-handled silver covered cup, 1710–1715, by Edward Winslow of Boston. (Yale University Art Gallery, Mabel Brady Garvan Collection)*

At the end of 1930, six months after his great gift to Yale, Garvan consigned a significant part of his remaining collection to auction. He sent a copy of the catalogue to Du Pont beforehand, assuring him that there was nothing *wrong* with the pieces, but that they were duplicates. The fact that Garvan had suffered financial losses in the Depression was almost surely a consideration.

The press gave the auction considerable attention. The Garvan collection, said *Art News*, had been brought to prominence through the display of many of its finest pieces at the Girl Scouts Exhibition in the fall of 1929. *The New*

York Times reported that the forthcoming sale would include, as well as furniture, rare seventeenth- and eighteenth-century silver, glass, Currier and Ives prints, and Oriental and English ceramics. When the three-day auction was over, the *Times* reported that the collection had brought $242,852, including $11,000 paid for "a Chippendale Highboy Attributed to Savery." This piece, which had been illustrated in Wallace Nutting's *Furniture Treasury*, was bought by the dealer Israel Sack along with a number of others. Nutting himself bought a New Jersey Queen Anne lowboy for $740. Among the silver, New York tankards brought the highest prices.[11]

Garvan's financial difficulties, followed by his death in 1937, prevented him from fully supporting the implementation of his grand plan for circulating antiques. But parts of the Yale collection were on loan to widely scattered museums and historic houses until the late 1950s. By then, displays of antiques had become so numerous throughout the country that the collection was gathered in to New Haven, where it has remained as a permanent monument to Garvan's enthusiasm and energy.

Even in sickness, Garvan did not lose his appetite for antiques. He told an interviewer that although he was bedridden for three years, "I had the collection on my mind continually, and some of the best pieces in it were added at that time." His law partner, concerned about the financial drain that resulted from Garvan's collecting mania, said to him at the end of one illness: "They've fixed you up physically. Now all you need is a cure for your antiquitis."[12]

Garvan's American antiques, installed in the Yale University Art Gallery about 1928.
(Yale University Art Gallery, Mabel Brady Garvan Collection)

Chapter 24

A Triumvirate
and One Lone Texan

THE MAJESTY OF LOUISE DU PONT CROWNINSHIELD, THE STYLE OF KATHARINE Prentis Murphy, and the distinction of Electra Havemeyer Webb contributed to their designation by a younger generation as the great Triumvirate of Collecting Ladies. Although their approaches showed considerable differences, and although Mrs. Murphy lacked the great affluence of the other two, in general they are representative of the ultra-rich collectors of their era. None of the three had a penchant for historical accuracy in arranging and decorating "period" rooms; it was the artistic impulse, much more than the associational, that underlay their activity. And despite their primary interest in American antiques, neither Mrs. Webb nor Mrs. Murphy was inclined to flout the tradition of their élite social class. Each continued to furnish her New York apartment with European objects, keeping her American collections elsewhere.

Electra Webb (1888–1960) had collecting in her blood. Her parents, the Henry Havemeyers of New York, were among the most avant-garde American collectors. But their time and money were expended in Europe, studying, talking to artists, and buying the best of the old masters as well as the work of the new, iconoclastic Impressionists. From the time she could walk, Electra accompanied her mother and their painter friend Mary Cassatt on European trips, in which art figured heavily.

Perhaps it was a reaction against this intensive exposure that caused Electra to find the art of the New World intriguing. For, having reached the age of independence, that is what she concentrated on. When Mrs. Havemeyer first saw her newly married daughter's Westbury, Long Island, house, she gasped in disbelief: "How can *you*, Electra, *you* who have been brought up with Rembrandts and Manets, live with this American trash?"[1]

Electra Havemeyer Webb. *Watercolor on paper, by Elizabeth Shoumatoff, 1964.* (*Courtesy, Shelburne Museum, Shelburne, Vermont*)

Mrs. Havemeyer should have resigned herself long before. Electra had grown up collecting—dolls, paintings, whatever took her fancy; and one day she showed up with a cigar-store Indian. Even then, her mother began to despair of her. The Indian was named Mary O'Connor, after a former nurse (Mrs. Webb always maintained that the wooden Mary was much more satisfactory than its flesh-and-blood namesake). It was relegated to the Havemeyers' Long Island residence, and—Mrs. Havemeyer hoped—to oblivion. Mary survived, however, and was moved eventually to the new home in Westbury that Electra and her husband bought shortly after their marriage in 1910.

By that time, Electra's rebellion had been confirmed. She went on from Mary O'Connor to buying early American art in all media, emphasizing folk art—hooked rugs, simple, sturdy furniture, pewter and tin, quilts, hatboxes—instead of high-style pieces. Somehow, she rose above the disapproval of family and wealthy friends, for she spent the rest of her life gathering that "American trash" with an intensity that became a passion.

Several of the ultra-rich collectors of American antiques prominent in the 1920s were among her friends, but she alone had a special affinity for folk art. Perhaps her childhood familiarity with the avant-garde work then being produced had set her apart; for those who were interested primarily in early American folk art during the twenties were also collecting—or actually creating—what was known at the time as modern painting. Both areas were characterized by simplicity of line, plain and bright colors, and bold, striking designs.

Electra's husband, J. Watson Webb, came from Vermont, where his family had a four-thousand-acre estate on Lake Champlain. His mother was a Vanderbilt. In the summer the young Webbs traveled to Vermont, acquiring one of the old farmhouses on the Webb property and doing it over in early American

A small sampling of Mrs. Webb's collection of thousands of dolls, begun in her childhood with dolls her grandmother made for her. (Courtesy, Shelburne Museum)

style. Aileen Saarinen, in a biographical sketch, speculated that Mrs. Webb's constant exposure to Great Art at home and in museums had made her long for simpler surroundings. "Perhaps when she came in after school and had to tiptoe past the somberly splashing fountain up the back stairs to avoid illustrious visitors in the music room or gallery she determined secretly that when she grew up *her* home would never be a 'museum.' "[2]

It was at the Webbs' place in Vermont, called then and now The Brick House, that Henry du Pont first realized how decorative and charming American antiques could be. Upon Mrs. Webb's death, her children presented to the Winterthur Museum the pine dresser and Staffordshire wares with which Du Pont had originally been smitten. Those antiques are still at Winterthur, appearing together just as Du Pont first saw them.

Whereas others began to collect as adults in order to furnish their houses, Mrs. Webb made her first purchases much earlier in life. Furthermore, she bought the wooden Mary O'Connor, for example, because (as she said) it "spoke to" her. She was probably responding directly and strongly to the sculptural aspects of the carved figure. In buying Mary O'Connor, she was collecting a form of art; and while other collectors came to regard their American antiques as important artistic pieces, most did not start out that way.

Electra Webb's energy was so formidable that over the years she collected enough American antiques to fill many houses. She never parted with any of them. Eventually they did, in fact, furnish houses, as well as other exhibition space at the Shelburne Museum in Vermont. The museum, founded by the Webbs in 1947, comprised a number of buildings, in addition to a steamboat, a lighthouse, and a covered bridge. The bridge, the last of its kind, was taken to Shelburne and installed at the expense of enormous amounts of both money and ingenuity.

What ultimately distinguished Mrs. Webb from other collectors was the catholicity of her tastes. For example, she retained her childhood doll collection and expanded it to the point where it became one of the museum's highlights. She was one of the first to collect and display attractively early American quilts, hatboxes, weathervanes, and other everyday objects. She installed at Shelburne an entire hunting camp, one of those luxurious dwellings that the very rich could still afford and maintain early in the century.

Mrs. Webb's innovative approach is evident throughout the Shelburne Museum. One of the major attractions is the huge paddlewheel steamer, also

Electra Webb's renowned collection of wooden Indians began with her first antique, "Mary O'Connor." (Courtesy, Shelburne Museum)

The Stencil House at the Shelburne Museum. (Courtesy, Shelburne Museum)

the last of its kind, which she salvaged. She was afraid to confess her folly to her husband, but finally screwed up her courage and said, "Pa, I've taken a terrible venture." When he asked, "WHAT?" she told him about the steamboat. "That's not so bad," he replied. "I think a lot of the other stuff you bought is much worse."[3]

She had more conventional interests, too. In her own houses, on Long Island and at Shelburne, she used early American furniture from the beginning, and the houses established at the museum were furnished in the period-room manner. The houses were from New England, unpretentious for the most part, found by Mrs. Webb and moved to Shelburne for preservation and exhibition.

The earliest was the Prentis House, built in 1733, a salt box which she discovered near Northampton, Massachusetts. Representing a very early style of American architecture, it was of special importance, for the form was becoming more and more scarce even in New England.

Finally, she never forgot the Manets and the Rembrandts. Her New York apartment was always furnished with the finest eighteenth-century French antiques and old-master paintings. Like most of the wealthy, socially élite Americans who turned to American antiques in the twenties, she used European furnishings for her home in the city. It was at the shore or in the country that these collectors assembled their American things. They seemed to derive considerably more pleasure from the latter; but in their circle it was fashionable and customary to live among European antiques, and they were not prepared to defy the fashion by substituting a Chippendale piece from Philadelphia for one from London.

Furnishings from Mrs. Webb's New York apartment were eventually moved to Shelburne and installed just as in New York. The variety of the museum was thus enriched, making it possible to observe the contrasts between European and American decorative arts of the same period. But Shelburne's forte is still the scope of its early Americana. Mrs. Webb's contribution to the understanding of that field was broader and more democratically oriented than that of any of her well-known contemporaries, with the exception of Henry Ford. She helped give respectability to the collecting of unpretentious American antiques that were unusual or unique. Perhaps most important, she acted to rescue and preserve some disappearing aspects of American life.

Louise du Pont Crowninshield (1877–1958) always claimed that she started her brother, Henry du Pont, on his collecting career. Early in the century, when he was at Harvard and she was living in Massachusetts, she took him with her to auctions. He started buying antiques then, she said, and continued during subsequent trips to Europe with their father. Henry, in turn, eventually influenced his sister to concentrate on American rather than European antiques. Once they had both become serious in the new field, they were terrific competitors. But in the end it was Henry, because of his vast wealth and his passionate energy, who became the almost mythical collector.

Mrs. Crowninshield furnished her seaside home at Peach's Point, Marblehead, Massachusetts, with exquisite examples of delicate early American furniture; but she once described Peach's Point as a "triumph of the second rate. I don't have the money to collect the way Harry does." She did, however, share his gift for creating beautifully integrated compositions of antiques. Although her house at Eleutherian Mills in Delaware was arranged more conventionally than her brother's, it was done with the same flair and delicacy of feeling for

*Louise du Pont Crownin-
shield. (Photograph
courtesy Eleutherian Mills
Historical Library)*

sympathetic lines, proportions, and colors. Her rooms were elegant and comfortable, filled with lovely things. Her drawing room, said a discriminating friend, "was the prettiest I ever saw." And Walter Muir Whitehill wrote that she was "a born collector who had the added gift of being able to blend possessions into a harmonious and unobtrusive whole. Her houses were packed with objects of rarity and intrinsic interest that quietly looked well together and were used with a freedom rare among collectors, to make daily life pleasanter." (Eleutherian Mills is now open to the public, arranged very much as it was in her day.)[4]

With troops of maids and everything of the finest quality, Mrs. Crowninshield lived in the grand manner. She seemed to assume that anyone of consequence lived in the same way, as is evident from a story told by one of Boston's leading collectors. The lady from Boston had a summer party at which Mrs. Crowninshield was among the guests. The table had been set for dinner inside, when Mrs. Crowninshield suddenly announced that it was a gorgeous night for outdoor dining. The hostess, considerably younger than her imperious guest, was all consternation; but she ordered the young temporary help to move the tables outside. Despite her visions of stumbling inexperienced maids and guttering candles, the al fresco meal went off beautifully. It was almost as if Mrs. Crowninshield had commanded it to do so.[5]

Her commanding presence was also observable on the boards to which she belonged for museums, historic houses, and other organizations devoted to the past. She was always helping with the thinking and planning, as well as financially. She would see immediately, according to Walter Whitehill, what was needed to make a room look *right*. He was a fellow member on the board of the Peabody Institute in Salem, and he described how she would suggest an improvement in an exhibition. If no one objected, she quickly implemented the change:

> . . . she would seat herself in the middle of the room and immediately, with staccato rapidity, issue orders for the removal of this and the shifting of that. In a few minutes the gallery seemed reduced to debris. Then with equally startling rapidity a new order emerged from the chaos as she directed the hanging of pictures and the placing of objects in locations that had obviously been in her mind's eye long before the shift had been ever so tentatively proposed. These excursions into museum installation were remarkable to watch, and they invariably came out right.[6]

The hallway at Eleutherian Mills. (*Eleutherian Mills Historical Library*)

Elegant American antiques furnish the drawing room of Mrs. Crowninshield's Delaware house, Eleutherian Mills. (*Eleutherian Mills Historical Library*)

Katharine Prentis Murphy.
(Photograph courtesy
Shelburne Museum)

Mrs. Crowninshield also had a sense of humor. She is reported to have said, in explaining her ownership of several Pekinese and poodles during her youth: "Young people can't afford old rugs. In our house we have lots of dogs. They antique our rugs."[7]

Although a very definite individual, Mrs. Crowninshield didn't strive to make dramatic statements with her antiques, as her brother and Mrs. Murphy did. Instead of trying to create her own three-dimensional picture of early American life, she lived with her antiques as she would have done with tasteful furnishings of any other country or age. Her influence on the collecting movement lay in helping to make American antiques eminently acceptable in the homes of wealthy aristocrats brought up to disdain them.

Katharine Prentis Murphy (1884–1967) has been remembered in the world of American antiques not for innovation, but for *style*. Big and round-faced, she was not a good-looking woman in her youth. But her enormous, overwhelming, undeniable style made up for what she lacked in looks and grace. She grew more attractive with age, and her personal magnetism increased until she had become the *grande dame* of the antiques world.

Mrs. Murphy went to Concord, New Hampshire, as the young bride of David Murphy, proprietor of the town's leading dry-goods store. When he died, leaving her a widow at an early age, Mrs. Murphy moved to New York, where her brother and sister-in-law lived, and settled into an apartment in the same building. With what means she had from her husband and what her very liberal brother provided (he was a successful contractor), Mrs. Murphy began to cut a swath. At her husband's funeral she had met young Katharine Howe Palmer, the wife of her lawyer and an enthusiast for American antiques. They became fast friends, and Mrs. Palmer introduced her to the delights of early American furniture.

Katharine Murphy bought a house in Connecticut, which she named Candlelight Farm. She "earlied it up," as one collector puts it, to provide a sympathetic setting for her William and Mary furniture and her late seventeenth- and early eighteenth-century accessories. Here Mrs. Murphy's style was at its most expressive; and what she accomplished at Candlelight Farm she reproduced in the numerous rooms she furnished at museums and historical societies from New Hampshire to Texas. It is impossible not to recognize a Murphy room. The elements are bold alternating black and white diamond-checked floors; curtains, fabrics, and bed hangings in dramatic flame-stitch patterns; and furniture with high arching curves, deep carving, and crisply turned legs and stretchers. The theme set by these striking patterns and shapes is then embellished with copious sets of pewter measures, plates, and mugs; numerous shining brass candlesticks; and ornamental hanging embroideries and prints. The whole effect is charming—and utterly unrelated to historical reality. Mrs. Murphy, like so many others of her generation, was seeking immortality through self-expression. She liked to think that prosperous eighteenth-century merchants might have lived in her period rooms, with heirlooms that came down through the family as well as objects imported, purchased in shops, made to order, or handmade in the home during the owner's lifetime.

On this large canvas, Mrs. Murphy painted an atmospheric and pleasing picture of early American life. But it was done with a very broad brush. The difficulty with such rooms is that they leave the impression that in the early eighteenth century *all* Americans lived this way. And of course few, if any, did.

Her rooms reflect not only a twentieth-century artistic vision and sensibility but also a projection of the twentieth-century ability to transport goods easily from one part of the world to another. Material things were very scarce before the nineteenth century, and available only through wealth or hard work. Every artifact made before the Machine Age represented untold hours of human labor. The generation of the 1920s was drawn to objects made and beautifully finished by hand. They had simply forgotten that the eighteenth century lacked the technology, machinery, and transportation facilities to make material goods widely available. The rooms these collectors created, chockablock with rich furnishings, could exist only in a mechanized world. Just finding all the furniture and accessories for a few rooms would have taken an incredible amount of time in the eighteenth century, when travel was painful and slow.

Mrs. Murphy personally supervised and supplied furnishings for period rooms all over the East and as far afield as Texas, where her good friend Miss Ima Hogg donated her own house to the Houston Museum. Her characteristically bold and vivid decoration may be seen at Shelburne in the Prentis House; at Wethersfield, Connecticut; at the White Horse Tavern in Newport; and at the New-York and New Hampshire Historical societies. And everywhere, amidst the colonial splendor, is the implication that only the *best* people would have occupied these houses in the eighteenth century. Many of Mrs. Murphy's fellow collectors and curators shared her desire to emphasize that taste and luxury existed in the early days of America. They still felt it necessary to combat the long-held view that early America had no art, culture, or taste worth preserving. Mrs. Murphy joined the combat with a vengeance, through her bold, vivid, evocative rooms; but they seem now like rooms with an artificial message, rather than accurate pictures of life in eighteenth-century America.

In her New York apartment, so often filled with interesting and attractive people, Mrs. Murphy lived with an eclectic assortment of ornate European antiques. These, too, were selected with an eye to their vividness or flamboyance, and Mrs. Murphy lived among them with panache. At dinner parties she liked to serve a large roast. When all the guests were seated, she would rise from the head of the table, brandish a razor-sharp knife, and demonstrate her consummate skill as a carver. Each slice was produced and laid to rest on its plate with one deft flourish. Samuel, Mrs. Murphy's faithful butler and factotum for many years, would solemnly carry the plates around.

The drama extended throughout the meal. After the main course, toasts

were proposed and drunk, the entire company rising with each one. One unfortunate guest, not realizing at first the difficulty of getting up quickly from a top-heavy William and Mary chair, dutifully continued to rise, sending his chair crashing backward to the floor on each occasion. Samuel, who saw how the land lay after one or two of these mishaps, stationed himself nearby and quietly returned the chair to an upright position each time it toppled. Throughout the commotion the hostess remained serene, as if this were a normal part of toasting.

In her late years, Mrs. Murphy was dressed by the French designer Givenchy—always in black. To his graceful gowns she added an enormous black hat, sometimes adorned with floating feathers. Her sense of drama stayed with her to the end.[8]

Left: *The parlor at the New Hampshire Historical Society, furnished and donated by Katharine Prentis Murphy. It is arranged very similarly to her country house, Candlelight Farm. (New Hampshire Historical Society)*

Below: *New England easy chair, maple, 1725–1735. The bold outlines and vivid upholstery of this chair proclaim Mrs. Murphy's love of dramatic William and Mary designs. (New Hampshire Historical Society)*

Ima Hogg. *Oil on canvas, by Robert Joy, 1971. In this idealized portrait, Miss Hogg is seated in a Philadelphia Queen Anne armchair. (The Museum of Fine Arts, Houston, The Bayou Bend Collection)*

Miss Ima Hogg (1882–1975), having grown up in Texas among "super-Americans," was perhaps easy to convince of the value of American antiques. Her original interest seems to have sprung from a patriotic feeling for objects made in colonial and early Federal times. It was reportedly triggered when, in the early twenties, she saw a Queen Anne chair used as a prop by the artist Wayman Adams in his New York studio. She tried to buy the chair, but he insisted on keeping it, so she went out and found her own in a shop. Years later, she said she didn't know what had been so special about the artist's chair, but when she finally acquired it from his estate she thought it much less interesting than her own. She called it a "dumb chair."[9]

Miss Ima, as she was called by many who knew her, and three brothers were the children of Texas governor James Hogg. Their fortune was in real estate, and in the oil discovered on their land after their father's death. Miss Ima's resources were therefore considerable, and she was an important part of the collecting scene in the 1920s. She lived in New York for part of the year, attending concerts and collecting. Having studied piano in Europe, she was friendly with many famous musicians of her day, as well as a faithful patron of the Houston Symphony. (During her later years, the pianist Van Cliburn sent her a huge poinsettia tree every Christmas.)

She and her brother Will joined Henry du Pont, Henry Ford, and Francis Garvan in bidding up prices at the most important auctions of the twenties. The antiques dealers considered her fair, and conscientious in dividing her purchases evenly among those she patronized. She was serious about quality, according to them, but missed out on much of importance because she was not a keen student like Harry du Pont. Even so, given the wealth of material available in the twenties and afterward, she was able to amass a first-rate collection. It can now be seen, charmingly arranged and lavishly appointed, at her former home in Houston.

After Miss Ima had begun her collection, her brother Will is said to have become so intrigued by it that he made some of the most important additions. Following his death in the early 1930s, Miss Ima let her collecting lag in favor of other interests. In the fifties, she decided to donate her family home, Bayou Bend, to the Houston Museum, as a series of period rooms illustrating the development of style in America from the seventeenth century to the early nineteenth. Before turning it over, she fitted it out down to the last mantel garnish. But afterward she had other commitments—to the Houston Symphony and the Hogg Foundation for Mental Health, for example; and before she died, she said: "What Bayou Bend needs now is a good philanthropist."

Unlike Du Pont, Miss Ima never felt compelled to have genuine old wood for interiors. Except in a few cases, what she had installed were reproduction woodwork and plasterwork. In the dining room, modeled in plaster, are four cherubs. Miss Ima always used to say that they represented her and three collecting friends—Du Pont, Murphy, and Henry Flynt (who began in the 1930s to restore Old Deerfield Village).

Katharine Murphy was the member of the Triumvirate of Collecting Ladies with whom Miss Ima was most friendly. When Bayou Bend was to be opened to the public, Mrs. Murphy went to Houston to help. Just as she

New England Queen Anne armchair—Miss Hogg's first antique. She was inspired to buy it by a similar Queen Anne chair which she saw in the New York studio of the artist Wayman Adams. (The Museum of Fine Arts, Houston, The Bayou Bend Collection)

arrived, Miss Ima contracted the flu and took to her bed. Undeterred, Mrs. Murphy gathered appropriate materials from the Hogg collection and set to work. When Miss Ima had recovered enough to venture downstairs, she found a parlor created at Bayou Bend exactly like one Mrs. Murphy had arranged at the New Hampshire Historical Society! It remains as a reminder of Mrs. Murphy's influence among her friends.

When asked why she hadn't collected early objects from her own Texas region, Miss Ima replied that no one had been able to find her any. It is true that antiques of a certain kind are difficult to locate as long as they are out of fashion; and in later life Miss Ima did restore and furnish the Winedale Tavern as representative of German life in early nineteenth-century Texas. But the primary reason for her concentration on the finest and rarest high-style pieces, made in the East, was probably that she wanted to live as elegantly as possible. Seeking the best that America had to offer, she would have been uncomfortable with anything less. Like Mrs. Crowninshield and Mrs. Murphy, she meant to absorb the early American spirit—but only from the very best of its representatives.

Queen Anne bedroom, Bayou Bend. This was Miss Hogg's own bedroom, filled with fine New England pieces from her favorite period. (The Museum of Fine Arts, Houston, The Bayou Bend Collection)

Chapter 25

Henry Ford

Reliving History Through Antiques

WHILE EASTERN COLLECTORS WERE PLANNING THE PERMANENT INSTALLA-
tion of elegant American antiques in plastered and paneled rooms, Henry Ford
(1863–1947) was restoring an ordinary old house in Michigan. Like so many
other Americans of the period during and after World War I, Ford had been
thinking about his roots—but much more actively than most. His mother had
died when he was quite young; according to an article in *The Mentor*, Ford's
nostalgia for the house of his birth impelled him to begin collecting: "The longing to restore objects similar to those his mother's hands had used and touched
led him to make journeys to numberless farms and villages."[1] Ford acquired
many more objects than he needed to furnish his restored childhood home; and
when the project was finished in 1919, he was still buying. He had become a
collector.

Ford's approach to collecting was quite different from that of others in the
ultra-rich class. Although he had risen to enormous power and wealth, his
vision was shaped by his modest origins. He was not intent upon establishing
the existence of an early American aristocracy, or a valid artistic tradition.
Ford wanted to document the pioneer spirit wherever it had arisen. He found

equally interesting expressions of that spirit in American objects of all kinds, from early to late and from crude to elegant.

In his concern for the rescue of furnishings, buildings, machines, tools—anything related to an American occupation or habit—Ford resembled more a museum man like George Francis Dow than a connoisseur like R. T. H. Halsey. He wanted to preserve the record of daily life among ordinary Americans—his own heritage—and his collection, unlike those of Halsey, Myers, Du Pont, and others, represented life on the farm as well as in the city. *House and Garden* for February 1931, in an article called "Kitchen Colonial," noted that museums and glamorous collectors of high-style pieces had passed over all but the most elegant aspects of early America:

> Until people began collecting Kitchen Colonial, it was customary to visualize the entire Early American scene as one of aristocracy, fine clothes and splendid furniture from which the taste filtered down to the classes below. Mr. Ford and those who collect the cruder implements and furnishings are reversing this process: they are beginning at the bottom, at the isolated farmer and his wife and their daily drudgery. They are entering the Early American home, not through the carved portal of an admirable Georgian facade, as most of us do, but they have gone around back, and come through the kitchen door.[2]

In 1923, Ford bought the Wayside Inn in Sudbury, Massachusetts. He was

Henry Ford (left) with Homer Eaton Keyes at Greenfield Village. (Photograph courtesy of Alice Winchester)

The Wayside Inn, c. 1900, some years before Ford bought it. (Ford Archives / Henry Ford Museum, Dearborn, Michigan)

attracted to the property by Longfellow's vivid and romantic description of it in *Tales of a Wayside Inn.* The next year he purchased the Botsford Inn near Detroit. He bought these historic buildings, he said, "to save them for America." In his book *Today and Tomorrow,* Ford described the Wayside Inn project, which foreshadowed what he was to do on a much larger scale at the Henry Ford Museum and Greenfield Village in Dearborn, Michigan:

> Having finished the Inn and bought all the surrounding land, we then began to put the whole neighborhood into somewhat of its former condition. We picked up two old sawmills of the time—one of them in Rhode Island. These we are reassembling. . . . [We have a] grist mill . . . an old blacksmith shop . . . coaches and rigs of the time . . . a collection of old ploughs and other farming tools . . . and oxen to draw them. . . .
>
> By the time we get through, we expect to have this section, not a museum of Revolutionary days, but a natural, working demonstration of how the people of those days lived. We have both lost and gained in the movement of modern industry. Our gains are many times greater than our losses; we can keep all of the gains and repair some of the losses.[3]

Ford's purchase of the inn had made front-page news, causing considerable trepidation among New Englanders as to what he planned to do with it. He went to Israel Sack, the famous dealer in American antiques, whose shop was then in Boston. "I just want to know how to furnish" the Wayside Inn, he said.

"Mr. Ford," Sack replied, "everybody knows you can afford to buy the best. If you give me the job, you shall have the best." Ford put himself in Sack's hands, and in two weeks the job was finished. Anxiety in New England was allayed. The Boston *Herald* expressed its relief:

[The Wayside Inn's] renown and its accessibility in this automobile age, which Mr. Ford himself had done so much to create, lent it readily to profanation and it was easy to foresee it transformed from top to bottom to a great restaurant, [with] Sunday dinner parties in every room. . . . It will probably be treated better than ever before. Mr. Ford's own hobby for old furniture and his invitation of men conspicuous in the preservation of New England antiquities to his recent housewarming seem evidence of the fitting kind of piety and the bringing on of his whole family to the event is surely a sign of warm, personal interest.[4]

The furnishing of the Wayside Inn was the beginning of a cordial relationship between Ford and Sack. In a recorded interview, the dealer remembered their association with satisfaction:

Antiques were plentiful then and I was a big operator. Things were coming and going, and if I had something I thought Henry Ford could use, I'd ship it. He didn't give me an order. He never said a word after the inn— it was a free-for-all. I'd send him a picture or send him a thing and I'd get an answer . . . Mr. Ford said "Yes" or he said "No." There were no "ifs" or "buts."

If I got anything historical, like I bought the Longfellow collection, Mr. Ford bought it. I bought the General Stark collection direct from his house. I bought it right from the family, from Mr. Stark, and Henry Ford bought it. Anything from John Hancock he bought.

It was just plain as day to me. He wanted the early American with a history. He came right into it. You get a Longfellow collection and you look at the bed and you look at the desk where Longfellow slept and worked; you've got Longfellow in your home already. He wanted something with a background.[5]

But "something with a background" encompassed far more than just associations with famous historical figures, although those associations always had a special appeal. Sack said in this interview that Ford had also been a very active buyer from small dealers—that he liked going out into the country and talking to them. Sometimes he would buy them out. Sack gave the offhand example of Ford's paying a country dealer $8,000 for his whole stock and never giving the transaction another thought. Ford enjoyed, Sack thought, contact and conversation with the small entrepreneur.

Devere Card, an upstate New York dealer who sold to many collectors and museums in the 1920s, recalls that Ford had his regional sales representatives looking for antiques as well as selling cars. Henry Tyler, the Eastern representative for the Ford Motor Company, would tour the countryside in a chauffered Lincoln Continental, scouting for his employer. Tyler had started out knowing nothing about the decorative arts, but he became so engrossed that he eventually gave up his job with Ford to be an antiques dealer.[6]

Because Ford was so wealthy, he could afford to contemplate "a stupendous scheme to put at the nation's disposal an illustrated course in comparative civilization." He began to collect "buildings as casually as he buys jugs and warming pans," said *The Mentor*. Ford moved the buildings to Dearborn, where he proposed to re-create in Greenfield Village life among ordinary Americans of the past:

> In the by-ways of the American Village, in shops where business and industry will proceed in the ancient manner, in homes where housewives will conduct their affairs according to methods long out-moded but endeared to

Parlor of the Wayside Inn, probably c. 1926, after Ford had hired Israel Sack to furnish the inn with American antiques. (Ford Archives / Henry Ford Museum, Dearborn, Michigan)

us all, in every cranny, on every corner, in recreations on the green, in school and church, will be the scene that was America.[7]

Set among the genuinely old buildings was one newly constructed for the complex, in colonial style. It was enormous, with a central portion modeled on Independence Hall. This was the Henry Ford Museum, where the chronological development of objects used in industry, on the farm, and in the home would be splendidly set forth. Ford recognized that the American Wing showed only a small part of life in early America; he was determined to present the whole picture, in all its variety.

Before the permanent display space was completed, Ford's collections were stored in a warehouse, crowding the floor and hanging from the ceiling:

> These hand-turned, rush-bottomed chairs are the middle-class cousins of Duncan Phyfe tables, Savery highboys, Sheraton desks, Chippendale cabinets stored elsewhere in protective wrappings. Some of them are association

Thomas Edison's Menlo Park, New Jersey, workshop. It was moved intact to Greenfield Village; photograph c. 1929. (Ford Archives/ Henry Ford Museum, Dearborn, Michigan)

pieces, many are from fine mansions. But the acquisition of mahogany, silver, luster and fine glass has not been Mr. Ford's main purpose. His aim is to show how the man of ordinary means furnished his house and maintained it. . . .[8]

As he continued to acquire objects of all descriptions, his collections filled the Henry Ford Museum and the buildings of Greenfield Village.

Ford also had an intense interest in individual inventors, and in others like himself whose enterprise had markedly affected American life. His great admiration for his friend Thomas Edison led him to name the entire Dearborn complex the "Edison Institute." Furthermore, he amassed one of the most comprehensive collections of lighting devices in the world; the display ranges from an old candlemaker's shop, in which candles are produced by hand, through a complete gamut of chandeliers and lamps. A related exhibit is Edison's laboratory and workshop, transported intact from Menlo Park, New Jersey. While the Institute was in process, Ford asked Edison to walk across a square of wet concrete so that his footsteps would be preserved; Edison's signature is also in the square, along with Luther Burbank's shovel.

With his awesome preservation effort, Ford hoped to rescue a tangible part of the past, just as Dow had set out to do (although on a much smaller scale) at the Essex Institute. Ford's famous statement "History is bunk!" referred to dry-as-dust textbooks. His guiding idea was that history could be comprehended much more effectively through objects and buildings:

> We ought to know more about the families who founded this nation, and how they lived and the force and courage they had. One way to do this is to reconstruct as nearly as possible the conditions under which they lived. Then we have a history that is intimate and alive, instead of something in a book.
>
> Here in Dearborn we are assembling a complete series of every article used or made by the first settlers in America, and in many instances we are extending the series down to the present time.
>
> * * *
>
> Improvements have been coming so quickly that the past is being lost to the rising generation, and it can be preserved only by putting it in a form where it may be seen and felt. That is the reason behind this collection.[9]

Henry Ford's dream was fulfilled when he opened the Edison Institute in 1929. It is the first American example of a museum with extensive indoor *and* outdoor components. All aspects of life in America, from the earliest days onward, were represented by the exhibits and houses, with emphasis on the everyday as opposed to the rich and luxurious. "When we are through," he said, "we shall have reproduced American life as lived; and that, I think, is the best way of preserving at least a part of our history and tradition."[10]

Chapter 26

Louis Guerineau Myers

and the Girl Scouts Loan Exhibition

Louis guerineau myers (1874–1932) epitomized the attitude of the most discriminating collectors of the twenties. He was interested almost exclusively in the artistic merit of his antiques—a completely different view from that of the earliest collectors. Myers would reject a desk used by George Washington if it lacked beauty, whereas Cummings Davis, for example, would have prized such a desk regardless of its aesthetic value.

Myers began collecting about 1904, because he needed a hobby: "It is a splendid thing for a business man to have a hobby," he commented. "It has been a life-saver for me. If a man is so busy that he has not a very great deal of time to devote to his hobby, so much the better for his purse—he has a chance to catch up with himself."[1]

Although Myers may have stopped at times to refill his purse, he had managed to gather more than seven hundred pieces by 1921 when he put his first collection up for auction. The two-day sale, held at the American Art Galleries, drew record crowds. *The New York Times* reported that every seat was taken. People sat on window seats and squeezed onto a stairway at the back of the galleries where, it was reported, "Bids were shouted from unseen buyers at the top." Many leading dealers and collectors attended, including Garvan, Lockwood, and Palmer. The *Times* explained that the auction represented a new trend: "It is said that a comparatively recent and now continually growing interest in American furniture, together with the fact of the beautiful examples shown in this sale, has brought the large number of buyers and which resulted in excellent prices."[2]

Louis Guerineau Myers.
(National Cyclopedia of American Biography)

The sale brought $89,068 for 709 objects. They comprised mainly furniture of the Queen Anne and Chippendale periods, plus a group of forty-five windsor chairs and a selection of glass. All of those collecting specialties had gained considerably in popularity by the time of the Girl Scouts show, eight and a half years later. Myers's friend Homer Keyes later commented on his ability to anticipate the market:

> In the field of antiques the wise buyer is one who does not follow the crowd. Either he keeps a few jumps ahead, or he follows sufficiently far behind to pick up the good things discarded by the faddists. Mr. Myers was one of those who maintained a constant position of leadership. While the attention of others was concentrated upon mahogany, he collected walnut. When most eyes were turned toward pre-Revolutionary Philadelphia, he busied himself with post-Revolutionary New York. It pleased him to pursue an independent course, and, in the end, it likewise profited him.[3]

A reporter once asked Myers if he did not mind selling what he had so painstakingly searched out. "Decidedly not," he said:

> One begins, in the first place, with the idea of beautifying one's home, I suppose. There is a desire to get something that other people do not have and to bring your collection up to a standard of perfection, but I think in buying you always have in mind that some time you will submit the things you have bought to the taste of others.[4]

The highest aesthetic standard was Myers's constant preoccupation. Keyes described his approach to antiques as follows:

> Form, proportion, quality of aged surfaces, finesse in workmanship were the attributes that he considered of prime importance. As he grew older he stressed them almost to the point of hypercriticism. Individuality, the occasional evidence of an original creative spirit in a piece of furniture, meant comparatively little to him unless it was manifested in terms of technical perfection.[5]

Myers was born and educated in Bayonne, New Jersey. After many years as secretary to George Foster Peabody, he became treasurer of the John D. Rockefeller Fund in New York City in 1913—a position he retained until his death nineteen years later. Since he and his wife were childless, he could devote himself to collecting with a singlemindedness impossible otherwise. According to Keyes, he formed several collections during his lifetime. Like all true collectors, he relished the chase and the capture, and he enjoyed numerous diverting experiences.

A mahogany and gilt mirror, described by Myers as having been made in England or America about 1735, provided material for one of his tales. He heard about the mirror from a dealer in Maine, who said its owner, a woman in Nova Scotia, could not be induced to part with it. Unable to resist the challenge, Myers asked the dealer to drive up to Nova Scotia with him. The mirror proved as beautiful as described, but Myers, too, was unsuccessful in buying it. Something changed the owner's mind soon after the visit, however, and Myers said, "I went up for it, and had to ride in an upper berth. The mirror was

Left: *"A fine and early American Chippendale walnut side chair, about 1775, sold to the [Metropolitan] Museum for $525,"* reported The New York Times *of the Myers sale in February 1921. (The Metropolitan Museum of Art; Rogers Fund, 1921)*

Right, above: *Myers's interest in American Federal furniture and American pewter and glass is evident in his dining room. (Photograph courtesy of the Photographic Archives of the National Gallery of Art)*

worth it."[6] He considered this to be the finest mirror in his collection, and at the 1921 auction the Metropolitan Museum paid the newsworthy sum of $950 for it.

Another time, a dealer told Myers of a Chippendale mahogany side table in a Virginia farmhouse. The two men took a night boat down the Potomac and, upon landing at five the next morning, walked three miles. "Then we came to a little bit of a house," said Myers, "and my heart sank. I didn't see how there could be anything worth while in a place like that, but the first thing I saw was the table, in a room where everything else was inconsequential. It had been treasured in the family for years. But they would not let me have it that day. Later they wrote that they were willing to give it up."[7]

Myers consistently demonstrated shrewdness in anticipating market trends. He was interested in American pewter and glass while both fields were still being generally ignored, and his book *Some Notes on American Pewterers* was published in 1926. Francis Garvan bought some of his pewter in the late twenties; the rest was sold at auction after his death in 1932. The related catalogue entries for that auction were prepared by the great pewter collector and author Ledlie Laughlin.

Like Halsey and a few others, Myers was collecting Phyfe-style furniture before it became the rage in New York. In 1922, the year after his first sale at auction, Myers lent several pieces to the Phyfe exhibition at the Metropolitan Museum. He also turned his attention to other craftsmen of the Federal period, collecting fine pieces from Philadelphia and Baltimore as well as New York.

Chippendale and Queen Anne continued to attract him, however; in 1929, he sold furniture from those periods to John D. Rockefeller for $44,650.[8] It was destined for Colonial Williamsburg, although most of the pieces had been made either in Philadelphia or in New England. Myers contended that they were nevertheless appropriate for a Southern restoration, because Northern cabinetmakers were known to have shipped furniture to the South during colonial times. Goodwin, and others involved in creating Colonial Williamsburg, disagreed. In their eyes, a Virginia restoration should reflect Southern, rather than Northern, culture.

Secretary from the Myers collection. Homer Keyes described it as having "delicacy of proportions and pervasive refinement of detail." (Photograph courtesy of The Magazine Antiques)

Myers discussed selling some of his other antiques, apparently of the Federal period, to Williamsburg. To William G. Perry, a fellow member of the restoration's furnishings committee, he wrote:

> I am wondering whether it would be at all interesting to you and the other members to come to Fair Haven, New Jersey—about an hour and ten minutes from New York—and see what I have done with a very small cottage in the way of furnishing it with not too expensive antiques. Part of these furnishings would be suitable for the Governor's Palace, if it were possible to run them into the Sheraton period, but as we are limited—and I think rightly—to the Chippendale period and earlier, this would be interesting only in connection with the other houses should they ultimately be furnished.[9]

Thus, Myers seems to have been anxious to do business with Colonial Williamsburg. Probably, however, he believed that his fine New England and Philadelphia furniture belonged there. It exemplified eighteenth-century America at its best; and that, in his opinion, was what Williamsburg was about. Susan Higginson Nash, who was assigned to oversee the furnishing of the houses, offers grudging confirmation of the sincerity of his motives:

> Some of the people connected with the Restoration over-emphasized their desire to have certain pieces bought. They truly thought such pieces should come to Williamsburg—certain pieces of Mr. Louis Myers, for example, which were very fine, but rather elaborate. I think he felt that I was not a great collector in the sense that he was. Therefore anything that he said should be bought, should be bought.
>
> *   *   *
>
> Theoretically Mr. Myers wasn't really a dealer; he was a collector who sold furniture occasionally. He operated as both agent and collector, but he was considered more of a collector than a dealer. In other words he had no office or shop that I know of.[10]

The Girl Scouts Loan Exhibition of American antiques, held in New York in 1929, was Louis Myers's greatest triumph. It was his wife, a member of the National Council of Girl Scouts, who conceived the project to raise funds. But his interests and insights shaped the exhibition and its catalogue, most of which he wrote. The show featured Queen Anne and Chippendale furniture of the very highest style; Federal furniture, with a definite emphasis on Duncan Phyfe; and glass. There were also sections for windsors, fabrics, and ceramics. Because of the quantity and the extraordinary quality of the examples included, and because of Myers's lucid text and captions, the illustrated catalogue is still a standard reference for American furniture.

Most of the objects were lent by private collectors. One of the reasons for the show was to put these privately owned pieces on public display for the first—and, some commentators said, perhaps the last—time. Another reason was to make available some of the Reifsnyder furniture, which had received such vast publicity the year before, to be seen by those who had missed the auction. *The New York Times* said:

> The homes of many of New York's foremost collectors of Americana will yield up cherished treasures to appear on display at the galleries of the American Art Association from Sept. 25 to Oct. 9, under the auspices of the National Council of Girl Scouts. From mansion, apartment and nearby country estate pieces will be assembled to re-create the surrounding of those colonists and citizens of the new republic who would have none but the best of their period.[11]

The antiques were not actually arranged in period-room displays, as the article implies, for there was too much. Since one of Myers's main goals was to begin isolating the characteristics of the regional schools of American cabinetmaking, furniture was grouped by period and style. In his text to the catalogue, Myers pointed out distinguishing marks of New England, Philadelphia, and Baltimore pieces. For New York he dealt with the characteristics only of Federal furniture, explaining that "one of the mysteries of furniture lore is the absence of any group in any period, until Phyfe's time, structurally identifiable with New York. . . ."[12]

In the Phyfe section he noted that the master could not possibly have made all the pieces attributed to him; to describe Phyfe's personal style, he relied on labeled or otherwise securely documented examples. Homer Keyes said that the Girl Scouts show brought Federal furniture to the fore, and in particular showed "what Duncan Phyfe furniture is, and what it is not."[13]

The catalogue illustrated and briefly discussed practically every piece of furniture in the exhibition. Myers tried to indicate what was important about it structurally, regionally, and artistically, instead of giving a dry list of facts as in previous catalogues. Myers's standards were so high that his own antiques, wrote Keyes, "will, I believe, be found virtually flawless."[14] In the catalogue, Myers was revealing to less discriminating collectors the fine points of furniture style and craftsmanship.

Right, above: *Sophisticated American Chippendale furniture from Philadelphia and New England at the Girl Scouts Exhibition, 1929. (Photograph courtesy of Wendy Cooper and the National Council of Girl Scouts)*

Right: *Duncan Phyfe furniture at the Girl Scouts Exhibition, 1929. (Photograph courtesy of Wendy Cooper and the National Council of Girl Scouts)*

Among the glittering list of lenders to the exhibition were the Garvans, Du Pont, Rockefeller (who had spent over $46,000 at the Reifsnyder sale and lent some of his outstanding purchases), and a number of New York collectors noted for their taste in American antiques: the Charles Hallam Keeps, the Andrew Varick Stouts, Mrs. J. Insley Blair, and Mrs. Harry Horton Benkard. Myers had asked Du Pont to oversee the actual placement of the furnishings. Mrs. Myers described the zeal with which he complied:

> One of the funniest things I ever saw in my life was Mr. Dupont, without his hat or coat, looking like a hod carrier. He was there working much harder than any of the others there to help him. He arranged the rooms, hanging pictures and straightening out things. He had a corps of perhaps eight or ten people under him but worked like a slave.[15]

Myers's ability to pick out areas still open to collectors of moderate means was reflected in the section on glass. George McKearin lent five hundred pieces

from his collection of over five thousand; American antique glass had never before received such serious attention in a major exhibition. Keyes called the glass section possibly the most individualistic feature of the exhibition, and said that its like might not be seen again. McKearin not only lent the glass, he also wrote the first careful outline of types, dates, makers, and regions for the catalogue. In this, he echoed Myers's scholarly effort in the furniture area.

The glass exhibit introduced many to a whole new collecting area at a most opportune time. The stock-market crash forced many omnivorous collectors to curb their appetites severely or to forego antiques altogether. Some who could no longer buy the finest furniture, however, could perhaps afford a choice piece of glass.

Myers's willingness to turn his pleasure to profit was manifest again after the Girl Scouts show, when he sold fourteen pieces of furniture and nine pieces of pewter to Du Pont. The last sale of his antiques occurred after his death. Upon viewing the collection at the galleries before the auction, Homer Keyes wrote this tribute:

> It was the collection with which Mr. Myers lived, it consummated his home surroundings, it signalized the culmination of his long development as a connoisseur. . . . For a little time . . . furniture, mirrors, porcelains, glass, pewter, prints will be assembled—a fleeting but impressive memorial of a great collector.[16]

The sale brought $101,000 during the throes of the Great Depression in 1932. Once again, Myers's hope had been realized: his taste was greatly appreciated.

American glass and windsor chairs at the Girl Scouts Exhibition, 1929. (Photograph courtesy of Wendy Cooper and the National Council of Girl Scouts)

Chapter 27

W. A. R. Goodwin

Restoring Colonial Williamsburg

THE REVEREND W. A. R. GOODWIN (1869–1939) HAD A VISION. *The Virginia Gazette* described him as the "man who can rightly be called 'the father of Williamsburg,' as it was he who for years, dreamed a dream which was finally made real by the restoration of this old colonial city to its former glory and splendor of the 17th and 18th centuries."[1] Like Halsey, Ford, and Garvan, Goodwin believed that America's true spirit would be revived for its people through historical sites and artifacts. For him, the artistic quality of those artifacts was secondary to their educational and inspirational value.

Goodwin was born and educated in Virginia. From 1902 to 1908, and again from 1926 to 1938, he was rector of Williamsburg's Bruton Parish Church, said to be the oldest Episcopal church in continuous use in America. As early as 1903, he led the membership in a project to return the building to its colonial appearance. His hope that other historic Williamsburg buildings might be restored began to become reality in 1926, when John D. Rockefeller visited the College of William and Mary. Dr. Goodwin, who was then on the faculty, told Rockefeller of his dream of a restored Williamsburg. When he mentioned that he had written Henry Ford to request help in the project, Rockefeller "immediately became interested, and asked me just what plan I had in mind."[2]

This competitive spirit among the very rich was important to the building of America's great collections in the 1920s.

Neglect had been the main agent of preservation in Williamsburg. Other colonial capitals like Boston, New York, and Philadelphia had been continually modernized, with the resultant destruction of many old buildings. So much colonial architecture survived in Williamsburg, however, that Dr. Goodwin's vision could take shape despite the shabbiness and the bleak corrugated-iron structures that had crept in here and there.

Because real-estate prices would have skyrocketed upon premature disclosure of Rockefeller's interest in the project, it was necessary to keep the whole thing secret. Goodwin told of preparing the original proposal for submission to Rockefeller:

> The preliminary plans were made from measurements of the streets and properties of Williamsburg taken by Mr. Perry and two assistants in the quiet darkness between midnight and dawn. . . . Photographs were taken from the air and pieced together. . . . Neither Mr. Perry nor the airplane photographer knew for what mysterious purpose these things were being done.[3]

The Reverend W. A. R. Goodwin. (Colonial Williamsburg photograph)

Late in 1927, Rockefeller agreed to back the project. To protect his anonymity, the pseudonym "Mr. David" was used in all related correspondence. Goodwin was given the title of Local Director, Williamsburg Restoration; and the Boston architectural firm of Perry, Shaw and Hepburn was retained to do the work, under the supervision of William G. Perry, the senior partner. *The Virginia Gazette* described the atmosphere of the preparations:

> Dr. Goodwin was requested to proceed with the purchase of the necessary properties. These were acquired gradually and much to the amazement of Williamsburg citizens—in spite of their being accustomed to innumerable surprises—properties along the Duke of Gloucester Street began to be sold and transferred to Dr. Goodwin. All of the deeds were first made out to Dr. Goodwin and Mrs. Goodwin and the city buzzed with great excitement as to the source of the Rector's extraordinary capacity for acquiring property. Still he kept his secret.
>
> It was not until a public meeting of the citizens of Williamsburg was held in the Court House on June 12, 1928, that Mr. Rockefeller's association with the Restoration was first announced.[4]

Williamsburg's main street, c. 1901, as it looked when Goodwin first saw it. (Colonial Williamsburg photograph)

Like Goodwin, Rockefeller was excited by the inspirational, patriotic possibilities of the work at Williamsburg. In undertaking the restoration, he found "a lasting challenge in the opportunity to preserve an entire historic area and, *more importantly* [italics added], the basic principles of American self-government and individual freedom founded in Williamsburg, and the opportunity to recall for the benefit of the people of the future the 'patriotism, high purpose, and unselfish devotion of our forefathers to the common good.' "[5] Rockefeller, like so many Americans of the twenties, felt the need to return to what he believed were basic American values; and he thought that visitors would be inspired by seeing where and how men who had led America's fight for independence had lived and worked.

This was an expansion on the idea, first implemented in the nineteenth century through exhibitions of relics, and later through period rooms, that objects could convey the spirit of the past. Goodwin and Rockefeller were restoring a whole town, and one of indisputable historic importance, to its eighteenth century appearance. Their project, with its drive for authenticity within a beautiful (but therefore limited) framework, was reminiscent of Halsey's American Wing—although to Goodwin and Rockefeller, the beauty was not an end in itself but rather a means of inspiration. They were attempting to provide visitors with the closest possible approximation of a colonial environment. The harmony and simplicity of the architecture, and the serene and charming atmosphere created by brick paths, dirt roads, old-fashioned gardens, and costumed guides, would serve as a pleasant antidote to a complicated and often ugly modern world.

In the largest sense, Goodwin and Rockefeller had reasons for reviving the past similar to those of Henry Ford. But Williamsburg focused on the élite culture of an important political center, while Greenfield Village was firmly devoted to the ordinary and practical elements of life.

At first, all efforts were concentrated on the architecture. Goodwin wrote:

In those early days of the restoration one never knew when he went to bed whose house he might meet in the morning moving down the street.

Sometimes it proved to be a colonial house on its way in to fill a vacant space, but more often it was a modern home exiled from the restoration area.[6]

To complete the illusion of an eighteenth-century town, however, furniture and accessories were necessary. By 1928 there was considerable discussion of interior decoration and the purchase of antiques. The attitudes and arguments of those involved in furnishing the Williamsburg houses shed substantial light on Americans' thinking in the twenties about antiques and their own past.

In May of 1928, Goodwin, Perry, and a man named Todd from Rockefeller's office were appointed with R. T. H. Halsey and Louis G. Myers (who was treasurer of the Rockefeller Fund) to a furnishings committee. The inclusion of Halsey and Myers made good sense—they were acknowledged experts —but also created potential problems. These two men were Northerners and connoisseurs; they did not understand Goodwin's overriding concern with historical authenticity, above everything else, including great craftsmanship.

Walnut desk and bookcase made in Williamsburg c. 1775. Said to have belonged to President John Tyler. Goodwin wrote in 1928: "I do think that if we are going into the matter of collecting interesting antiques we ought to get the Tyler desk. . . ." (Colonial Williamsburg photograph)

Still, Goodwin was the pivotal figure in these early years. He was especially impressed with Halsey's credentials, and both Halsey and Myers had some influence. But it was Goodwin's vision that held sway. Recognizing the importance of procuring objects that related to Williamsburg and to the South, he worked hard to keep Northerners from creating a Northern restoration. His feelings were set forth in a report of the furnishings committee in July 1928:

> He expressed himself as opposed to the purchase, at a premium, of any object which derived its excess value from historical association with localities other than Williamsburg, but urged the serious consideration of the Committee of objects, whatever their cost might be, of rare and unreplaceable character with distinct local historic association. . . . every opportunity should be taken in an intelligent and comprehensive way to provide for the expression of early Virginia life through the furnishings of the buildings which it is proposed to restore and recreate. Further, that the Williamsburg Restoration would be hollow and meaningless if such expressive documents are not made a part of the whole. The soul of the Restoration will lie in the expression of the contact of the ancient time with the new, through the possession of objects known to have played their part in early Colonial Williamsburg.[7]

That same month Goodwin wrote Perry a letter about the kind of furniture suitable for the restoration, expressing doubts as to Myers's and Halsey's qualifications for this particular project:

> With reference to furniture there is one matter which should, I think, be especially considered, and that is as to whether the Williamsburg cabinet makers—and there were a great many of them—can be certainly assumed to have followed the patterns and designs familiar to the students of New England and Pennsylvania furniture. The old *Virginia Gazette* makes mention of a number of cabinet makers here. We find invoices of large importations of mahogany. We further find records of cabinet makers brought over from England. But I am just wondering if those expert in pieces of New England and Pennsylvania furniture, would be entirely safe in judging some piece that might have been made by one of these cabinet makers located in Virginia, brought over from England.[8]

Almost exactly fifty years after this, Goodwin was vindicated. An article entitled "Furniture of Williamsburg and Eastern Virginia" appeared in the August 1978 issue of *The Magazine Antiques*, documenting the existence of a flourishing and sophisticated cabinetmaking trade in eighteenth-century Williamsburg: "Written evidence and surviving examples indicate . . . that even the wealthiest of the colonial aristocracy patronized Virginia cabinetmakers—most often for the vast majority of their furniture."[9]

Halsey and Myers tended to ignore the possible importance of work by local craftsmen, in favor of furniture exported from North to South. Rather than regarding Williamsburg as a regional museum, they wanted to emphasize the best craftsmanship the American colonies had been able to muster. Susan Higginson Nash, a member of Perry's staff who oversaw (as previously noted) much of the original furnishing, gave her impression of the two men:

> The records may look as though furniture purchases first went to the committee on furnishings and were stamped and approved by that committee. I don't know exactly how the idea ever sprang up—that feeling of the Furnishings Committee being important. They certainly weren't important to me! . . . I don't think that Mr. Myers or Mr. Halsey [ever saw a piece of furniture until it was installed at Williamsburg], unless it was some piece of furniture *they* wished to sell. . . .
>
> * * *
>
> Mr. Halsey at that time was very much interested in Duncan Phyfe, and always was, I believe. I think that was the period in which he particularly specialized, and he could see no logical reason why we couldn't use Duncan Phyfe furniture in Williamsburg. It didn't seem to matter to him that Duncan Phyfe built his furniture after 1800. It was beautiful furniture, and that was important to Mr. Halsey.
>
> In other words, I think Mr. Halsey cared more about beautiful furniture than he did about Williamsburg. I don't think in his mind he pictured Williamsburg very clearly as a pre-Revolutionary town in its most important era—which is what I did when I thought out the restoration. After the Revolution Williamsburg had ceased to exist as the town Mr. Rockefeller was restoring.[10]

Goodwin, not surprisingly, had reservations when Myers sold Rockefeller more than $44,000 worth of furniture, mostly from New England and Pennsylvania, for the restoration. In a letter to Colonel Arthur Woods, president of the Rockefeller Foundation and much involved in the Williamsburg project, Goodwin said that he had signed the purchase form for the furniture only because Perry had also signed it. "I am strongly of the opinion that all of the rest of the furniture which we buy should be either of English make or furniture known to have been made in or south of Baltimore."[11]

Although Goodwin protested to Perry about the purchase of an Empire chandelier for a colonial restoration, Perry and Susan Nash seem to have been generally in accord with him. They stressed the importance of Southern and English influences on the town, and stood firmly against the acquisition of too much furniture that was neither Southern nor English. Perry described the touching resolution of his own disagreement with Myers on the question:

Mr. Louis Myers . . . wanted us to buy a forty to fifty thousand—perhaps more than that—collection of Duncan Phyfe furniture. I wouldn't have a piece in Williamsburg, not a solitary piece.

* * *

One day I heard he was ill and that he was at Johns Hopkins Hospital. I went up there and asked the nurse if I could see him. . . . I sat down and had a nice talk with him.

He put his hand out and he said, "William, I don't think I ever understood that restoration you were attempting to do. We specialists, you know, have to look out a little bit for mistakes and pitfalls that we might fall into. It's a little bit wider, you know, than a mere specialty: you were trying to interpret a civilization down there; we were trying to sell you fine pieces. You knew that there were fine pieces down there but not every piece down there was a fine piece. We made a mistake. . . ."

And he died the next day.[12]

Myers's "mistake," which he recognized only at the very end, was one made by many of his fellow collectors. It resulted from the desire to show early American art and life at their best, and not in all their variety. Dr. Goodwin's vision was broader, yet in its own way, it too focused on the best. Goodwin sought historical authenticity, but emphasized the important men who had lived, written, and debated in Williamsburg. Just as Halsey wanted to establish the validity of American art, Goodwin wanted to confirm the intelligence and effectiveness of early American statesmen, and to demonstrate that their rationality had emerged in beautifully harmonious surroundings. He strove for accuracy and believed the restoration had achieved it, yet he was as romantic as his contemporaries. He overlooked all but the harmony and beauty of colonial life.

More recently, researchers and archeologists have turned up new facts to correct even Goodwin's relatively narrow picture. To the extent that these findings make life at the highest levels seem more pedestrian, Dr. Goodwin would probably have regarded them with some regret. Much as he supported the substitution of fact for tradition, he was sorry to see the romance of history diminish. In 1937, he wrote dryly:

To the Restoration's department of research, truth is so dear that it often has to be purchased at the price of romance. . . . Counting the traditional nights spent by Washington in homes scattered far and wide, the department checks to see if there were that many nights on the calendar or if there were any nights left for him to spend at home, as history records he sometimes did.[13]

Epilogue

IT SEEMS APPROPRIATE TO END THIS COLLECTING SAGA AT 1930. THE PRECEDING decade had been one of extraordinary significance in the world of American antiques; the collectors and permanent museum exhibitions of that period have influenced our thinking about the American past and its artifacts ever since.

Until the 1920s, collecting American antiques had been a rather solitary pastime, or one confined to limited geographical areas like Hartford. Then the American Wing opened, to a public ready to be convinced that American antiques have artistic and historical value, and ideas took hold that have continued until recently to govern our understanding of home life in early America. Those ideas were more romantic than archeologically correct, but their romanticism was necessary to capture the national imagination. For, in spite of growing acceptance, there was still a good deal of skepticism about the artistic value of American antiques. Museum men and collectors of the twenties therefore arranged those antiques, with imported accessories, in rooms that were irresistibly elegant and charming.

One of the most widely held ideas was that good taste was intrinsic to the early American interior. Colors and forms always harmonized; symmetry prevailed in both objects and their arrangement; order and serenity were ever present. Exhibiting an unrestored object, or presenting a period room cluttered with family belongings—as Dow had done nearly twenty years earlier in Salem —was unacceptable to many collectors and museum people. They wanted to show early American arts and crafts at their peak, to demonstrate to the world at large that those crafts embodied—in artistically valid ways—the best of the American character. Simplicity of form and restraint in ornamentation, which for so long had seemed to make American decorative arts inferior to their ornate European counterparts, now appeared as outstanding expressions of the national taste and culture. Our ideas of what is beautiful were changing.

Curators and wealthy collectors were determined to present American arts in the most attractive settings possible, to prove that American antiques could be arranged as charmingly, comfortably, and even luxuriously as European ones. This was particularly true of such collectors as Henry du Pont, his sister Louise Crowninshield, Katharine Murphy, and Ima Hogg. They had been accustomed to living in beautifully arranged and appointed rooms, among ob-

Left to right: *Katharine Murphy, Ima Hogg, and curator John Graham, c. 1952, at an early Williamsburg Forum. (Colonial Williamsburg Foundation)*

jects of rarity and beauty, and they brought these same expectations to furnishing with American antiques. Their eminently successful rooms delighted all who entered.

The period-room concept was crucial in firing the imaginations of these collectors, and then enabling them to make their visions tangible. Without the period room, collecting American antiques would probably not have become such an enormously popular pastime. And because of it, the twenties generation of collectors and curators was the first to have a widespread impact. Each of the earlier generations had learned from and built on preceding ones; but collecting American antiques had remained a specialized pursuit, engaged in by a relative few.

In the 1920s, however, the contagious idea of period rooms produced beautifully decorated museums and private houses filled with masterpieces of early American craftsmanship. All was polished and gleaming, all was meticulously arranged. Dust and dirt were banished. They charmed the observer, the rooms of these gifted collectors and curators—they caught and held the imagination, and they inspired respect and appreciation for American heirlooms. From the 1920s onward, countless period rooms were lovingly assembled by those whose frame of reference was the augustly elegant American Wing or the opulent and seemingly unending chain of perfection at Winterthur. When Williamsburg opened to the public, these influences were reinforced. Here was a whole *town* radiating serenity, taste, simplicity, and order. Few could resist these havens from a troubled and often ugly modern world; for four decades, no one even tried.

Recently, as a result of new research and discoveries, we have come to consider the early period rooms as expressions of a personal and romantic vision rather than historically accurate re-creations. The symphonies of color and form imitated by thousands are giving way to arrangements that are more austere, less comfortable, and less conventionally pleasing to the twentieth-century eye. The task of proving the worth of American antiques has been completed, and we are now free to engage in serious inquiry into just how our ancestors *did* live, rather than creating the charming imaginary settings in which we *wish* they had lived.

The legacy of the original period rooms, and of the grand collections that took shape during the twenties, is our enthusiasm and appreciation for native arts and crafts. The early period-room advocates, who were the first sweeping influence on the American collecting movement, left us a zest for collecting and a love of the objects that are with us still. Our perception of the past need not agree with theirs for us to share their passion for American antiques. We caught the essence of their vision, and it enriches our own.

Notes

SOURCES CITED FREQUENTLY THROUGHOUT THE NOTES ARE GIVEN HERE WITH FULL BIBLIO-graphical information; thereafter they will be referred to by their short titles. Sources cited often within only one chapter will be fully listed the first time and referred to by a shortened title thereafter.

Walpole Society *Note Books* and other publications are given without place of publication, because they were privately printed by a variety of presses in small editions.

Short Titles

Henry Wood Erving, "Random Recollections of an Early Collector," *The Twenty-fifth Anniversary Meeting of the Walpole Society* (Walpole Society, 1935), hereinafter referred to as "Random Recollections."

Richard Henry Saunders, "American Decorative Arts Collecting in New England, 1840–1920" (unpublished Master's thesis, University of Delaware, 1973), hereinafter referred to as "Collecting in New England."

Lawrence C. Wroth, *The Walpole Society, Five Decades* (Walpole Society, 1960), hereinafter referred to as *Five Decades*.

PART I

Introduction

1. Allan Nevins and Milton Halsey Thomas, eds., *The Diary of George Templeton Strong* (New York: The Macmillan Co., 1952), Vol. II, p. 197.

2. *Autumn*, quoted in Frances Clary Morse, *Furniture of the Olden Time* (New York: The Macmillan Co., 1917), title page.

3. *The House of the Seven Gables, a*

Romance (Boston: Ticknor, Reed, & Fields, 1851), p. 9.

4. Vol. LII, No. CCIX, pp. 313–28.
5. Henry W. B. Howard, ed., *The Eagle and Brooklyn* (Brooklyn, N.Y.: The Brooklyn Eagle, 1893), Part 3, p. 152.
6. Quoted in *History of the Brooklyn and Long Island Fair, Feb. 22, 1864* (Brooklyn, N.Y.: 1864), p. 73.
7. *The Drum Beat*, 26 Feb. 1864, p. 4.
8. *The Drum Beat*, 24 Feb. 1864, p. 4.
9. P. 75.
10. Quoted in Saunders, "Collecting in New England," p. 13.
11. *Ibid.*, p. 21.
12. Quoted in *ibid.*, p. 22.
13. See the *Catalogue of Antique Articles on Exhibition at Plummer Hall, Salem, 1875* (hereinafter referred to as Plummer Hall catalogue; Salem, Mass.: Press of the Salem Gazette, 1875); Saunders, "Collecting in New England," includes some discussion of Waters, Curwen, and Moulton.
14. *Frank Leslie's Illustrated Newspaper*, New York, 22 Jan. 1876, p. 324.
15. Plummer Hall catalogue, No. 127; No. 666.
16. Quoted in Dee Brown, *The Year of the Centennial* (New York: Charles Scribner's Sons, 1966), p. 130.
17. Quoted in Robert C. Post, ed., *1876 A Centennial Exhibition* (hereinafter referred to as *1876*; Washington, D.C.: Smithsonian Institution, 1976), p. 15.
18. Quoted in Brown, *The Year*, p. 131.
19. Saunders, "Collecting in New England," pp. 39, 40; John Maass, "The Centennial Success Story," *1876*, p. 23.
20. Rodris Roth, "The Colonial Revival and Centennial Furniture," *Art Quarterly*, XXVII, No. 1 (1964), pp. 57–81; quoted in Rodris Roth, "Furniture," *1876*, p. 103.
21. "The Centennial," *Frank Leslie's Illustrated Weekly Newspaper*, 10 June 1876, p. 217.
22. Oliver Larkin, *Art and Life in America* (New York: Rinehart & Co., 1957), p. 242.

Chapter 1: The First Collectors

1. Dean A. Fales, Jr., "The Furnishings of the House," *Essex Institute Historical Collections*, Vol. XCVII, No. 2 (April 1961), pp. 111–12.
2. Huldah M. Smith, "Some Aspects of William Bentley as Art Collector and Connoisseur," *ibid.*, pp. 154–6.
3. William Bentley, *Diary* (Salem, Mass.: The Essex Institute, 1905), Vol. II, p. 172.
4. *Ibid.*
5. Philadelphia: E. L. Carey & A. Hart; New York: G. & C. & H. Carvill, 1830.
6. "John F. Watson: First Historian of American Decorative Arts," *The Magazine Antiques*, Vol. LXXXIII, No. 3 (March 1963), p. 302.
7. Rodris Roth discusses these and other examples of relic furniture in "Pieces of History," *The Magazine Antiques*, Vol. CI, No. 5 (May 1972), pp. 874–8.

Chapter 2: Cummings Davis

1. Mrs. Hans Miller of Concord most generously shared with me her genealogical and other notes on Davis, which she collected over a period of many years from manuscripts and other sources at the Concord Antiquarian Society and the Concord Free Library. She acquired more facts and impressions of Davis through conversations with early members of the society. My descriptions of Davis's life in Concord are based importantly on Mrs. Miller's research and recollections.
2. Russell Kettell, *Cummings E. Davis and His Concord Furniture* (Concord, Mass.: Concord Antiquarian Society, n.d.), p. 4.
3. Allen Franch, "The New House and Old Collection of the Concord Antiquarian Society," *Old-Time New England*, Vol. XXI, No. 4 (April 1931), pp. 147–8.
4. *The Quest of the Colonial* (New York: The Century Co., 1907), pp. 216, 219.
5. "Summer Correspondence of the

Transcript" [Concord, Mass.],
Transcript, August 1870.

6. *The Quest of the Colonial*, p. 220.
7. *Catalogue of a Portion of the Collection of the Concord Antiquarian Society* (Concord, Mass.: Concord Antiquarian Society, 1911), p. vi.
8. Kettell, *Cummings E. Davis*, p. 6.

Chapter 3: Ben: Perley Poore

1. In the files of the Society for the Preservation of New England Antiquities (hereinafter referred to as SPNEA).
2. Clipping from the Exeter (Mass.) *News-Letter*, 6 June 1887, SPNEA files.
3. Hesketh Pearson, *Sir Walter Scott* (New York: Harper & Brothers, 1954), p. 150.
4. Clipping dated 10 April 1920, SPNEA files.
5. 6 June, SPNEA files.
6. "Ben: Perley Poore of Indian Hill" (hereinafter referred to as "Poore"), *Essex Institute Historical Collections*, Vol. LXXXIX, No. 1 (January 1953), pp. 11–12.
7. *The New York Times*, 29 May 1887.
8. Driver, "Poore," pp. 12–13.
9. Unidentified newspaper clipping, SPNEA files.
10. Clipping of a newspaper article by Leonard Woodman Smith dated 10 April 1925, SPNEA files.
11. Driver, "Poore," p. 12.
12. Newspaper clipping dated 23 June 1941, SPNEA files.
13. Cartoon depicting Poore wheeling

his barrow, with explanatory caption, published 1856, SPNEA files.
14. Smith, 10 April 1925; *ibid*.
15. Clipping from the Salem (Mass.) *Evening News*, 13 Jan. 1940, SPNEA files; Driver, "Poore," pp. 10, 11.
16. Clipping from the Boston *Globe*, 27 July 1941, SPNEA files.

Chapter 4: Edward Lamson Henry

1. In the Henry Collection at the New York State Museum, Albany, New York (hereinafter referred to as NYSM).
2. Francis L. Henry, "A Memorial Sketch: E. L. Henry, N.A., His Life and His Life Work," in *The Life and Work of Edward Lamson Henry N.A. 1841–1919*, by Elizabeth McClausland, NYSM *Bulletin*, No. 339 (September 1945), p. 342.
3. *Catalogue of the Collection of Mr. E. L. Henry N.A.* (New York: Ortgies & Co., March 2, 1887).
4. *Ibid.*
5. McClausland, *Henry*, p. 50.
6. Quoted in *ibid*., p. 39.
7. Quoted in *ibid*., p. 344.
8. *Ibid.*, p. 51.
9. Quoted in Walter Knight Sturgis, "Arthur Little and the Colonial Revival," *Journal of the Society of Architectural Historians*, Vol. XXXII (May 1973), p. 148. I am indebted to Alice Winchester for this and other Henry material.
10. Quoted in *Henry*, p. 48.
11. *Ibid.*, pp. 49, 324.
12. Quoted in *ibid*., p. 65.

PART II

Introduction

1. Irving Whitall Lyon, *The Colonial Furniture of New England* (Boston and New York: Houghton Mifflin Co., 1924), p. iii.
2. Reprinted in Clarence P. Hornung, *Treasury of American Design* (New York: Harry N. Abrams, Inc., n.d.), p. xxv.

3. Thurlow Weed Barnes, ed. (Albany, N.Y., 1886), pp. xvii–xviii.
4. *Catalogue of Arts, Relics, and Curiosities at the Brooklyn Sanitary Fair* (Brooklyn, N.Y.: 1864), Nos. 57 and 94; *Catalogue of Albany's Bicentennial Loan Exhibition* (Albany, N.Y.: 1886), No. 72.

5. Clarence Winthrop Bowen, ed. (New York: D. Appleton & Co., 1892), pp. 406, 134–5.
6. *Ibid.*, pp. 147–8.
7. *Harper's Weekly*, 27 April 1889, pp. 331, 332.
8. (New York: G. P. Putnam's Sons, 1875), Vol. II, p. 189.
9. *The Pocket History of the United States* (New York: Pocket Books, Inc., 1945), p. 333.
10. Frederick Lewis Allen, *The Big Change* (New York: Harper & Row, 1952), pp. 25–6.
11. *The House Beautiful* (New York: Charles Scribner's Sons, 1878), p. 164.
12. Vol. XCIII (September), pp. 577–86.
13. James Wilson Pierce, *Photographic History of the World's Fair* (Baltimore: R. H. Woodward and Co., 1893), p. 276.
14. Quoted in Pierce, *Photographic History*, p. 491.
15. (New York: The New American Library, 1964), p. 20.

Chapter 5: Clarence Cook

1. (New York: The New American Library, 1964), p. 194.
2. *The House Beautiful* (New York: Charles Scribner's Sons), p. 188.
3. Quoted in Saunders, "Collecting in New England," p. 29.
4. *The House Beautiful*, p. 162.
5. *Ibid.*, p. 16.
6. *Ibid.*, p. 222.
7. *Ibid.*, p. 163.
8. A. J. Downing, *The Architecture of Country Houses* (New York: D. Appleton & Co., 1850; Dover reprint, 1969), p. ix.
9. Dumas Malone, ed., *Dictionary of American Biography* (New York: Charles Scribner's Sons, 1934), p. 371.
10. *Ibid.*
11. *The House Beautiful*, p. 190.

Chapter 6: Old China

1. "Random Recollections," p. 41.
2. New York: Charles Scribner's Sons; reprinted, Rutland, Vermont, and Tokyo, Japan: Charles E. Tuttle Co., Inc., 1973.
3. *Ibid.*, p. 3.
4. (New York: Harper & Brothers), p. 410.
5. *Ibid.*, p. 23.
6. Annie Trumbull Slosson, *China Hunters Club* (New York: Harper & Brothers, 1878), p. 255.
7. Dover reprint, 1969, p. 233.
8. (New York: Frederick A. Stokes Co.), p. 39.
9. *Ibid.*
10. *China Collecting*, pp. 18–19.
11. XVI (September), No. 5, p. 677.
12. *China Collecting*, pp. 412–13.
13. "Random Recollections," p. 31; Henry Wood Erving, Hartford, 31 Jan. 1940, letter to W. L. McAtlee, Arlington, Virginia, Gurdon Trumbull file, Registrar's Office, Wadsworth Atheneum, Hartford, Conn.
14. *China Collecting*, p. 413.
15. Erving to McAtlee.

Chapter 7: Irving W. Lyon

1. Boston and New York: Houghton Mifflin Co.
2. Interview with Mrs. Stephen T. Keiley, Lyon's granddaughter, 17 March 1977. I am indebted to Mrs. Keiley for information and reminiscences about her grandfather and her father, Irving P. Lyon, and for photographs of objects in the former's collection; *Colonial Furniture*, p. iii.
3. I. W. Lyon, London, 28 Nov. 1879, letter to Mrs. Lyon, Hartford, Conn., Lyon papers, Joseph Downs Manuscript Collection, H. F. du Pont Winterthur Museum (hereinafter referred to as Winterthur), No. 76x99.36.
4. London, 28 Nov. 1879, letter to Mrs. Lyon, Winterthur No. 76x99.36.
5. Winterthur No. 76x99.30.
6. London, 25 May, 20 June, and 25 June 1881, letters to Mrs. Lyon, Winterthur No. 76x99.35.
7. I. W. Lyon, handwritten "Notes from Inventories on Old Furniture, etc." (hereinafter referred to as

"Notes"), 1883, Winterthur No. 76x99.17.

8. "Notes," pp. 77–9.

9. "Notes," pp. 74–5, 96.

10. France, 20 June 1881, London, 30 June 1881, Worcester, 21 May 1881, letters to Mrs. Lyon, Winterthur No. 76x99.35.

11. London, 2 May 1886, letter to Mamie Lyon, Hartford, Conn., Winterthur No. 76x99.38.

12. See London, 7 May 1886, letters to Mrs. Lyon and I. P. Lyon, Winterthur No. 76x99.39.

13. Obituary clipping signed George Leon Walker, Hartford, Conn., 6 March 1896, sent to me by Mrs. Keiley; clipped review from the *Public Ledger*, 4 Dec. 1891, Winterthur No. 76x99.34; clipped review from the Hartford *Courant*, 19 Nov. 1891, Winterthur No. 76x99.34.

14. See Saunders, "Collecting in New England," pp. 65–6.

15. 13 Nov. 1891, Winterthur No. 76x99.39.

16. March 1892, 413–14; 4 March 1892, Winterthur No. 76x99.39; scrapbook, Winterthur No. 76x99.34.

17. Unidentified newspaper clipping in the possession of Mrs. Keiley.

18. 28 Nov. 1892, Winterthur No. 76x99.38.

19. 9 June 1895; 9 July 1895, Winterthur No. 76x99.38.

20. "In Praise of Antiquaries," Walpole Society *Note Book* (1931), pp. 11–13.

21. "Living with Antiques, The Connecticut Home of Mr. and Mrs. C. Sanford Bull," Vol. XLVI, No. 4 (April 1944), p. 190.

22. Buffalo, New York, 30 Oct. 1909, letter to Henry Kent, New York, Hudson-Fulton file, Metropolitan Museum Archives.

23. Winterthur No. 76x99.38; 4 Sept. 1895, Winterthur No. 76x99.44.

Chapter 8: Henry Wood Erving

1. "Henry Wood Erving" (hereinafter referred to as "Erving"), Walpole Society *Note Book* (1941), pp. 10–11.

2. Henry Wood Erving, *Random Notes on Colonial Furniture* (hereinafter referred to as *Random Notes*; Topsfield, Mass.: The Wayside Press, 1931), p. 30.

3. "Random Recollections," p. 30.

4. *Ibid.*, p. 31.

5. *Ibid.*, pp. 32–3.

6. *Ibid.*, pp. 41–2.

7. *Ibid.*, pp. 33–4.

8. *Ibid.*, pp. 36–7.

9. *Ibid.*, pp. 37–8.

10. *Ibid.*, p. 40.

11. *Random Notes*, pp. 9, 45.

12. "Erving," p. 10.

13. "Henry Wood Erving, A Collector's Portrait," *American Collector* (hereinafter referred to as *American Collector*), Vol. IV, No. 3 (25 July 1935), p. 5.

14. Hartford, Conn., 14 Sept. 1939, letter to Chauncey Cushing Nash, Boston, printed in the Walpole Society *Note Book* (1942), p. 52.

15. "Random Recollections," p. 41; *American Collector*, p. 5.

16. *American Collector*, p. 5; *Random Notes*, p. 30.

17. "Random Recollections," p. 43.

Chapter 9: George Dudley Seymour

1. 24 Dec., Joseph Downs Manuscript Collection, Winterthur Museum, No. 76x99.34.

2. Chauncey C. Nash, "Charles Hitchcock Tyler, Antiquarian," Walpole Society *Note Book* (1932), p. 30.

3. *A History of the Seymour Family*, compiled and arranged for publication under direction of George Dudley Seymour by Donald Lines Jacobus (New Haven, Conn.: 1939), p. 1.

4. "George Dudley Seymour" (hereinafter referred to as "Seymour"), Walpole Society *Note Book* (1945), pp. 34–5.

5. *Ibid.*, p. 34.

6. *Ibid.*

7. *Ibid.*, pp. 36, 34.

8. *George Dudley Seymour's Furniture Collection in The Connecticut*

Historical Society (hereinafter referred to as Seymour catalogue; Hartford, Conn.: The Connecticut Historical Society, 1958), pp. 39, 40.

9. Irving W. Lyon, *The Colonial Furniture of New England* (Boston and New York: Houghton Mifflin Co., 1924), p. v; Seymour catalogue, p. 112.

10. Seymour catalogue, p. 20.

11. Erving, "Random Recollections," pp. 35–6.

12. *A History of the Seymour Family*, pp. 416–17.

13. "Seymour," p. 36.

14. *Ibid.*, p. 35.

15. *A History of the Seymour Family*, pp. 417–18.

16. "The Hale Federal Stamp," Walpole Society *Note Book* (1938), p. 77.

17. "Seymour," pp. 39–40.

Chapter 10: Horace Eugene Bolles and Charles Hitchcock Tyler

1. Boston, Mass., 29 Oct. 1909, letter to Henry W. Kent, New York, N.Y., Bolles correspondence, Metropolitan Museum of Art Archives (hereinafter referred to as MMA Archives).

2. "Notes," *Bulletin of the Metropolitan Museum of Art*, Vol. XI, No. 6 (June 1916), p. 134.

3. Hudson-Fulton correspondence, MMA Archives. In explaining that he knows these prices seem high, Bolles wrote: "Although the table board may look worse than a carpenter's bench, I could not afford to lose from my collection the oldest American table known, and the only example of its kind found in this country, for $750; and so with the Peregrine White chair, which, in addition to some sentimental value from the fact that it probably belonged to him, is, in my opinion, the rarest and most distinguished American chair yet found."

4. "Horace Eugene Bolles" (hereinafter referred to as "Bolles"), Walpole Society *Note Book* (1950), p. 89.

5. *Ibid.*, p. 90.

6. 12 April 1910, letter to Henry W. Kent, New York, N.Y., Bolles corres., MMA Archives.

7. From Bolles's notes, which accompanied his furniture to the museum, Bolles corres., MMA Archives.

8. Letter to the Walpole Society, *The Twenty-fifth Anniversary Meeting of the Walpole Society* (1935), pp. 7–8.

9. Bolles's notes, Bolles corres., MMA Archives.

10. 27 Dec. 1909, Bolles corres., MMA Archives.

11. 11 Feb. 1910, letter to Kent, Bolles corres., MMA Archives.

12. Bolles's notes, Bolles corres., MMA Archives.

13. Bolles corres., MMA Archives.

14. Clipped newspaper article by Mary Fifield King, probably from the summer of 1920, Bolles corres., MMA Archives.

15. 18 Jan. 1932, letter to Ida M. Tarbell, New York, N.Y., Bolles corres., MMA Archives; 10 Jan. 1910, Bolles corres., MMA Archives; "Bolles," p. 90.

16. "George Shepard Palmer," Walpole Society *Note Book* (1934), p. 63.

17. 18 Jan. 1932, letter to Ida M. Tarbell, Bolles corres., MMA Archives; Richard H. Randall, Jr., *American Furniture in the Museum of Fine Arts, Boston* (Boston: The Museum of Fine Arts, 1965), p. xiii.

18. "Charles Hitchcock Tyler," 7 Dec. 1931, Boston *Evening Transcript*, reprinted in the Walpole Society *Note Book* (1931), p. 29.

19. Wroth, *Five Decades*, p. 49.

20. Hollis French, "Charles Hitchcock Tyler," Walpole Society *Note Book* (1932), p. 32; Chauncey Cushing Nash, "Charles Hitchcock Tyler, Antiquarian," Walpole Society *Note Book* (1932), pp. 31–2.

21. 18 Jan. 1932, letter to Ida M. Tarbell, Bolles corres., MMA Archives; Kathryn Buhler, personal interview with the author at the Museum of Fine Arts, Boston, 25 Sept. 1976.

Chapter 11: Dwight Blaney

1. Quoted in Henry W. Kent, "Dwight Blaney" (hereinafter referred to as "Blaney"), Walpole Society *Note Book* (1945), p. 26.
2. *Ibid.*, p. 25.
3. Mrs. G. Frank Cram, letter, 25 Sept. 1976, to the author.
4. "Blaney," p. 30.
5. *Ibid.*, p. 28.
6. May, letter in the possession of Mrs. Cram.
7. Wroth, *Five Decades*, p. 59.
8. 29 Dec. 1935.
9. No date, letter in the possession of Mrs. Cram.
10. *Five Decades*, p. 59.
11. "Blaney," pp. 28–9.
12. *Ibid.*, p. 30.
13. *Ibid.*, p. 26.
14. "Mr. Walpole's Friends in Boston," reprinted in the Walpole Society *Note Book* (1966), p. 15.

Chapter 12: Canfield, Perry, and Pendleton

1. Quoted in Cleveland Amory, *The Last Resorts* (New York: Harper & Brothers, 1951), p. 437.
2. *Ibid.*, pp. 435–6.
3. *Ibid.*, p. 437.
4. *Ibid.*, p. 436.
5. Quoted in *ibid.*, p. 437.

6. Clarence S. Brigham, "Reminiscences of Early Members Such as He Knew Fifty Years Ago" (hereinafter referred to as "Reminiscences"), Walpole Society *Note Book* (1955), p. 20.
7. Quoted in Wroth, *Five Decades*, p. 16.
8. 12 Dec. 1914.
9. *Ibid.*
10. Wroth, *Five Decades*, pp. 16–17.
11. "Marsden J. Perry" (hereinafter referred to as "Perry"), Walpole Society *Note Book* (1935), p. 31.
12. "Reminiscences," p. 22.
13. Quoted in *Grolier 75* (New York: The Grolier Club, 1959), p. 62; Wroth, *Five Decades*, p. 46.
14. "Perry," p. 32.
15. *Yale Class of 1869 Sexennial* (1875).
16. Hedy B. Landman, "The Pendleton House at the Museum of Art, Rhode Island School of Design," *The Magazine Antiques*, Vol. CVII, No. 5 (May 1975), p. 924.
17. Vol. V, No. 1 (January 1910), p. 14.
18. Saunders, "Collecting in New England," p. 104.
19. Luke Vincent Lockwood, *The Pendleton Collection* (Providence, R.I.: The Rhode Island School of Design, 1904), p. 10.
20. Landman, "Pendleton House," p. 925.
21. *Ibid.*, p. 931.

PART III

Introduction

1. 9 Oct. 1906.
2. *Historic Silver of the Colonies and Its Makers* (New York: The Macmillan Co., 1917), p. 2.
3. Pp. 42–3.
4. *American Silver The Work of 17th and 18th Century Silversmiths, Exhibited at the Museum of Fine Arts June to November 1906* (Boston: The Museum of Fine Arts), p. 31.
5. "Richard Townley Haines Halsey" (hereinafter referred to as "Halsey"), Walpole Society *Note Book* (1942), p. 21.
6. P. 10.

7. *Annual Report* (Boston: The Museum of Fine Arts, 1911), pp. 122–3; *American Church Silver of the 17th and 18th Centuries with a Few Pieces of Domestic Plate* (Boston: The Museum of Fine Arts).
8. "Halsey," pp. 22–3.
9. *Ibid.*
10. Edward Hagaman Hall, *The Hudson-Fulton Celebration, Fourth Annual Report of the Hudson-Fulton Celebration Commission . . .* (Albany, N.Y.: J. B. Lyon Co., 1910), p. 58.
11. *Old New York from the Battery to*

Bloomingdale (New York: G. P. Putnam's Sons, 1875), p. 211.

12. Hall, *The Hudson-Fulton Celebration*, p. 120.

13. "Young America at the Metropolitan," Vol. I, No. 9 (July 1910), pp. 252–7.

14. Vol. XVII, No. 2 (November 1909), p. 140.

15. (New York: Metropolitan Museum of Art), p. 299; *ibid.*, Preface, p. ix; *Bulletin of the Metropolitan Museum of Art*, Vol. XVII, No. 11 (November 1922), Part II, p. 10.

16. Henry Watson Kent and Florence N. Levy, *The Hudson-Fulton Celebration, Catalogue of an Exhibition of American Paintings, Furniture, Silver, and Other Objects of Art, 1625–1825*, Vol. II (New York: Metropolitan Museum of Art).

Chapter 13: Judge A. T. Clearwater

1. Clearwater correspondence, MMA Archives.

2. *The New York Herald Tribune*, 24 Sept. 1933.

3. 11 July 1931, letter in Clearwater corres., MMA Archives.

4. "Recollections," *Bulletin of the Metropolitan Museum of Art*, Vol. XXVI, No. 7 (July 1931), pp. 174–5.

5. Quoted in *The New York Herald Tribune*, 24 Sept. 1933.

6. *Ibid.*

7. "Recollections," p. 175.

8. 11 Feb. 1910, letter to Edward Robinson, Assistant Director of the Metropolitan Museum, Clearwater corres., MMA Archives.

9. 20 Oct. 1911, letter to the MMA Staff, Clearwater corres., MMA Archives; Clearwater, 10 Nov. 1911, letter to Robinson, Clearwater corres., MMA Archives.

10. 21 March 1913, Joseph Downs Manuscript Collection, Winterthur Museum, No. 69x83.40, 41.

11. 19 June 1931, letter to Winifred Howe of the Metropolitan Museum, Clearwater corres., MMA Archives.

12. 14 March 1911, letter, Winterthur No. 69x83.768; 15 March 1911, Winterthur No. 69x83.767.

13. 10 April 1911, letter, Winterthur No. 69x83.540-a&b.

14. 24 Sept. 1919, letter, Clearwater corres., MMA Archives.

15. 28 Dec. 1928, letter to Winifred Howe, Clearwater corres., MMA Archives.

16. "The Clearwater Collection of Colonial Silver," *Bulletin of the Metropolitan Museum of Art*, Vol. XI, No. 1 (January 1916), pp. 5–6.

17. 24 Nov. 1911, letter to John H. Buck, Curator of Silver, Metropolitan Museum, Clearwater corres., MMA Archives.

18. 11 Dec. 1912, letter to John H. Buck, Clearwater corres., MMA Archives.

19. 16 Oct. 1911, letter to Edward Robinson, Clearwater corres., MMA Archives.

20. 24 May 1932, letter to H. E. Winlock, Director of the Metropolitan Museum, Clearwater corres., MMA Archives.

21. 17 July 1922, letter to Winifred Howe, Clearwater corres., MMA Archives.

Chapter 14: Francis Hill Bigelow

1. New York: The Macmillan Co.; hereinafter referred to as *Historic Silver*.

2. *Colonial Furniture, the Superb Collection of Mr. Francis Hill Bigelow of Cambridge, Mass.* (New York: Anderson Galleries, 1924).

3. John Cotton Dana, "Mr. Walpole's Friends in Boston," reprinted in the Walpole Society *Note Book* (1966), p. 18.

4. *Historic Silver*, pp. 2–3; E. Alfred Jones, *The Old Silver of American Churches* (Letchworth, England: National Society of Colonial Dames of America).

5. 8 Aug. 1911, letter to Judge Alphonso T. Clearwater, Kingston, New York, Joseph Downs Manuscript Collection, Winterthur Museum, No. 69x83.899.

6. 19 Dec. 1916, letter in the Bigelow correspondence, American Arts

Office, Yale University Art Gallery.
7. 29 Dec., Bigelow corres., Yale.
8. 5 Jan. 1917, Bigelow corres., Yale;
12 Jan 1917, Bigelow corres., Yale.
9. 6 Nov. 1929, Bigelow corres., Yale.
10. Wroth, *Five Decades*, pp. 47–8.
11. *Ibid.*, p. 68; "Hollis French: Walpolean," Walpole Society *Note Book* (1940), p. 60; Wroth, *Five Decades*, p. 69.
12. Hudson-Fulton corres., Bigelow to Henry W. Kent, 18 March 1909, MMA Archives.
13. 10 May 1916, Bigelow corres., Yale; 19 Dec. 1916, Bigelow corres., Yale.

Chapter 15: George Francis Dow

1. "Report of the Secretary," *Annual Report of the Essex Institute* (Salem, Mass.: The Essex Institute, 1906), p. 17.
2. "Report of the Secretary," *Annual Report of the Essex Institute* (Salem, Mass.: The Essex Institute, 1908), p. 9; "Report of the Secretary," *Annual Report of the Essex Institute* (Salem, Mass.: The Essex Institute, 1911), p. 20.
3. "Report of the Secretary" (1906).
4. Quoted in Charles B. Hosmer, Jr., *Presence of the Past* (New York: G. P. Putnam's Sons, 1965), p. 215.
5. Quoted in *ibid.*, p. 216; Edward P. Alexander, "Artistic and Historical Period Rooms," *Curator*, Vol. VII, No. 4 (1964), p. 267.
6. Wroth, *Five Decades*, pp. 42–3.
7. "Report of the Secretary," *Annual Report of the Essex Institute* (Salem, Mass.: The Essex Institute, 1900).
8. Chauncey C. Nash, Walpole Society *Note Book* (1947), p. 21.

Chapter 16: Henry Watson Kent

1. 21 Sept. 1918, Palmer corres., MMA Archives.
2. *What I Am Pleased to Call My Education* (hereinafter referred to as *My Education*; New York: The Grolier Club, 1949), p. 1.
3. *Ibid.*, p. 2.
4. *Ibid.*, p. 10.
5. *Ibid.*, p. 12.

6. *Ibid.*, p. 49.
7. *Ibid.*, p. 79.
8. *Ibid.*, pp. 82–3.
9. *Ibid.*, p. 113.
10. *Ibid.*, pp. 135–6.
11. *Ibid.*, pp. 143–4.
12. *Ibid.*, p. 84.
13. *Ibid.*, pp. 83–4.
14. 7 Aug. and 9 Aug. 1907, Bolles corres., MMA Archives.
15. 10 Aug. 1907, Bolles corres., MMA Archives.
16. 16 Mar. 1909, Bolles corres., MMA Archives.
17. *My Education*, pp. 160–1.
18. Henry W. Kent, 18 Jan. 1932, letter to Ida M. Tarbell, Bolles corres., MMA Archives; 5 Jan. 1910, Bolles corres., MMA Archives.
19. Vol. V, No. 1, pp. 15–16.
20. 23 Dec. 1908, Hudson-Fulton corres., MMA Archives; 29 Oct. 1909, Bolles corres., MMA Archives; *My Education*, p. 163.
21. Wroth, *Five Decades*, p. 72.
22. Quoted in *ibid.*, p. 74.

Chapter 17: The Walpole Society

1. Theodore Sizer, "Our Golden Anniversary," Walpole Society *Note Book* (1960), p. 12.
2. Henry W. Kent, "The Walpole Society, 1910–1935," *The Twenty-fifth Anniversary Meeting of the Walpole Society* (1935), p. 21.
3. "Random Recollections," pp. 42–3; letter to the membership published in the *Twenty-fifth . . .*, pp. 7–8.
4. Undated letter to Chauncey C. Nash, secretary of the Walpole Society, published in the Walpole Society *Note Book* (1940), p. 12.
5. *A Walpole Society Pilgrimage* (1921), pp. 8–9.

Chapter 18: Edwin AtLee Barber

1. "Preface to the Combined Editions," in the reprinted *The Pottery and Porcelain of the United States* (New York: Feingold & Lewis, 1976), p. 4.
2. P. iv.

3. *Pottery and Porcelain*, pp. 428–9.
4. "Preface," *Pottery and Porcelain*, p. 10.
5. *Pottery and Porcelain*, pp. 429–31.
6. 14 July 1909, letter in the Hudson-Fulton corres., MMA Archives; 26 March 1909, letter in the Hudson-Fulton corres., MMA Archives.
7. *Ceramic Collectors' Glossary* (New York: Printed for The Society, 1914), Preface.
8. P. 74.
9. *The Knickerbocker Press*, 24 June 1911.
10. "Extracts from an Address at Hartford by Mr. E. A. Barber of Philadelphia on the Fuller-Terry Collections in the Wadsworth Atheneum," typewritten notes in the Registrar's Office, Wadsworth Atheneum, Hartford, Connecticut, p. 1.
11. (Hartford, Conn.: printed for Mrs. Albert Hastings Pitkin by the Case, Lockwood, & Brainard Co.), p. 8.
12. *Ibid.*, pp. 81–2; Hudson-Fulton corres., MMA Archives.
13. 24 June 1911.

14. 29 June 1911.
15. *Ibid.*
16. "Preface," *Pottery and Porcelain*, p. 11.

Chapter 19: George Shepard Palmer

1. Quoted in Saunders, "Collecting in New England," p. 83.
2. "George Shepard Palmer" (hereinafter referred to as "Palmer"), Walpole Society *Note Book* (1934), p. 69.
3. *Ibid.*, pp. 65–6.
4. Quoted in Saunders, p. 77.
5. "Palmer," p. 63.
6. *Ibid.*, p. 61.
7. *Ibid.*, p. 64.
8. *Ibid.*, p. 68.
9. *Ibid.*, pp. 66–7.
10. *Bulletin of the Metropolitan Museum of Art*, Vol. XIII, No. 12 (December 1918), p. 252.
11. Quoted in Saunders, p. 103.
12. *What I Am Pleased to Call My Education*, p. 71.
13. "Palmer," p. 69.

PART IV

Introduction

1. *Days of the Phoenix, The Nineteen Twenties I Remember* (New York: E. P. Dutton, 1951), pp. 2–3.
2. *Period Furniture* (Framingham, Mass.: n.d.), p. 6.
3. *Ibid.*, p. 5.
4. 2 July, Palmer correspondence, MMA Archives.
5. 27 June 1918, Palmer corres., MMA Archives.
6. "An Exhibition of Furniture from the Workshop of Duncan Phyfe," *Bulletin of the Metropolitan Museum of Art*, Vol. XVII, No. 10 (October 1922), pp. 213–14.
7. *Ibid.*, p. 206; 10 Nov. 1922, to Kent, Phyfe exhibition files, MMA Archives.
8. "The Clearwater Collection of Colonial Silver," *Bulletin of the Metropolitan Museum of Art*, Vol. XI, No. 1 (January 1916), p. 3.

9. "Exhibition of Americana at the Brooklyn Museum," Vol. VIII, No. 3 (March 1917), pp. 130–6. I am grateful to Donald Peirce for calling this article to my attention.
10. Circular with Kent's penciled notation, Bolles files, MMA Archives.
11. "Impressions," typescript in the files of the Department of Decorative Arts, Brooklyn Museum, New York.
12. *The Homes of Our Ancestors* (Garden City, N.Y.: Doubleday, Doran and Co., 1925), p. 238.
13. *The Proper Bostonians* (New York: E. P. Dutton, 1947), p. 23.
14. Alice Winchester, Editorial, *The Magazine Antiques*, Vol. CI, No. 1 (January 1972), p. 146. Much of the information about Mr. Keyes and *Antiques* included here is based on conversations with Miss Winchester, as well as on her writings.

15. *Ibid.*
16. *Fruits of the Shaker Tree of Life, Memoirs of Fifty Years of Collecting and Research* (Stockbridge, Mass.: The Berkshire Traveller Press, 1975), p. 22.
17. Editorial, p. 146.
18. "Cobwebs & Dust," Vol. II, No. 1 (July 1922), p. 7.
19. 14 March 1925, p. 13.
20. "Shop Talk," *The Magazine Antiques*, Vol. XVII, No. 2 (February 1930), p. 155; Walpole Society *Note Book* (1926), pp. 25–6.
21. "Shop Talk" (February 1930), pp. 155–6.
22. 15 Sept. 1929.
23. 28 Sept. 1929.

Chapter 20: R. T. H. Halsey

1. Halsey papers, Joseph Downs Manuscript Collection, H. F. du Pont Winterthur Museum No. 75x80.1.
2. "R. T. H. Halsey," Preface, *A Handbook of the American Wing* (7th ed., New York: Metropolitan Museum of Art, 1942), p. xiii.
3. Speech given at the Baltimore Museum of Art, 21 Feb. 1925, Halsey papers, Winterthur No. 75x80.15.
4. "Richard Townley Haines Halsey" (hereinafter referred to as "Halsey"), Walpole Society *Note Book* (1942), p. 19; Albert Ten Eyck Gardner, "Huntington's Franklins," *Bulletin of the Metropolitan Museum of Art*, Vol. XV (Summer 1956), p. 22. I am indebted to Clare Le Corbeiller, Associate Curator, Department of Western Decorative Art, Metropolitan Museum, for finding and sharing this article with me.
5. *Handbook of the American Wing*, p. xii.
6. "Halsey," p. 20.
7. *Historic Silver of the Colonies and Its Makers*, p. 2.
8. Henry W. Kent, 13 Oct. 1906, letter to Halsey, MMA Archives; "Halsey," p. 24.

9. *Handbook of the American Wing*, p. xiii.
10. 4 Feb. 1932, letter in the Halsey corres., MMA Archives.
11. Wroth, *Five Decades*, pp. 71–2.
12. "Those American Things," Metropolitan Museum of Art *Journal*, Vol. III (1970), pp. 230–1.
13. Quoted in R. T. H. and Elizabeth Tower Halsey, *The Homes of Our Ancestors* (Garden City, N.Y.: Doubleday, Page & Co., 1925), p. vii.
14. *Ibid.*, p. 238.
15. "The New Metropolitan Wing," *The Magazine Antiques*, Vol. VII, No. 4 (April 1925), p. 182.
16. Quoted in "Those American Things," p. 231.

Chapter 21: Luke Vincent Lockwood

1. Dr. Jane Lockwood, personal interview with the author, 23 July 1976.
2. "Luke Vincent Lockwood, A Collector's Portrait," *American Collector*, Vol. IV, No. 11 (June 27, 1935), p. 7.
3. *The Celebrated Collection Formed by the Late Mr. and Mrs. Luke Vincent Lockwood* (New York: Parke-Bernet Galleries, Inc., May 13, 14, 15, 1954).
4. "Preface to the First Edition" (reprinted New York: Castle Books, 1951), p. ix.
5. 1 Dec. 1929, clipping in the files of the Decorative Arts Department, Brooklyn Museum. I am indebted to Diane Pilgrim, Curator, and Donald Peirce, Associate Curator, for making this and other material available to me.
6. Donald Peirce pointed out Lockwood's interest in documented furniture and discussed Lockwood's contribution to the field in several valuable conversations with me.
7. Albany *Times Union*, 1 Dec. 1929.
8. 30 Nov. 1929.
9. "Shop Talk," *The Magazine Antiques*, Vol. XVII, No. 1 (January 1930), p. 60.
10. Walpole Society *Note Book* (1951), pp. 57–9.

Chapter 22: Henry Francis du Pont

1. This is from an unpublished version of Du Pont's "Foreword" to Joseph Downs, *American Furniture, Queen Anne and Chippendale Periods* (hereinafter referred to as Downs; New York: The Viking Press, 1952). The typescript is in the Winterthur Archives, H. F. du Pont Winterthur Museum.
2. "The Reminiscences of Henry Francis du Pont" (hereinafter referred to as "Reminiscences"), unpublished transcript of a tape-recorded interview with Dr. Harlan B. Phillips (n.p.: Archives of American Art, 1962), p. 13.
3. "Foreword," Downs, p. vi.
4. Unpublished "Foreword," p. 2.
5. *Ibid.*, p. 3.
6. "Foreword," Downs, p. vi.
7. 13 Nov., to Sleeper, Registrar's Office, H. F. du Pont Winterthur Museum.
8. "Reminiscences," p. 25.
9. Providence *Sunday Journal*, 12 Sept. 1976.
10. Henry Davis Sleeper, 22 Oct. 1926, letter to Du Pont, Registrar's Office, Winterthur Museum; 25 March 1962, letter to Dr. Harlan Phillips, Registrar's Office, Winterthur.
11. Quoted in Charles F. Montgomery, "Henry Francis du Pont" (hereinafter referred to as Montgomery), Walpole Society *Note Book* (1969), p. 21.
12. Samuel W. Woodhouse, Jr., "Further Notes on the Invasion [of Long Island]," Walpole Society *Note Book* (1940), p. 56.
13. Quoted in Wesley Towner, *The Elegant Auctioneers* (New York: Hill & Wang, 1970), p. 452; "Shop Talk," *The Magazine Antiques*, Vol. XVII, No. 2 (February 1930), p. 155; "Furniture Items from the Year's Sales," *Antiques*, Vol. XVII, No. 4 (April 1930), p. 328.
14. "Shop Talk," *Antiques* (February 1930), p. 156; "Furniture Items from the Year's Sales," *Antiques* (April

1930), Fig. 6, p. 331, and Fig. 5, p. 330.
15. Albert J. Collings, New York, letter, 21 June 1929, to H. F. du Pont, Registrar's Office, Winterthur Museum; minutes of the Girl Scouts' Board of Directors' meeting, 4 Nov. 1929, National Council of Girl Scouts files. I am indebted to Wendy Cooper for directing me to both these sources, and for conversations about collecting attitudes in the 1920s.
16. 22 Aug. 1933, letter, to Thomas T. Waterman, Registrar's Office, Winterthur Museum.
17. "The Meeting at Winterthur," Walpole Society *Note Book* (1932), p. 22.
18. C[hauncey] C[ushing] N[ash], W[illiam] D[avis] M[iller], N[orman] M[orrison] I[sham], Walpole Society *Note Book* (1932), p. 26.
19. Wilmarth S. Lewis, quoted in Montgomery, p. 21.
20. "The Meaning of the Museum," *The Magazine Antiques*, Vol. LX, No. 5 (November 1951), pp. 407–8.
21. Roger Butterfield, "The Treasure House of Henry du Pont," *The Saturday Evening Post* (3 Nov. 1951).

Chapter 23: Francis Patrick Garvan

1. *The New York Times*, 22 June 1930.
2. *The New York Sun*, 26 July 1930.
3. *The New York Times*, 22 June 1930.
4. A brief discussion of this and other aspects of Garvan's professional career is included in his *New York Times* obituary, 8 Nov. 1937.
5. Jay Robert Nash, *Bloodletters and Badmen* (New York: M. Evans & Co., Inc., 1973), p. 542.
6. Telephone conversation 20 Sept. 1976, with John Kirk, director of the New England Studies Program, Boston University, who very kindly shared this and other stories he had heard during his years on the staff of the Garvan and Related Collections, Yale University Art Gallery. As

Mr. Kirk pointed out, it is impossible to know whether the stories are fact or folklore.

7. *The New York Sun*, 26 July 1930.

8. "Garvan Furniture at Yale," reprinted from *The Connoisseur Year Book* (n.p.: 1960), p. 1.

9. Kathryn Buhler and Graham Hood, *American Silver, Garvan and Other Collections in the Yale University Art Gallery* (New Haven, Conn.: Yale University Art Gallery, 1970), p. xi.

10. 27 Feb. 1930, letter in the Registrar's Office, Winterthur Museum.

11. *The New York Times*, 11 Jan. 1931.

12. *The New York Sun*, 26 July 1930; the late Charles Montgomery, Curator of the Garvan Collection, personal interview with the author, 23 July 1976, in New Haven. I am indebted to Mr. Montgomery, as well, for Xeroxes of many newspaper clippings and magazine articles about Garvan and the collection, and for discussions on the nature of the American antiques collecting movement as a whole.

Chapter 24: A Triumvirate and One Lone Texan

1. Quoted in Aline B. Saarinen, *The Proud Possessors* (New York: Random House, 1958), pp. 288–9.

2. *Ibid.*, p. 291.

3. Undated typescript of a talk Mrs. Webb gave at the Williamsburg Forum, p. 25. Maggie Moody, Registrar of the Shelburne Museum in 1978, very kindly supplied me with a Xerox of the typescript.

4. John A. H. Sweeney, Coordinator of Research, H. F. du Pont Winterthur Museum, Winterthur, Delaware, personal interview with the author at the museum, 9 June 1976; Walter Muir Whitehill, "Louise du Pont Crowninshield" (Winterthur, Del.: privately printed, 1960), p. 4.

5. Nina Fletcher Little, Brookline, Mass., personal interview with the author in Brookline, 21 April 1976.

6. Whitehill, "Louise du Pont Crowninshield," p. 21.

7. *Ibid.*, p. 17.

8. I am indebted to Mrs. Warren Heddon, daughter of the early New Hampshire collector Katharine Howe Palmer, for her reminiscences about the collecting activities of her mother and Mrs. Murphy. Much of the material included here is based on my conversations with Mrs. Heddon, 8 April 1977 and 6 May 1978, in Hopkinton, New Hampshire.

9. Dean Failey, Curator, Society for the Preservation of Long Island Antiquities, personal interview with the author in Stony Brook, New York, 10 December 1976. I am indebted to Mr. Failey, who worked at Bayou Bend, for this and other stories and information included here.

Chapter 25: Henry Ford

1. Ruth Kedzie Wood, "Henry Ford's Great Gift to the American People," Vol. XVII, No. 5 (June 1929), p. 4.

2. Richardson Wright, "Americana Through the Back Door—an Explanation of Kitchen Colonial," Vol. LIX, p. 38.

3. Wood, "Ford's Great Gift," p. 10 (Garden City, N.Y.: Doubleday, Page & Co., 1926), pp. 226–7.

4. "The Reminiscences of Mr. Israel Sack," interview with Owen Bombard, Dearborn, Michigan, 2 Nov. 1953, Ford Motor Co. Archives, Oral History Section, p. 25. Harold Sack, president of Israel Sack, Inc., very kindly allowed me to read the firm's copy of the typescript of this interview (hereinafter referred to as "Reminiscences"); Lucia Ames Mead, "How the Old Wayside Inn Came Back," *Old-Time New England*, Vol. XXII, No. 1 (July 1931), p. 44.

5. "Reminiscences," pp. 28–30.

6. Personal interview with the author in Hamilton, New York, 21 June 1976.

7. Ford, "Ford's Great Gift," p. 9.
8. *Ibid.*
9. *Ibid.*, p. 1.
10. *Ibid.*

Chapter 26: Louis Guerineau Myers

1. "Hunting Rare Furniture," *The New York Times*, 27 March 1921.
2. 27 Feb. 1921.
3. *The Magazine Antiques*, Vol. XXI, No. 5 (May 1932), p. 236.
4. *The New York Times*, 27 March 1921.
5. "The Louis Guerineau Myers Collection," *The Magazine Antiques*, Vol. XXI, No. 4 (April 1932), p. 180.
6. *The New York Times*, 27 March 1921.
7. *Ibid.*
8. Louis G. Myers, New York, letter, 30 Oct. 1929, to William G. Perry, Boston. Furnishings Committee files, Archives, Colonial Williamsburg.
9. The Colonial Williamsburg Foundation Archives, Dr. W. A. R. Goodwin records, Furnishings—Myers, L.G.—General, Louis G. Myers to William G. Perry, 17 June 1929.
10. Williamsburg Archives, Oral History Collection, Susan Higginson Nash, "The Reminiscences of Susan Higginson Nash," transcript of interview 18, 19, and 20 June 1956, pp. 36, 92.
11. 15 Sept. 1929.
12. "American Queen Anne and Chippendale," *Loan Exhibition of Eighteenth and Early Nineteenth Century Furniture and Glass* (New York: American Art Galleries, Sept. 25 to Oct. 9, 1929).
13. *The Magazine Antiques*, Vol. XVI, No. 5 (November 1929), p. 366.
14. *The Magazine Antiques*, Vol. XXI, No. 4 (April 1932), p. 180.
15. Mrs. Louis G. Myers, Minutes of a Meeting of the Board of Directors of the National Council of Girl Scouts, 4 Nov. 1929, p. 42. I am indebted to Wendy Cooper for this source.

16. *The Magazine Antiques* (April 1932), p. 184.

Chapter 27: W. A. R. Goodwin

1. 8 Sept. to 15 Sept. 1939. I am grateful to Bland Blackford, Archivist, Colonial Williamsburg, for her help in finding this and other material relating to Colonial Williamsburg.
2. Williamsburg, Virginia, The Colonial Williamsburg Foundation Archives, Dr. W. A. R. Goodwin records, Restoration—Its Conception—John D. Rockefeller, Jr., Dr. W. A. R. Goodwin to Dr. James H. Dillard, 20 April 1926.
3. "The Restoration of Colonial Williamsburg," *The National Geographic Magazine*, Vol. LXXI, No. 4 (April 1937), p. 426.
4. 15 September 1939, p. 7.
5. "News from Colonial Williamsburg," press release dated 18 Jan. 1977, p. 2.
6. "The Restoration," p. 441.
7. Williamsburg Archives, General Correspondence records, Furnishings—General, "Report of Meeting of Committee on Purchase of Antiques and Historical Objects," 9 July 1928, p. 1.
8. Williamsburg Archives, Dr. W. A. R. Goodwin records, Furnishings—Committee for Purchases of Antiques, Dr. W. A. R. Goodwin to Mr. William G. Perry, 17 July 1928.
9. Vol. CXIV, No. 2, p. 282.
10. Williamsburg Archives, Oral History Collection, Susan Higginson Nash, "The Reminiscences of Susan Higginson Nash," transcript of interview, 18, 19, and 20 June 1956, pp. 91–93.
11. Williamsburg Archives, General Correspondence records, Furnishings—General, Dr. W. A. R. Goodwin to Colonel Arthur Woods, 20 November 1929.
12. Williamsburg Archives, Oral History Collection, William G. Perry, "The Reminiscences of William G. Perry," transcript of interview, 14–16 August 1956, pp. 39–40.
13. "The Restoration," p. 432.

Index

Page numbers in italics denote illustrations.

A Note About the Author

Elizabeth Stillinger was born in Waukesha, Wisconsin. After receiving her B.A. from Smith College in 1960, she worked as Assistant Editor for the *Hudson Review*. From 1963 to 1972 she edited and wrote for *The Magazine Antiques*. Since 1972 she has been a free-lance writer, lecturer, and teacher. She lives with her two daughters in Blauvelt, New York. She is the author of *The* ANTIQUES *Guide to Decorative Arts in America, 1600–1875* (1972).

A Note on the Type

This book was set on the Linotype in Janson, a recutting made direct from type cast from matrices long thought to have been made by the Dutchman Anton Janson, who was a practicing type founder in Leipzig during the years 1668–87. However, it has been conclusively demonstrated that these types are actually the work of Nicholas Kis (1650–1702), a Hungarian, who most probably learned his trade from the master Dutch type founder Dirk Voskens. The type is an excellent example of the influential and sturdy Dutch types that prevailed in England up to the time William Caslon developed his own incomparable designs from them.

Composing by The Maryland Linotype Composition Corporation, Baltimore, Maryland. Printing and Binding by The Murray Printing Company, Forge Village, Massachusetts. Design by Karolina Harris.